Taste of Home

WHAT'S FOR DINNER?

358 DISHES THAT MAKE MEALTIME A SNAP

TASTE OF HOME BOOKS • RDA ENTHUSIAST BRANDS, LLC • MILWAUKEE, WI

**KUNG PAO
SLOPPY JOES, P. 106**

Visit us at **tasteofhome.com** for other Taste of
Home books and products.

International Standard Book Number:
979-8-88977-051-0

Chief Content Officer: Jason Buhrmester
Content Director: Mark Hagen
Creative Director: Raeann Thompson
Associate Creative Director: Jami Geittmann
Senior Editor: Christine Rukavena
Senior Art Director: Courtney Lovetere
Assistant Art Director: Jazmin Delgado
Manager, Production Design:
Satyandra Ragnav
Senior Print Publication Designer:
Bipin Balakrishnana
Project Coordinator: Sierra Schuler
Production Artist: Nithya Venkatakrishnan
Deputy Editor, Copy Desk: Ann M. Walter
Copy Editor: Rayan Naqash

Photographer: Dan Roberts
Set Stylist: Stephanie Marchese,
Stacey Genaw
Food Stylist: Sue Draheim

Pictured on front cover: Easy Ziti Bake, p. 94;
Honey Chicken Stir-Fry, p. 127; Cheeseburger
Cups, p. 105

Pictured on back cover: Pressure-Cooker
Penne with Meat Sauce, p. 248; Pressure-
Cooker Sonoran Clam Chowder, p. 53; Grilled
Pork Chops with Smokin' Sauce, p. 146; Taco
Cornbread Casserole, p. 219; Farmer's Market
Street Tacos, p. 188

Printed in China
1 3 5 7 9 10 8 6 4 2

MEAL SOLUTIONS AT THE READY

In today's fast-paced world, the question "What's for dinner?" quickly raises flags for home cooks. Between work, school and home life, figuring out what to make for dinner can be as overwhelming as actually preparing it.

That's why the team at *Taste of Home* created this collection of 358 easy recipes. With *What's for Dinner?* cookbook at your side, deciding what to serve is a breeze. Take a look inside, and you'll see that there's always time to prepare a quick dinner bursting with flavor. In fact, 240 of the recipes are ready in less than 30 minutes!

Whether you're a seasoned chef or a kitchen novice, you're sure to love the meal-in-one sheet-pan dinners, bowls and entree salads, comfy casseroles, pasta favorites and the hundreds of other dinner solutions you'll find here. You'll even enjoy fun chapters such as "Breakfast for Dinner" and "Snacks for Supper."

To make your meal solutions even easier, serving suggestions are scattered throughout, and a bonus chapter offers 10-minute dinner additions.

The next time you find yourself asking what you can make for supper, simply reach for this all-new cookbook. After all, with *What's for Dinner?* at your fingertips, the answer is always delicious!

WATCH FOR THESE AT-A-GLANCE ICONS

🕐 These **fast-to-fix recipes** are table-ready in just 30 minutes or less.

🍲 A **slow cooker**—one of the most convenient kitchen tools—does the cooking while you do other things.

🍲 The handy **Instant Pot**® icon signals the timesaving recipes that use this popular appliance.

🍳 For the flavor and crispness of fried but without added fat, try these family-favorite **air-fried** dishes.

5i These recipes use **five or fewer ingredients**. (They may also call for water, salt, pepper, oils or optional items.)

WHAT'S FOR DINNER? HOW ABOUT ...

MORE WAYS TO CONNECT WITH US: 📘 📷 📌 🎵

CHAPTER 1

BREAKFAST FOR DINNER

P. 21

P. 17

P. 18

P. 20

CHILES RELLENOS
CROQUE-MADAME

CHILES RELLENOS CROQUE-MADAME

A traditional croque-madame is a heartier version of a croque-monsieur because it's served with an egg on top of the sandwich. Instead of bechamel and Gruyere, this playful version has pepper jack, chiles and chipotle.
—*Lauren Wyler, Dripping Springs, TX*

TAKES: 30 min. • **MAKES:** 4 servings

- 1 can (7 oz.) whole green chiles, drained
- 8 slices country-style white bread
- 3 Tbsp. chipotle mayonnaise
- 4 slices pepper jack cheese
- ½ lb. sliced deli ham
- 5 Tbsp. butter, softened, divided
- 1 cup shredded sharp cheddar cheese
- 4 large eggs
- ⅛ tsp. salt
- ⅛ tsp. pepper
  Fresh minced chives, optional

1. Slice chiles into long strips; pat dry with paper towels and set aside. Spread 4 bread slices with chipotle mayonnaise. Layer with pepper jack cheese, ham and chiles; top with remaining 4 bread slices. Spread outside of the sandwiches with 4 Tbsp. butter.
2. On a griddle, toast sandwiches over medium heat until bottom is golden brown, 2-3 minutes. Flip and sprinkle with cheddar cheese. Cover and cook until bottom is golden brown and cheese just starts to melt, 2-3 minutes longer.
3. Meanwhile, for eggs, heat remaining 1 Tbsp. butter in a large nonstick skillet over medium-high heat. Break the eggs, 1 at a time, into pan. Reduce heat to low. Cook until the whites are set and yolks begin to thicken, turning once if desired. Sprinkle with salt and pepper. Top the sandwiches with the eggs. Sprinkle with chives if desired.
1 SANDWICH 709 cal., 48g fat (23g sat. fat), 308mg chol., 1529mg sod., 34g carb. (6g sugars, 2g fiber), 35g pro.

MAPLE BACON FRENCH TOAST BAKE

MAPLE BACON FRENCH TOAST BAKE

Our family loves Sunday brunch. Each season I try to bring a different flavor to the table. This French toast reminds us of fall. Whole or 2% milk works best, but I use regular almond milk because I can't have dairy and it works perfectly well.
—*Peggie Brott, Milford, KS*

PREP: 35 min. + chilling • **BAKE:** 50 min.
MAKES: 12 servings

- 8 cups cubed bread
- 8 large eggs
- 2 cups 2% milk
- ½ cup packed brown sugar
- ⅓ cup maple syrup
- ½ tsp. ground cinnamon
- 1 lb. bacon strips, cooked and crumbled

1. Place the bread in a greased 13x9-in. baking dish. In a large bowl, whisk eggs, milk, brown sugar, syrup and cinnamon. Pour over the bread. Sprinkle with the bacon. Refrigerate, covered, 4 hours or overnight.
2. Remove the casserole from the refrigerator 30 minutes before baking. Preheat oven to 350°. Bake, uncovered, until a knife inserted in center comes out clean, 50-60 minutes. Let stand for 5-10 minutes before serving.
1 PIECE 256 cal., 10g fat (3g sat. fat), 141mg chol., 426mg sod., 29g carb. (18g sugars, 1g fiber), 12g pro.

PRESSURE-COOKER DENVER OMELET FRITTATA

Pepper, onion and ham go into this classic dish. It's the perfect recipe to serve company after church or another early outing.
—*Connie Eaton, Pittsburgh, PA*

PREP: 25 min. • **COOK:** 35 min. + releasing
MAKES: 6 servings

- 1 Tbsp. olive oil
- 1 medium Yukon Gold potato, peeled and sliced
- 1 small onion, thinly sliced
- 1 cup water
- 12 large eggs
- 1 tsp. hot pepper sauce
- ½ tsp. salt
- ¼ tsp. pepper
- 8 oz. sliced deli ham, chopped
- ½ cup chopped green pepper
- 1 cup shredded cheddar cheese, divided

1. Select saute setting on a 6-qt. electric pressure cooker and adjust for medium heat; then heat oil. Add potato and onion; cook and stir 4-6 minutes or until the potato is lightly browned. Press cancel. Transfer to a greased 6- or 7-in. souffle or round baking dish (1½-qt.). Wipe the pressure cooker clean; pour in water.
2. In a large bowl, whisk eggs, pepper sauce, salt and pepper; stir in the ham, green pepper and ½ cup cheese. Pour over potato mixture. Top with remaining cheese. Cover the baking dish with foil and place on a trivet with handles; lower into the pressure cooker. Lock lid; close pressure-release valve.
3. Adjust to pressure-cook on high for 35 minutes. Allow pressure to naturally release for 10 minutes, then quick-release any remaining pressure.
1 SERVING 320 cal., 19g fat (7g sat. fat), 407mg chol., 822mg sod., 12g carb. (3g sugars, 1g fiber), 25g pro.

MUSHROOM & EGG TACOS

Breakfast tacos aren't unusual, but a rich and flavorful mushroom sauce takes simple tacos from ordinary to extraordinary in no time.
—*Kathleen Gill, Las Vegas, NV*

TAKES: 30 min. • **MAKES:** 6 servings

- 1 lb. sliced fresh mushrooms
- 1 cup slivered almonds
- 2 Tbsp. dried minced onion
- 1 Tbsp. minced garlic
- 2 Tbsp. olive oil
- ½ tsp. salt
- ½ tsp. pepper
- 1 Tbsp. butter
- 4 large eggs, lightly beaten
- 12 mini flour or whole wheat tortillas
  Minced fresh tarragon, optional

1. In a nonstick skillet, cook mushrooms over medium heat until reduced in size and starting to brown, 8-10 minutes, stirring occasionally. Add almonds, onion and garlic; cook until the nuts are toasted and fragrant, 1-2 minutes. Transfer mixture to a blender or food processor. Add the oil, salt and pepper; process until smooth. Set aside.
2. Meanwhile, heat butter in same skillet over medium heat. Pour in the eggs; cook and stir until eggs are thickened and no liquid egg remains. Divide the mushroom puree among tortillas; top with eggs, and tarragon if desired. Serve immediately.
2 TACOS 360 cal., 23g fat (6g sat. fat), 129mg chol., 468mg sod., 25g carb. (3g sugars, 5g fiber), 14g pro.

PRESSURE-COOKER DENVER OMELET FRITTATA

BLUEBERRY OAT WAFFLES

I truly enjoy recipes that make enough for the two of us, such as this one for yummy waffles. Instead of blueberries, you can slice ripe strawberries on top or use the batter to make pancakes.
—*Ruth Andrewson, Leavenworth, WA*

TAKES: 25 min. • **MAKES:** 4 waffles

⅔ cup all-purpose flour
½ cup quick-cooking oats
1 Tbsp. brown sugar
1 tsp. baking powder
½ tsp. salt
1 large egg, room temperature
⅔ cup 2% milk
¼ cup canola oil
½ tsp. lemon juice
¼ cup ground pecans
½ cup fresh or frozen blueberries
 Optional: Additional blueberries, chopped pecans, maple syrup and butter

1. In a bowl, combine flour, oats, brown sugar, baking powder and salt. In another bowl, combine egg, milk, oil and lemon juice; stir into dry ingredients just until combined. Fold in ground pecans and blueberries. Let stand for 5 minutes.
2. Bake mixture in a preheated waffle iron according to the manufacturer's directions until golden brown. If desired, top with additional blueberries and chopped pecans, and serve with maple syrup and butter.
2 WAFFLES 691 cal., 44g fat (5g sat. fat), 100mg chol., 907mg sod., 64g carb. (15g sugars, 5g fiber), 14g pro.

BLUEBERRY OAT WAFFLES

SHAKSHUKA

Shakshuka is a dish made of poached eggs with tomatoes, onion and cumin. I learned it while traveling, and it's now my favorite way to eat eggs.
—*Ezra Weeks, Calgary, AB*

TAKES: 30 min. • **MAKES:** 4 servings

- 2 Tbsp. olive oil
- 1 medium onion, chopped
- 1 garlic clove, minced
- 1 tsp. ground cumin
- 1 tsp. pepper
- ½ to 1 tsp. chili powder
- ½ tsp. salt
- 1 tsp. Sriracha chili sauce or hot pepper sauce, optional
- 2 medium tomatoes, chopped
- 4 large eggs
   Chopped fresh cilantro
   Whole pita breads, toasted

1. In a large cast-iron or other heavy skillet, heat the oil over medium heat. Add the onion; cook and stir until tender, 4-6 minutes. Add garlic, seasonings and, if desired, chili sauce; cook 30 seconds longer. Add tomatoes; cook until mixture is thickened, stirring occasionally, 3-5 minutes.

2. With back of spoon, make 4 wells in vegetable mixture; break 1 egg into each well. Cook, covered, until egg whites are completely set and yolks begin to thicken but are not hard, 4-6 minutes. Sprinkle with cilantro; serve with pita bread.

1 SERVING 159 cal., 12g fat (3g sat. fat), 186mg chol., 381mg sod., 6g carb. (3g sugars, 2g fiber), 7g pro. **DIABETIC EXCHANGES** 1½ fat, 1 medium-fat meat, 1 vegetable.

SHAKSHUKA

BLUEBERRY-CINNAMON CAMPFIRE BREAD

A neighboring camper made a bread so tempting, I had to ask for the details. Here's my version, best enjoyed with a steaming cup of coffee by the campfire. —Joan Hallford, Fort Worth, TX

PREP: 10 min. • **COOK:** 30 min. + standing
MAKES: 8 servings

- 1 loaf (1 lb.) cinnamon-raisin bread, sliced
- 6 large eggs
- 1 cup 2% milk or half-and-half cream
- 2 Tbsp. maple syrup
- 1 tsp. vanilla extract
- ½ cup chopped pecans, toasted
- 2 cups fresh blueberries, divided

1. Prepare campfire or grill for low heat. Arrange the bread slices on a greased double thickness of heavy-duty foil (about 24x18 in.). Bring foil up the sides, leaving the top open. Whisk eggs, milk, syrup and vanilla. Pour over the bread; sprinkle with nuts and 1 cup blueberries. Fold edges over top, crimping to seal.
2. Place on a grill grate over campfire or grill until eggs are cooked through, 30-40 minutes. Remove from heat; let stand 10 minutes. Sprinkle with remaining blueberries; serve with additional maple syrup if desired.
2 PIECES 266 cal., 10g fat (2g sat. fat), 142mg chol., 185mg sod., 36g carb. (14g sugars, 5g fiber), 12g pro. **DIABETIC EXCHANGES** 2 starch, 1 medium-fat meat, ½ fruit, ½ fat.
OVEN DIRECTIONS Preheat oven to 350°. Place foil packet on a 15x10x1-in. baking pan. Bake 25-30 minutes or until heated through? Let stand 10 minutes before serving. Sprinkle with remaining blueberries; serve with syrup.

COASTAL CAROLINA MUFFIN-TIN FRITTATAS

Incorporating the flavors of a Lowcountry South Carolina crab boil, these tasty frittatas are easy to make and fun to eat. If you have leftover cooked potatoes (roasted or boiled), try dicing them and substituting them for the refrigerated shredded potatoes in this recipe. —Shannon Kohn, Summerville, SC

PREP: 15 min. • **BAKE:** 30 min.
MAKES: 1 dozen

- ½ cup mayonnaise
- 1 Tbsp. lemon juice
- 2 tsp. sugar
- 1 tsp. seafood seasoning
- 1⅓ cups refrigerated shredded hash brown potatoes
- 1 cup smoked sausage, chopped
- 1 can (8 oz.) jumbo lump crabmeat, drained
- ¼ cup chopped roasted sweet red peppers
- 6 large eggs
- ½ cup heavy whipping cream
- 2 tsp. Louisiana-style hot sauce
- ½ tsp. salt
- 6 bacon strips, cooked and crumbled
- ¼ cup thinly sliced green onions

1. Preheat oven to 350°. In a small bowl, combine mayonnaise, lemon juice, sugar and seafood seasoning. Refrigerate until serving.
2. Meanwhile, in a large bowl, combine the potatoes, sausage, crab and red peppers. Divide among 12 greased muffin cups. In another large bowl, whisk the eggs, cream, hot sauce and salt. Pour over the potato mixture. Top with the bacon.
3. Bake until a knife inserted in center comes out clean, 30-35 minutes. Serve with sauce and green onion.
1 FRITTATA 223 cal., 18g fat (6g sat. fat), 135mg chol., 604mg sod., 5g carb. (2g sugars, 0 fiber), 10g pro.

GOES GREAT WITH ...
Shakshuka can be served with any breakfast potato or vegetable.

TOASTY PUMPKIN WAFFLES

QUINOA BOWL

This is such a bright and healthy way to enjoy quinoa!
—Karen Kelly, Germantown, MD

TAKES: 30 min. • **MAKES:** 1 serving

- ⅔ cup water
- ⅓ cup quinoa, rinsed
- ¼ tsp. salt, divided
- ¼ tsp. pepper, divided
- 1 large egg
- ½ cup grape tomatoes, halved
- ¼ cup loosely packed basil leaves
- ½ medium ripe avocado, peeled and sliced
  Balsamic glaze

1. Place the water in a small saucepan. Bring to a boil; add the quinoa and ⅛ tsp. each salt and pepper. Reduce heat; cover and simmer until tender, 12-15 minutes.
2. Meanwhile, heat a small nonstick skillet over medium-high heat. Break the egg into pan; reduce the heat to low. Sprinkle with the remaining ⅛ tsp. salt and ⅛ tsp. pepper. Cook egg until white is set and yolk begins to thicken, turning once if desired.
3. Fluff quinoa with a fork; place in a serving bowl. Top with tomatoes, basil, avocado and cooked egg. Drizzle with balsamic glaze or serve on the side.

1 BOWL 411 cal., 19g fat (3g sat. fat), 186mg chol., 674mg sod., 46g carb. (4g sugars, 10g fiber), 17g pro.

TOASTY PUMPKIN WAFFLES ✓

When I really want to have comfort food, I serve these waffles. They are beautiful with a fresh sprig of mint atop the sweet butter. It was my most requested recipe when I owned a bed and breakfast.
—Brenda Ryan, Marshall, MO

TAKES: 30 min.
MAKES: 3 servings (1 cup butter)

- 1½ cups all-purpose flour
- 1 Tbsp. brown sugar
- 1 tsp. baking powder
- ¼ tsp. salt
- 1 large egg, lightly beaten, room temperature
- 1¼ cups whole milk
- ⅔ cup canned pumpkin
- 4½ tsp. butter, melted
- ⅓ cup chopped pecans

MAPLE CRANBERRY BUTTER
- ½ cup fresh or frozen cranberries
- ¼ cup maple syrup
- 1 cup butter, softened
  Additional maple syrup, optional

1. In a large bowl, combine flour, brown sugar, baking powder and salt. Whisk the egg, milk, pumpkin and butter; stir into dry ingredients until blended. Fold in pecans.
2. Bake in a preheated waffle maker according to manufacturer's directions until golden brown.
3. Meanwhile, in a small saucepan, combine the cranberries and syrup. Cook over medium heat until berries pop, about 10 minutes. Transfer to a small bowl; cool slightly. Beat in butter until blended.
4. Serve waffles with maple cranberry butter, and syrup if desired. Refrigerate or freeze leftover butter.

1 WAFFLE WITH 2 TSP. BUTTER 595 cal., 30g fat (13g sat. fat), 115mg chol., 557mg sod., 69g carb. (15g sugars, 5g fiber), 14g pro.

TEST KITCHEN TIP
Adding pumpkin spice seasoning is a quick way to increase the pumpkin flavor in these waffles.

QUINOA BOWL

SHEET-PAN BACON & EGGS

I re-created this recipe from inspiration I found on social media, and it was a huge hit! Use any cheeses and spices you like; you can even try seasoned potatoes.
—*Bonnie Hawkins, Elkhorn, WI*

PREP: 20 min. • **BAKE:** 40 min.
MAKES: 8 servings

10	bacon strips
1	pkg. (30 oz.) frozen shredded hash brown potatoes, thawed
1	tsp. garlic powder
1	tsp. dried basil
1	tsp. dried oregano
½	tsp. salt
½	tsp. crushed red pepper flakes
1½	cups shredded pepper jack cheese
1	cup shredded cheddar cheese
8	large eggs
¼	tsp. pepper
¼	cup chopped green onions

1. Preheat oven to 400°. Place bacon in a single layer in a 15x10x1-in. baking sheet. Bake until partially cooked but not crisp, about 10 minutes. Remove to paper towels to drain. When cool enough to handle, chop bacon.
2. In a large bowl, combine potatoes and seasonings; spread evenly into drippings in pan. Bake until golden brown, 25-30 minutes.
3. Sprinkle with the cheeses. With the back of a spoon, make 8 wells in the potato mixture. Break 1 egg in each well; sprinkle with pepper and bacon. Bake until egg whites are completely set and yolks begin to thicken but are not hard, 12-14 minutes. Sprinkle with chopped green onion.

1 SERVING 446 cal., 30g fat (13g sat. fat), 246mg chol., 695mg sod., 22g carb. (2g sugars, 1g fiber), 22g pro.

SHEET-PAN BACON & EGGS

**PANCAKES WITH
PEANUT MAPLE SYRUP**

HAM & CHEESE SLIDERS

I turned one of my favorite sliders into a breakfast sandwich, then exchanged the regular mustard for spicy brown to give it more zip. I added the same mustard to the eggs, and the recipe is now a mainstay. When we host overnight guests, I make these sandwiches the night before and finish them in the morning before popping them into the oven to bake.
—*Jill Landis, Shinnston, WV*

TAKES: 30 min. • **MAKES:** 1 dozen

- ½ cup butter, cubed, plus 1 Tbsp. butter, divided
- 2 Tbsp. brown sugar
- 2 Tbsp. spicy brown mustard, divided
- 1 tsp. Worcestershire sauce
- 12 dinner rolls, split *hawiian*
- 6 slices deli ham, halved
- 6 large eggs
- 2 Tbsp. 2% milk
- 6 slices cheddar cheese, halved

1. Preheat oven to 350°. In a small saucepan, combine ½ cup butter, brown sugar, 1 Tbsp. mustard and Worcestershire sauce; bring to a boil. Cook and stir until sugar is dissolved, 1-2 minutes. Remove from the heat.
2. Place roll bottoms, cut side up, in an ungreased 13x9-in. baking dish. Top each with 1 piece of ham.
3. In a large bowl, whisk eggs, milk and remaining 1 Tbsp. mustard until blended. In a large nonstick skillet, heat remaining 1 Tbsp. butter over medium heat. Pour in egg mixture; cook and stir until eggs are thickened and no liquid egg remains. Spoon scrambled eggs evenly over ham. Top with the cheese. Replace roll tops. Brush the butter mixture over roll tops. Bake, uncovered, until cheese is melted, 10-15 minutes.
1 SLIDER 299 cal., 18g fat (10g sat. fat), 154mg chol., 524mg sod., 22g carb. (4g sugars, 1g fiber), 12g pro.

PANCAKES WITH
PEANUT MAPLE SYRUP

My family loves eating s'mores around the campfire when we vacation at the lake. Campfire pancakes are my tribute to those happy times.
—*Cheryl Snavely, Hagerstown, MD*

TAKES: 20 min.
MAKES: 8 pancakes (¼ cup syrup)

- 1 pkg. (6½ oz.) chocolate chip muffin mix
- ⅔ cup 2% milk
- 1 large egg, lightly beaten, room temperature
- ½ cup miniature marshmallows
- ¼ cup butterscotch chips
- ¼ cup maple syrup
- 1 Tbsp. chunky peanut butter

1. In a large bowl, combine muffin mix, milk and egg; stir just until moistened. Fold in marshmallows and chips.
2. Lightly grease a griddle; heat over medium heat. Pour batter by ¼ cupfuls onto griddle. Cook until bubbles on top begin to pop and bottoms are golden brown. Turn; cook until second side is golden brown.
3. Meanwhile, in a microwave-safe bowl, microwave the maple syrup and peanut butter in 10-to-20-second intervals until heated through. Serve with pancakes.
2 PANCAKES WITH 1 TBSP. SYRUP MIXTURE 407 cal., 13g fat (7g sat. fat), 50mg chol., 386mg sod., 63g carb. (43g sugars, 2g fiber), 8g pro.

EVERYTHING
BREAKFAST SLIDERS

GOES GREAT WITH ...
Blueberry
Cantaloupe Salad
(p. 304) makes
a tasty side for
these sliders.

EVERYTHING BREAKFAST SLIDERS

These breakfast sliders combine all your favorite morning foods—eggs, bacon and bagels—into one tasty package. Try them for lunch and dinner too!
—*Rashanda Cobbins, Aurora, CO*

PREP: 30 min. • **BAKE:** 15 min.
MAKES: 8 servings

- 8 large eggs
- ¼ cup 2% milk
- 2 green onions, thinly sliced
- ¼ tsp. pepper
- 8 Tbsp. spreadable chive and onion cream cheese
- 8 miniature bagels, split
- 8 slices cheddar cheese, halved
- 8 slices Canadian bacon
- 8 cooked bacon strips, halved

GLAZE
- 2 Tbsp. butter, melted
- 1½ tsp. maple syrup
- ⅛ tsp. garlic powder
- 2 Tbsp. everything seasoning blend

1. Preheat oven to 375°. Heat a large nonstick skillet over medium heat. In a large bowl, whisk eggs, milk, green onion and pepper until blended; pour into skillet. Cook and stir until eggs are thickened and no liquid egg remains; remove from heat.
2. Spread cream cheese over bagel bottoms; place in a greased 13x9-in. baking dish. Layer each with 1 piece of cheese and 1 slice of Canadian bacon. Spoon scrambled eggs over top. Layer with remaining cheese slices and cooked bacon. Replace bagel tops. Stir together butter, maple syrup and garlic powder; brush over bagel tops. Sprinkle with the everything seasoning blend.
3. Bake until tops are golden brown and cheese is melted, 12-15 minutes.

1 SLIDER 415 cal., 26g fat (13g sat. fat), 253mg chol., 1070mg sod., 18g carb. (4g sugars, 1g fiber), 24g pro.

CREAMY PESTO & BACON EGGS BENEDICT

CREAMY PESTO & BACON EGGS BENEDICT

One of my favorite dishes is eggs Benedict. I adore the traditional version, but I also have fun using other flavors. This is my Italian take using a semi-homemade creamy pesto sauce.
—*Jenn Tidwell, Fair Oaks, CA*

TAKES: 25 min. • **MAKES:** 4 servings

- 2 Tbsp. butter
- 1 Tbsp. all-purpose flour
- 1 cup 2% milk
- 1 cup grated Parmesan cheese
- 3 Tbsp. prepared pesto
- ⅛ tsp. ground nutmeg
- ⅛ tsp. pepper
- 4 large eggs
- 2 onion bagels, split and toasted
- 8 cooked bacon strips

1. In a small saucepan, melt butter over medium heat. Stir in flour until smooth; gradually whisk in milk. Bring to a boil, stirring constantly; cook and stir until slightly thickened, 3-5 minutes. Stir in cheese, pesto, nutmeg and pepper. Keep warm.
2. Place 2-3 in. water in a large saucepan or skillet with high sides. Bring to a boil; adjust heat to maintain a gentle simmer. Break 1 egg into a small bowl; holding bowl close to surface of water, slip egg into water. Repeat with remaining eggs.
3. Cook, uncovered, until whites are completely set and yolks begin to thicken but are not hard, 3-5 minutes. Using a slotted spoon, lift eggs out of water.
4. Top each bagel half with 2 slices of bacon, 1 poached egg and sauce. Serve immediately.

1 SERVING 537 cal., 30g fat (13g sat. fat), 246mg chol., 1255mg sod., 38g carb. (8g sugars, 1g fiber), 28g pro.

BAKED BLUEBERRY GINGER PANCAKE

My kids just love pancakes, so I came up with this baked version that saves a lot of time in the morning. They always gobble these ginger-kissed breakfast squares right up!
—Erin Wright, Wallace, KS

TAKES: 30 min. • **MAKES:** 9 servings

- 2 large eggs, room temperature
- 1½ cups 2% milk
- ¼ cup butter, melted
- 2 cups all-purpose flour
- 2 Tbsp. sugar
- 3 tsp. baking powder
- 1½ tsp. ground ginger
- ½ tsp. salt
- 2 cups fresh or frozen unsweetened blueberries
  Maple syrup

1. Preheat the oven to 350°. Combine eggs, milk and butter. Whisk the next 5 ingredients; add to the egg mixture. Spoon batter into a 9-in. square baking pan coated with cooking spray. Sprinkle blueberries over top.

2. Bake until a toothpick inserted in center comes out clean, 20-25 minutes. Cut into squares. Serve squares with warm maple syrup.

1 PIECE 213 cal., 7g fat (4g sat. fat), 58mg chol., 368mg sod., 31g carb. (8g sugars, 2g fiber), 6g pro. **DIABETIC EXCHANGES** 2 starch, 1½ fat.

TEST KITCHEN TIP
If your family isn't big on ginger, feel free to scale it back or substitute something else, such as ground cinnamon or grated lemon zest.

BAKED BLUEBERRY GINGER PANCAKE

CORNMEAL PANCAKES

These fluffy blueberry cornmeal pancakes are one of my family's favorites. Grandma's standby of store-bought corn muffin mix makes quick work of the job.
—Carolyn Eskew, Dayton, OH

TAKES: 30 min. • **MAKES:** 10 pancakes

- 1 pkg. (8½ oz.) cornbread/muffin mix
- 1 cup fresh or frozen blueberries
- ⅓ cup canned white or shoepeg corn
  Maple syrup

In a large bowl, prepare muffin mix according to package directions. Gently stir in blueberries and corn. Lightly grease a griddle; warm over medium heat. Pour batter by ¼ cupfuls onto griddle; flatten slightly. Cook until bottoms are golden brown. Turn; cook until second sides are golden brown. Serve with syrup.

2 PANCAKES 251 cal., 7g fat (2g sat. fat), 39mg chol., 454mg sod., 41g carb. (14g sugars, 4g fiber), 6g pro.

GREEK SALAD-INSPIRED QUICHE

GREEK SALAD-INSPIRED QUICHE

I love using my cast-iron skillet to create this meatless, family-sized Greek quiche for a quick meal. Just add a green salad and some pita bread, and dinner is on the table with little fuss and no extra dishes to wash!
—*Donna M Ryan, Topsfield, MA*

PREP: 20 min. • **BAKE:** 20 min. + standing
MAKES: 6 servings

- 1   Tbsp. olive oil
- 1   cup cherry tomatoes, halved
- 2/3 cup finely chopped green pepper
- 1/2 cup thinly sliced red onion
- 2/3 cup chopped fresh spinach
- 2   garlic cloves, minced
- 1   cup crumbled feta cheese
- 1/2 cup pitted Greek olives, sliced
- 6   large eggs
- 1   cup 2% milk
- 1   Tbsp. minced fresh oregano or 1 tsp. dried oregano
- 1/2 tsp. salt
- 1/8 to 3/4 tsp. crushed red pepper flakes

1. Preheat the oven to 375°. In a 9-in. cast-iron or other ovenproof skillet, heat oil over medium-high heat. Add tomatoes, green peppers and onion; cook and stir until the vegetables are tender, 6-7 minutes; drain. Add spinach and garlic; cook and stir until spinach is wilted, 1-2 minutes. Remove from heat and stir in feta and olives.
2. In a large bowl, whisk eggs, milk, oregano, salt and pepper flakes until blended. Pour over vegetables.
3. Bake until a knife inserted in center comes out clean, 20-25 minutes. Let stand 10 minutes before serving.
1 PIECE 354 cal., 22g fat (9g sat. fat), 175mg chol., 778mg sod., 25g carb. (5g sugars, 2g fiber), 12g pro.

TEST KITCHEN TIP
Add sliced mushrooms to the tomatoes, pepper and onion.

OMELET WAFFLES WITH SAUSAGE CHEESE SAUCE

This waffle-omelet mashup is topped with sausage, onions and sweet peppers, and is finished with a chunky cheesy sauce. This dish is fun and satisfying to eat in the morning or evening.
—*Ronna Farley, Rockville, MD*

PREP: 30 min. • **COOK:** 5 min./batch
MAKES: 4 servings

- 1 lb. bulk pork sausage
- ½ lb. whole fresh mushrooms, chopped
- ½ cup chopped onion
- ½ cup chopped sweet red pepper
- 2 Tbsp. all-purpose flour
- 2 cups half-and-half cream, divided
- 1 tsp. seasoned salt, divided
- 1 cup shredded sharp cheddar cheese
- 8 large eggs, room temperature
- 1 Tbsp. minced fresh parsley

1. Preheat waffle maker. In a large skillet, cook sausage, mushrooms, onion and red pepper over medium heat until sausage is no longer pink and vegetables are tender, 8-10 minutes, breaking sausage into crumbles; drain. Remove from heat and keep warm.
2. Meanwhile, in a large saucepan, whisk flour, 1¾ cups cream and ½ tsp. seasoned salt until smooth. Bring to a boil, stirring constantly; cook and stir until thickened, 2-3 minutes. Stir in cheese and 1 cup sausage mixture until cheese is melted. Remove from heat and keep warm.
3. In a large bowl, whisk the eggs and remaining ¼ cup cream and ½ tsp. seasoned salt until blended. Bake in a well-greased waffle maker until golden brown, 2-3 minutes. Serve with sausage mixture and cheese sauce; sprinkle with parsley.

2 WAFFLES 734 cal., 56g fat (24g sat. fat), 521mg chol., 1461mg sod., 15g carb. (7g sugars, 1g fiber), 38g pro.

OMELET WAFFLES WITH SAUSAGE CHEESE SAUCE

GOES GREAT WITH ...
Slice up some oranges for a no-fuss side.

SWEET POTATO & EGG SKILLET
(PICTURED ON PAGE 5)

I try to incorporate nutritious sweet potatoes in meals as often as possible. I came up with this recipe to feed my family a healthy, hearty meal—and it worked!
—Jeanne Larson, Rancho Santa Margarita, CA

TAKES: 25 min. • **MAKES:** 4 servings

- 2 Tbsp. butter
- 2 medium sweet potatoes, peeled and shredded (about 4 cups)
- 1 garlic clove, minced
- ½ tsp. salt, divided
- ⅛ tsp. dried thyme
- 2 cups fresh baby spinach
- 4 large eggs
- ⅛ tsp. coarsely ground pepper

1. In a large cast-iron or other heavy skillet, heat the butter over low heat. Add sweet potatoes, garlic, ¼ tsp. salt and thyme; cook, covered, until potatoes are almost tender, 4-5 minutes, stirring occasionally. Stir in spinach just until wilted, 2-3 minutes.
2. With the back of a spoon, make 4 wells in potato mixture. Break 1 egg into each well. Sprinkle eggs with pepper and remaining ¼ tsp. salt. Cook, covered, over medium-low heat until egg whites are completely set and yolks begin to thicken but are not hard, 5-7 minutes.
1 SERVING 224 cal., 11g fat (5g sat. fat), 201mg chol., 433mg sod., 24g carb. (10g sugars, 3g fiber), 8g pro. **DIABETIC EXCHANGES** 1½ starch, 1½ fat, 1 medium-fat meat.

TEST KITCHEN TIP
If you like your eggs sunny-side up, leave the pan uncovered while they cook.

TEX-MEX QUICHE

I discovered this recipe many years ago, and it's still one of my favorites today. It's quick and easy, yet very tasty. It's also a good dish to take to potlucks or to serve as an appetizer.
—Hazel Turner, Houston, TX

325°

PREP: 10 min. • **BAKE:** 45 min. + cooling
MAKES: 6 servings

- 1 tsp. chili powder
- 1 pastry shell (9 in.), unbaked
- 1 cup shredded cheddar cheese
- 1 cup shredded Monterey Jack cheese
- 1 Tbsp. all-purpose flour
- 3 large eggs, beaten
- 1½ cups half-and-half cream
- 1 can (4 oz.) chopped green chiles, well drained
- 1 can (2¼ oz.) sliced ripe olives, drained
- 1 tsp. salt
- ¼ tsp. pepper

1. Sprinkle chili powder over the inside of the crust. Combine cheeses with flour and place in crust.
2. Combine eggs, cream, chiles, olives, salt and pepper. Pour over cheese.
3. Bake at 325° for 45-55 minutes or until a knife inserted in the center comes out clean. Cool for 10 minutes before cutting into wedges.
1 PIECE 438 cal., 30g fat (17g sat. fat), 180mg chol., 985mg sod., 23g carb. (4g sugars, 1g fiber), 15g pro.

CHAPTER 2

SNACKS FOR SUPPER

P. 29

P. 33

P. 30

P. 37

PEPPERONI-ZUCCHINI ROUNDS

PEPPERONI-ZUCCHINI ROUNDS

This simple recipe is the perfect, low-carb way to satisfy your pizza cravings on busy nights.
—Taste of Home *Test Kitchen*

TAKES: 20 min. • **MAKES:** about 2 dozen

- 1   large zucchini (about 11 oz.), cut diagonally into ¼-in. slices
- ⅛ tsp. salt
- ⅛ tsp. pepper
- ⅓ cup pizza sauce
- ¾ cup shredded part-skim mozzarella cheese
- ½ cup miniature pepperoni slices
     Minced fresh basil

1. Preheat the broiler. Arrange zucchini in a single layer on a greased baking sheet. Broil 3-4 in. from heat just until crisp-tender, 1-2 minutes per side.
2. Sprinkle zucchini with salt and pepper; top with sauce, cheese and pepperoni. Broil until the cheese is melted, about 1 minute. Sprinkle with basil.

1 MINI PIZZA 29 cal., 2g fat (1g sat. fat), 5mg chol., 108mg sod., 1g carb. (1g sugars, 0 fiber), 2g pro.

SOUTHWESTERN EGG ROLLS

SOUTHWESTERN EGG ROLLS

At my church potluck, these crispy, spicy snacks went fast thanks to the triple kick from the Italian sausage, Mexicorn and chiles. Sour cream and guacamole are tasty additions too.
—Jacqueline Bower, Washington, IA

TAKES: 30 min. • **MAKES:** 1½ dozen

- 1   lb. bulk hot Italian sausage
- 1   can (15 oz.) black beans, rinsed and drained
- 1   can (11 oz.) Mexicorn, drained
- 1   can (10 oz.) diced tomatoes and green chiles, undrained
- 1   pkg. (8.8 oz.) ready-to-serve Spanish rice
- 18 egg roll wrappers

   Oil for frying
   Optional: Sour cream and guacamole

1. In a large skillet, cook sausage over medium heat 6-8 minutes or until no longer pink, breaking it into crumbles; drain. Stir in beans, Mexicorn, tomatoes and chiles, and rice; bring to a boil. Reduce heat; simmer, uncovered, 5 minutes, stirring occasionally.
2. With 1 corner of an egg roll wrapper facing you, place ⅓ cup filling just below center. (Cover remaining wrappers with a damp paper towel until ready to use.) Fold bottom corner over filling; moisten remaining wrapper edges with water. Fold side corners toward center over filling. Roll up tightly, pressing at tip to seal. Repeat.

3. In an electric skillet, heat 1 in. oil to 375°. Fry the egg rolls, 2 at a time, 1-2 minutes or until golden brown, turning occasionally. Drain on paper towels. If desired, serve with sour cream and guacamole.

1 EGG ROLL 333 cal., 19g fat (4g sat. fat), 21mg chol., 643mg sod., 31g carb. (2g sugars, 2g fiber), 10g pro.

TEST KITCHEN TIP

We recommend frying these Tex-Mex egg rolls in peanut or canola oil. Refined oils such as these are the best for frying because they can withstand a high smoke point.

CHICKEN SKEWERS WITH COOL AVOCADO SAUCE

I'm always looking for lighter recipes to take on tailgate outings—and this one works fabulously for grilling.
—*Veronica Callaghan, Glastonbury, CT*

PREP: 25 min. + marinating
GRILL: 10 min.
MAKES: 16 skewers (¾ cup sauce)

- 1   lb. boneless skinless chicken breasts
- ½   cup lime juice
- 1   Tbsp. balsamic vinegar
- 2   tsp. minced chipotle pepper in adobo sauce
- ½   tsp. salt

SAUCE

- 1   medium ripe avocado, peeled and pitted
- ½   cup fat-free sour cream
- 2   Tbsp. minced fresh cilantro
- 2   tsp. lime juice
- 1   tsp. grated lime zest
- ¼   tsp. salt

1. Flatten chicken to ¼-in. thickness; cut lengthwise into sixteen 1-in.-wide strips. In a large bowl, combine the lime juice, vinegar, chipotle pepper and salt; add the chicken and turn to coat. Cover and refrigerate for 30 minutes.
2. Meanwhile, for the sauce, place the remaining ingredients in a food processor; cover and process until blended. Transfer to a serving bowl; cover and refrigerate until serving.
3. Drain chicken, discarding marinade. Thread meat onto 4 metal or soaked wooden skewers. On a lightly oiled rack, grill skewers, covered, over medium heat (or broil 4 in. from the heat) for 8-12 minutes or until no longer pink, turning frequently. Serve with sauce.

1 SKEWER WITH ABOUT 2 TSP. SAUCE
59 cal., 3g fat (0 sat. fat), 17mg chol., 74mg sod., 3g carb. (1g sugars, 1g fiber), 6g pro.
DIABETIC EXCHANGES 1 lean meat, ½ fat.

SWEET POTATO & BEAN QUESADILLAS

This recipe is special to me because it's healthy, easy, fast, fun and delicious!
—*Brittany Hubbard, St. Paul, MN*

TAKES: 30 min. • **MAKES:** 4 servings

- 2   medium sweet potatoes
- 4   whole wheat tortillas (8 in.)
- ¾   cup canned black beans, rinsed and drained
- ½   cup shredded pepper jack cheese
- ¾   cup salsa

1. Scrub sweet potatoes; pierce several times with a fork. Place on a microwave-safe plate. Microwave, uncovered, on high, turning once, until very tender, 7-9 minutes.
2. When cool enough to handle, cut each potato lengthwise in half. Scoop out pulp. Spread onto half of each tortilla; top with beans and cheese. Fold other half of the tortilla over filling.
3. Heat a cast-iron skillet or griddle over medium heat. Cook the quesadillas until golden brown and the cheese is melted, 2-3 minutes on each side. Serve with the salsa.

1 QUESADILLA WITH 3 TBSP. SALSA
306 cal., 8g fat (3g sat. fat), 15mg chol., 531mg sod., 46g carb. (9g sugars, 6g fiber), 11g pro.

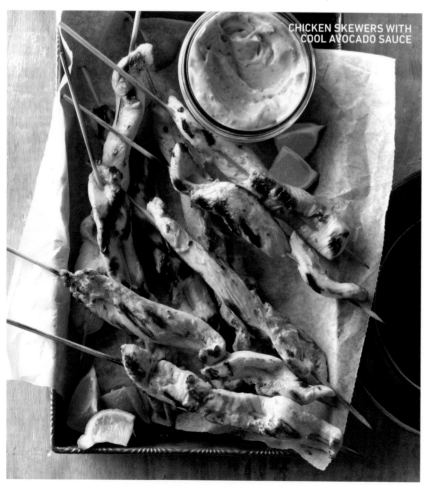

CHICKEN SKEWERS WITH COOL AVOCADO SAUCE

PIZZA MUFFIN CUPS

PIZZA MUFFIN CUPS

I just baked these mini pizzas, and the kids are already asking for more. The no-cook pizza sauce and refrigerated dough make this meal a snap.
—Melissa Haines, Valparaiso, IN

PREP: 25 min. • **BAKE:** 10 min.
MAKES: 8 servings

1   can (15 oz.) tomato sauce
1   can (6 oz.) tomato paste
1   tsp. dried basil
½   tsp. garlic salt
¼   tsp. onion powder
¼   tsp. sugar
1   tube (11 oz.) refrigerated thin pizza crust
1½   cups shredded part-skim mozzarella cheese

OPTIONAL TOPPINGS
    Pepperoni, olives, sausage, onion, green pepper, Canadian bacon, pineapple, tomatoes, fresh basil and crushed red pepper flakes

1. Preheat the oven to 425°. In a small bowl, mix the first 6 ingredients.
2. Unroll pizza dough; cut into 16 squares. Press squares onto bottoms and up sides of 16 ungreased muffin cups, allowing corners to hang over edges.
3. Spoon 1 Tbsp. sauce mixture into each cup. Top with the cheese; add optional toppings as desired. Bake 10-12 minutes or until crust is golden brown. Serve pizzas with remaining sauce mixture.

FREEZE OPTION Freeze cooled baked pizzas in a resealable freezer container. To use, reheat pizzas on a baking sheet in a preheated 425° oven until heated through.

2 PIZZAS WITH 2 TBSP. SAUCE 209 cal., 8g fat (3g sat. fat), 14mg chol., 747mg sod., 26g carb. (5g sugars, 2g fiber), 10g pro.

ARTICHOKE & SPINACH DIP PIZZA

If you love artichoke-spinach dip, this easy pizza is for you. Serve it as a quick dinner or a hearty appetizer.
—*Shelly Bevington, Hermiston, OR*

TAKES: 20 min. • **MAKES:** 24 pieces

- 1   prebaked 12-in. pizza crust
- 1   Tbsp. olive oil
- 1   cup spinach dip
- 1   cup shredded part-skim mozzarella cheese
- 1   jar (7½ oz.) marinated quartered artichoke hearts, drained
- ½   cup oil-packed sun-dried tomatoes, patted dry and chopped
- ¼   cup chopped red onion

1. Preheat oven to 450°. Place crust on an ungreased pizza pan; brush with oil. Spread spinach dip over top. Sprinkle with the cheese, artichokes, tomatoes and onion.
2. Bake until cheese is melted and edge is lightly browned, 8-10 minutes. Cut into 24 pieces.

1 PIECE 127 cal., 9g fat (2g sat. fat), 6mg chol., 213mg sod., 10g carb. (1g sugars, 0 fiber), 3g pro.

GREAT GARLIC
Garlic oil is a tasty substitute for the olive oil in this recipe. Give it a try, and you will find lots of uses for it.

ARTICHOKE & SPINACH DIP PIZZA

PIZZA PUFFS ✓

What's more fun than a pizza puff? You can substitute any meat or vegetable for the pepperoni and any cheese for the mozzarella.
—*Vivi Taylor, Middleburg, FL*

TAKES: 30 min. • **MAKES:** 20 puffs

- 1 loaf (1 lb.) frozen pizza dough, thawed
- 20 slices pepperoni
- 8 oz. part-skim mozzarella cheese, cut into 20 cubes
- ¼ cup butter
- 2 small garlic cloves, minced
  Dash salt
  Marinara sauce, warmed
  Optional: Crushed red pepper flakes and grated Parmesan cheese

1. Preheat oven to 400°. Shape dough into 1½-in. balls; flatten into ⅛-in.-thick circles. Place 1 pepperoni slice and 1 cheese cube in center of each circle; wrap dough around pepperoni and cheese. Pinch edges to seal; shape into a ball. Repeat with the remaining dough, pepperoni and cheese. Place seam side down on greased baking sheets; bake until light golden brown, 10-15 minutes. Cool slightly.
2. Meanwhile, in a small saucepan, melt butter over low heat. Add garlic and salt, taking care not to brown butter or garlic; brush over puffs. Serve with marinara sauce, and sprinkle with red pepper flakes and Parmesan cheese if desired.
FREEZE OPTION Cover and freeze unbaked pizza puffs on waxed paper-lined baking sheets until firm. Transfer to a freezer container; seal and return to freezer. To use, preheat oven to 400°; bake pizza puffs on greased baking sheets as directed, increasing time as necessary until golden brown.
1 PIZZA PUFF 120 cal., 6g fat (3g sat. fat), 15mg chol., 189mg sod., 11g carb. (1g sugars, 0 fiber), 5g pro.

REUBEN ROUNDS

Fans of the classic Reuben sandwich will go crazy for delicious baked pastry spirals of corned beef, Swiss cheese and sauerkraut. They're so easy to make, and bottled Thousand Island dressing makes the perfect dipping sauce.
—*Cheryl Snavely, Hagerstown, MD*

TAKES: 30 min. • **MAKES:** 16 rounds

- 1 sheet frozen puff pastry, thawed
- 6 slices Swiss cheese
- 5 slices deli corned beef
- ½ cup sauerkraut, rinsed and well drained
- 1 tsp. caraway seeds
- ¼ cup Thousand Island salad dressing

1. Preheat oven to 400°. Unfold puff pastry; layer with cheese, corned beef and sauerkraut to within ½-in. of edges. Roll up jelly-roll style. Trim ends and cut crosswise into 16 slices. Place rolls on greased baking sheets, cut side down. Sprinkle with caraway seeds.
2. Bake until golden brown, 18-20 minutes. Serve with salad dressing.
1 REUBEN ROUND 114 cal., 7g fat (2g sat. fat), 8mg chol., 198mg sod., 10g carb. (1g sugars, 1g fiber), 3g pro.

TOT-CHOS

3. Bake, uncovered, 10 minutes. Sprinkle with the jalapenos, cilantro and green onions. Top with avocado and tomato. Serve with sour cream.
1 SERVING 378 cal., 23g fat (9g sat. fat), 45mg chol., 1152mg sod., 29g carb. (5g sugars, 5g fiber), 13g pro.

GRILLED GLAZED DRUMMIES
My family prefers these mild, slightly sweet chicken wings to the traditional hot wings. They're truly a favorite.
—*Laura Mahaffey, Annapolis, MD*

PREP: 10 min. + marinating
GRILL: 15 min.
MAKES: about 24 drummies

- 1 cup ketchup
- ⅓ cup reduced-sodium soy sauce
- 4 tsp. honey
- ¾ tsp. ground ginger
- ½ tsp. garlic powder
- 3 lbs. fresh or frozen chicken drumettes, thawed
  Optional: Sliced green onions and ranch dressing

1. In a small bowl, combine the first 5 ingredients. Pour 1 cup marinade into a large shallow dish. Add the chicken; turn to coat. Cover and refrigerate for at least 4 hours or overnight. Cover and refrigerate remaining marinade for basting.
2. Drain chicken, discarding marinade. Grill, covered, over medium heat until juices run clear, 15-20 minutes, turning and basting occasionally with reserved marinade. If desired, top with sliced green onions and serve with ranch dressing.
1 DRUMMY 141 cal., 9g fat (2g sat. fat), 43mg chol., 311mg sod., 3g carb. (3g sugars, 0 fiber), 11g pro.

TOT-CHOS
This is an easy, versatile party appetizer that everyone loves for dinner too! If you can't find chorizo, ground beef or chicken are terrific too. Top as desired!
—*Connie Krupp, Racine, WI*

PREP: 15 min. • **BAKE:** 50 min.
MAKES: 12 servings

- 1 pkg. (32 oz.) frozen Tater Tots
- 7 oz. fresh chorizo or bulk spicy pork sausage
- 1 can (14½ oz.) diced tomatoes with mild green chiles, undrained
- 12 oz. Velveeta, cubed
- 1 can (15 oz.) black beans, rinsed and drained
- ½ cup pickled jalapeno slices
- ¼ cup minced fresh cilantro
- ⅓ cup thinly sliced green onions
- 1 medium ripe avocado, cubed
- 1 medium tomato, chopped
- ½ cup sour cream

1. Preheat oven to 425°. Place Tater Tots in an ungreased 13x9-in. baking dish. Bake, uncovered, 40 minutes.
2. Meanwhile, in a large skillet, cook the chorizo over medium heat until meat is no longer pink, breaking into crumbles; drain. Remove from pan and set aside. In same skillet, add the tomatoes and chiles and cheese. Cook, uncovered, over medium heat until blended and the cheese is melted, stirring occasionally. Pour over Tater Tots. Sprinkle with the chorizo and black beans.

GRILLED GLAZED DRUMMIES

CHEESEBURGER WAFFLE FRIES

These loaded fries are perfect for game-day grazing and no-fuss dinners alike. Load them up with all the toppings or let everyone claim part of the platter that they can top with their faves.
—Taste of Home *Test Kitchen*

TAKES: 25 min. • **MAKES:** 8 servings

- 1   pkg. (22 oz.) frozen waffle fries
- 1   lb. ground beef
- ⅔   cup water
- 1   envelope taco seasoning
- 1   cup shredded cheddar cheese
- 8   bacon strips, cooked and crumbled
- ½   cup dill pickle slices
- ¾   cup shredded lettuce
- 1   medium tomato, seeded and chopped
- ¼   cup secret burger sauce
- ¼   cup ketchup
- 1   Tbsp. prepared mustard

1. Bake fries according to the package directions. Meanwhile, in a large skillet, cook the beef over medium heat until no longer pink, 5-7 minutes, breaking into crumbles; drain. Return to the pan. Add water and taco seasoning. Cook and stir until sauce thickens, about 3 minutes.
2. Transfer the fries to a 10-in. cast-iron or other ovenproof skillet. Top with the seasoned ground beef, shredded cheese and bacon. Return to the oven until the cheese is melted, about 5 minutes. Top with pickles, lettuce and tomato. Drizzle with secret sauce, ketchup and mustard.
1 CUP 407 cal., 24g fat (11g sat. fat), 71mg chol., 1082mg sod., 27g carb. (3g sugars, 3g fiber), 22g pro.

TEST KITCHEN TIP
For best results, bake fries until they're nice and crispy so they don't get soggy once the toppings are added.

CHEESEBURGER
WAFFLE FRIES

SALSA STEAK
GARLIC TOASTS

CHICKEN CHILI NACHOS

Spicy nachos with plenty of chicken and two kinds of beans make a fun and filling snack as well as a quick and easy dinner!
—Karen Horning, Rockford, IL

TAKES: 25 min. • **MAKES:** 8 servings

- 1 lb. boneless skinless chicken breasts, cubed
- 1 can (10 oz.) diced tomatoes and green chiles, undrained
- 1 can (16 oz.) kidney beans, rinsed and drained
- 1 can (16 oz.) chili beans, undrained
- 1 tsp. paprika
- 1 tsp. ground cumin
- ½ tsp. cayenne pepper
- 1 pkg. (13½ oz.) tortilla chips
- 1½ cups shredded Mexican cheese blend

1. In a large skillet coated with cooking spray, saute chicken until no longer pink. Add the tomatoes and chiles; cook over medium-high heat for 3 minutes or until the tomato juice is reduced. Stir in beans, paprika, cumin and cayenne; cook for 5 minutes or until heated through.
2. Arrange the tortilla chips on 2 large microwave-safe plates; sprinkle each with ¼ cup cheese. Top with chicken mixture and the remaining cheese. Microwave, uncovered, on high 25-30 seconds or until the cheese is melted.
½ CUP 484 cal., 19g fat (7g sat. fat), 50mg chol., 754mg sod., 54g carb. (2g sugars, 8g fiber), 26g pro.

SALSA STEAK GARLIC TOASTS ✓

These open-faced steak sandwiches play up the popular combo of steak and garlic bread. The salsa, sour cream and garnish elevate them into quick, satisfying meals. Substitute the chopped green onions or chives for cilantro if desired.
—Arlene Erlbach, Morton Grove, IL

TAKES: 25 min. • **MAKES:** 4 servings

- 4 slices frozen garlic Texas toast
- 1 Tbsp. olive oil
- 1 beef top sirloin steak (1 lb.), thinly sliced
- 1½ cups salsa
  Sour cream and chopped fresh cilantro

1. Prepare garlic toast according to the package directions.
2. Meanwhile, in a large skillet, heat oil over medium heat. Saute steak until no longer pink, 3-5 minutes; drain. Stir in salsa; cook and stir until heated through. Serve over toast. Top with sour cream and cilantro.
1 GARLIC TOAST WITH ¾ CUP STEAK MIXTURE 375 cal., 16g fat (4g sat. fat), 52mg chol., 721mg sod., 27g carb. (5g sugars, 1g fiber), 29g pro.

🕐 5️⃣

BUFFALO CHICKEN POCKETS

Here's my idea of pub food made easy: biscuits flavored with Buffalo wing sauce and blue cheese. They're my Friday night favorite.
—*Maria Regakis, Saugus, MA*

TAKES: 30 min. • **MAKES:** 8 pockets

- ¾ lb. ground chicken
- ⅓ cup Buffalo wing sauce
- 1 tube (16.3 oz.) large refrigerated buttermilk biscuits
- ½ cup shredded cheddar cheese
  Blue cheese salad dressing, optional

1. Preheat oven to 375°. In a large skillet, cook chicken over medium heat until no longer pink, 5-7 minutes, breaking into crumbles; drain. Remove from heat; stir in wing sauce.
2. On a lightly floured surface, roll each biscuit into a 6-in. circle and top each with ¼ cup chicken mixture and 2 Tbsp. cheese. Fold dough over filling; pinch edge to seal.
3. Transfer to an ungreased baking sheet. Bake until golden brown, 12-14 minutes. If desired, serve with blue cheese dressing.
FREEZE OPTION Freeze cooled pockets in a freezer container. To use, reheat pockets on an ungreased baking sheet in a preheated 375° oven until heated through.
1 POCKET 258 cal., 12g fat (5g sat. fat), 35mg chol., 987mg sod., 25g carb. (3g sugars, 1g fiber), 12g pro.

ROASTED CHICKEN & BRIE BITES

Featuring a symphony of sweet fig, roasted apple, melted brie and tangy garlic mayonnaise, these open-faced sandwiches are wonderful appetizers. Try them for a meal alongside a salad or bowl of soup.
—*Terri Gilson, Calgary, AB*

PREP: 20 min. • **BROIL:** 5 min. + cooling
MAKES: 24 mini sandwiches

- 1 French bread baguette (10½ oz.)
- ¼ cup mayonnaise
- 1½ tsp. garlic paste
- 12 slices deli chicken, halved
- ¼ cup apple jelly
- ¼ cup fig preserves
- 24 fresh baby spinach leaves
- 4 oz. mini Brie cheese wheel
- ⅓ cup sweetened dried cranberries

1. Preheat the broiler. Cut the baguette into 24 slices; place on foil-lined baking sheets. Combine mayonnaise and garlic; spread evenly over baguette slices. Add 1 piece of chicken to each. Combine apple jelly and fig preserves; spread evenly over chicken.
2. Add 1 baby spinach leaf to each slice. Standing the Brie wheel on end, cut crosswise into 6 narrow slices. Lay the slices flat; cut each into 4 wedges. Add 1 cheese wedge to each baguette. Top with 3 cranberries. Broil 3-4 in. from heat until cheese is melted, 1-2 minutes. Cool 5 minutes before serving.
1 MINI SANDWICH 98 cal., 3g fat (1g sat. fat), 11mg chol., 233mg sod., 13g carb. (6g sugars, 1g fiber), 4g pro.

SO-EASY STICKY CHICKEN WINGS

My neighbor once shared these tangy wings with me at a potluck, and they have been a family favorite ever since.
—*Jo Vanderwolf, Lillooet, BC*

PREP: 20 min. • **COOK:** 3 hours
MAKES: 40 pieces

- 4 lbs. chicken wings
- 1 cup barbecue sauce
- 1 cup soy sauce
- 6 green onions, chopped, divided
- 1 Tbsp. sesame seeds

Using a sharp knife, cut through the 2 joints on each wing; discard wing tips. Place remaining wing pieces in a 4- or 5-qt. slow cooker. Stir in the barbecue sauce, soy sauce and ¼ cup chopped green onions. Cook, covered, on high 3-4 hours or until tender. Sprinkle with the sesame seeds and remaining green onions.

1 PIECE 68 cal., 4g fat (1g sat. fat), 14mg chol., 452mg sod., 3g carb. (2g sugars, 0 fiber), 6g pro.

SO-EASY STICKY CHICKEN WINGS

ITALIAN PINWHEELS

ITALIAN PINWHEELS ✓

These treats taste a lot like rolled up pizza. With crispy pepperoni and lots of mozzarella and Parmesan, what's not to love?
—*Dorothy Smith, El Dorado, AR*

TAKES: 25 min. • **MAKES:** 8 pinwheels

- 1 tube (13.8 oz.) refrigerated pizza crust
- 1 cup shredded part-skim mozzarella cheese
- ¼ cup grated Parmesan cheese
- 1 cup chopped pepperoni (about 64 slices)
- ½ cup spaghetti sauce, warmed, optional

1. Preheat oven to 400°. On a lightly floured surface, roll dough into a 16x10-in. rectangle. Sprinkle with cheeses and pepperoni.
2. Roll up jelly-roll style, starting with a long side. Cut into 2-in. slices. Place cut side down in a greased 15x10x1-in. baking pan; lightly press down to flatten.
3. Bake for 8-10 minutes or until golden brown. Serve with spaghetti sauce if desired.

1 PINWHEEL 265 cal., 13g fat (5g sat. fat), 26mg chol., 776mg sod., 24g carb. (3g sugars, 1g fiber), 12g pro.

TEST KITCHEN TIP ✳
Feel free to use homemade pizza dough or frozen pizza dough that has been thawed in the refrigerator overnight.

SAUSAGE WONTON CUPS

SAUSAGE WONTON CUPS ✓

Here's a tasty bite for all those parties that feature fun finger foods. I've made this recipe several times, and the savory cups always disappear so fast. They're really easy as well.
—*Shirley Van Allen, High Point, NC*

TAKES: 30 min. • **MAKES:** 24 cups

- 1 lb. Italian turkey sausage links, casings removed
- 1 can (15 oz.) tomato sauce
- ½ tsp. garlic powder
- ½ tsp. dried basil
- 24 wonton wrappers
- 1 cup shredded Italian cheese blend

1. In a large skillet, cook the sausage over medium heat until no longer pink; drain. Stir in the tomato sauce, garlic powder and basil. Bring to a boil. Reduce heat; simmer, uncovered, until thickened, 8-10 minutes.
2. Meanwhile, press wonton wrappers into 24 miniature muffin cups coated with cooking spray. Bake at 350° until lightly browned, 8-9 minutes.
3. Spoon the sausage mixture into the cups. Sprinkle with cheese. Bake until cheese is melted, 5-7 minutes longer. Serve warm.

FREEZE OPTION Cool appetizers; freeze them in freezer containers, separating layers with waxed paper. To use, reheat wonton cups in coated muffin pans in a preheated 350° oven until crisp and heated through.

1 WONTON CUP 68 cal., 3g fat (1g sat. fat), 15mg chol., 270mg sod., 6g carb. (0 sugars, 0 fiber), 5g pro. **DIABETIC EXCHANGES** ½ starch, ½ fat.

CHAPTER 3

SOUPS & STEWS

P. 53

P. 54

P. 43

P. 42

WEEKNIGHT GOULASH

GOES GREAT WITH ...
Savor this dish alongside Grilled Naan (p. 297).

WEEKNIGHT GOULASH ✓

With this slow-cooker recipe, you can put in a full day's work, run some errands and still get dinner on the table in hardly any time. Make it extra special by serving the meat sauce over spaetzle.
—*Cyndy Gerken, Naples, FL*

PREP: 25 min. • **COOK:** 8½ hours
MAKES: 2 servings

- 1 lb. beef stew meat
- 1 Tbsp. olive oil
- 1 cup beef broth
- 1 small onion, chopped
- ¼ cup ketchup
- 1 Tbsp. Worcestershire sauce
- 1½ tsp. brown sugar
- 1½ tsp. paprika
- ¼ tsp. ground mustard
- 1 Tbsp. all-purpose flour
- 2 Tbsp. water
   Hot cooked egg noodles or spaetzle

1. In a large skillet, brown beef in oil; drain. Transfer to a 1½-qt. slow cooker. Combine the broth, onion, ketchup, Worcestershire sauce, brown sugar, paprika and mustard. Pour over beef. Cover and cook on low 8-10 hours, until meat is tender.
2. In a small bowl, combine flour and water until smooth. Gradually stir into beef mixture. Cover and cook on high until thickened, about 30 minutes longer. Serve with noodles.
1 CUP 478 cal., 23g fat (7g sat. fat), 141mg chol., 1005mg sod., 20g carb. (14g sugars, 1g fiber), 45g pro.

EASY MOROCCAN CHICKPEA STEW

EASY MOROCCAN CHICKPEA STEW

When I'm invited to a potluck, I easily double or triple this healthy vegetarian recipe to treat the crowd to an exotic dish of enticing, bold flavors.
—*Heather Demeritte, Scottsdale, AZ*

TAKES: 30 min. • **MAKES:** 4 servings

- 1 Tbsp. olive oil
- 2 cups cubed peeled butternut squash (½-in. cubes)
- 1 large onion, chopped
- 1 large sweet red pepper, chopped
- 1 tsp. ground cinnamon
- ½ tsp. pepper
- ¼ tsp. ground ginger
- ¼ tsp. ground cumin
- ¼ tsp. salt
- 1 can (15 oz.) chickpeas or garbanzo beans, rinsed and drained
- 1 can (14½ oz.) diced tomatoes, undrained
- 1 cup water
   Chopped cilantro, optional

1. In a Dutch oven, heat oil over medium-high heat. Add the squash, onion and red pepper; cook and stir until the onion is translucent and red pepper is crisp-tender, about 5 minutes. Stir in seasonings until blended.
2. Add chickpeas, tomatoes and water; bring to a boil. Reduce heat; cover and simmer until squash is tender, about 8 minutes. If desired, top with cilantro.
1½ CUPS 217 cal., 6g fat (1g sat. fat), 0 chol., 455mg sod., 38g carb. (11g sugars, 9g fiber), 7g pro.

TEST KITCHEN TIP

This is an adaptable recipe, so feel free to experiment by swapping out the butternut squash for another winter squash, such as sugar pumpkin. And though it's called chickpea stew, you could easily use a substitute like navy beans.

EASY SHRIMP & SCALLOPS RAMEN SOUP

This recipe is delicious and so easy to make at home on a weeknight. You can add any vegetables, seafood or meat that you have on hand.
—Aleni Salcedo, East Elmhurst, NY

TAKES: 30 min.
MAKES: 6 servings (2¼ qt.)

½ lb. sea scallops
½ lb. uncooked shrimp (16-20 per lb.), peeled and deveined
2 pkg. (3 oz. each) shrimp ramen noodles
2 tsp. sesame oil
2 garlic cloves, minced
2 cartons (32 oz. each) chicken broth
2 Tbsp. lime juice
3 cups fresh bean sprouts

Optional toppings: Fresh cilantro leaves, black and white sesame seeds and lime wedges

1. Sprinkle scallops and shrimp with contents of 1 seasoning packet from the noodles (discard second packet or save for another use). In a Dutch oven, heat the sesame oil over medium heat. In batches, cook scallops and shrimp until scallops are firm and opaque and shrimp turn pink. Remove and keep warm. To the same pan, add garlic; cook 1 minute longer.
2. Add broth and lime juice. Bring to a boil; reduce heat. Add noodles. Cook for 3 minutes. Add bean sprouts. Return scallops and shrimp to pan; heat through. Top as desired.
1½ CUPS 231 cal., 8g fat (3g sat. fat), 59mg chol., 1603mg sod., 24g carb. (4g sugars, 1g fiber), 17g pro.

SHORTCUT MEATBALL & TORTELLINI MINESTRONE SOUP

This hearty soup is quick to prepare with shortcut ingredients and ready in less than an hour. Add a salad and a warm, crusty loaf of bread or breadsticks to round out the meal.
—Joan Hallford, Fort Worth, TX

TAKES: 30 min.
MAKES: 8 servings (2¾ qt.)

2 cans (14½ oz. each) beef broth
1 jar (24 oz.) marinara sauce
3 cups frozen mixed vegetables, thawed
1 can (15½ oz.) navy beans, rinsed and drained
24 frozen fully cooked Italian meatballs, thawed
5 oz. frozen chopped spinach, thawed and squeezed dry (about ½ cup)
1 pkg. (9 oz.) refrigerated cheese tortellini
Shredded Parmesan cheese

In a Dutch oven, combine broth, marinara sauce and mixed vegetables. Bring to a boil; add beans, meatballs and spinach. Simmer, uncovered, for 5 minutes. Stir in the tortellini; cook 7 minutes longer. Serve with Parmesan cheese.
1⅓ CUPS 384 cal., 15g fat (6g sat. fat), 36mg chol., 1467mg sod., 44g carb. (7g sugars, 9g fiber), 21g pro.

EASY SHRIMP & SCALLOPS RAMEN SOUP

COWBOY STEW

I came up this beef stew back in the early 1970s, when I was down to very little food in the house. Since it's a combination of barbecue sauce, hamburger, hot dogs and beans, this one-skillet meal makes both children and adults happy.
—*Val Rananawski, Millville, NJ*

TAKES: 30 min. • **MAKES:** 11 servings

2 lbs. ground beef
4 cans (16 oz. each) baked beans
8 hot dogs, sliced
½ cup barbecue sauce
½ cup grated Parmesan cheese

In a Dutch oven, cook beef over medium heat until no longer pink; drain. Stir in remaining ingredients. Bring to a boil. Reduce heat; cover and simmer for 4-6 minutes or until flavors are blended.
1 CUP 469 cal., 23g fat (9g sat. fat), 84mg chol., 1256mg sod., 39g carb. (5g sugars, 9g fiber), 28g pro.

TEST KITCHEN TIP
Add some heat to the stew by using a spicy sausage, such as chorizo or andouille. Or toss in some pickled jalapenos or spicy chipotle peppers.

COWBOY STEW

SPICY LENTIL & CHICKPEA STEW

This recipe came to me from a friend and former co-worker at a health food store. I changed a few things until I found a version my family loves. My son doesn't like things too spicy, so I make the stew milder for him and add a sprinkle of extra spice in mine. My husband, who farms, works outdoors for long hours at a time and finds this soup hearty enough to keep him satisfied.
—Melanie MacFarlane, Bedeque, PE

PREP: 25 min. • **COOK:** 8 hours
MAKES: 8 servings (2¾ qt.)

- 2   tsp. olive oil
- 1   medium onion, thinly sliced
- 1   tsp. dried oregano
- ½   tsp. crushed red pepper flakes
- 2   cans (15 oz. each) garbanzo beans or chickpeas, rinsed and drained
- 1   cup dried lentils, rinsed
- 1   can (2¼ oz.) sliced ripe olives, drained
- 3   tsp. smoked paprika
- 4   cups vegetable broth
- 4   cans (8 oz. each) no-salt-added tomato sauce
- 4   cups fresh baby spinach
- ¾   cup fat-free plain yogurt

1. In a small skillet, heat the oil over medium-high heat. Add onion, oregano and pepper flakes; cook and stir until onion is tender, 8-10 minutes. Transfer to a 5- or 6-qt. slow cooker.
2. Add the chickpeas, lentils, olives and paprika; stir in broth and tomato sauce. Cook, covered, on low 8-10 hours, until lentils are tender. Stir in spinach. Top servings with yogurt.

1⅓ CUPS 266 cal., 4g fat (0 sat. fat), 0 chol., 712mg sod., 45g carb. (11g sugars, 10g fiber), 14g pro. **DIABETIC EXCHANGES** 2 starch, 2 vegetable, 1 lean meat.

SPICY LENTIL
& CHICKPEA STEW

VEGAN TORTILLA SOUP

Quinoa may be an unconventional ingredient but it adds protein in this vegan tortilla soup, making it hearty enough for a main dish.
—Taste of Home *Test Kitchen*

TAKES: 30 min.
MAKES: 8 servings (3 qt.)

- 1 Tbsp. olive oil
- 1 medium onion, chopped
- 4 garlic cloves, minced
- 1 jalapeno pepper, seeded and chopped
- 8 cups vegetable broth
- 1 cup quinoa, rinsed
- 2 tsp. chili powder
- ½ tsp. ground cumin
- ½ tsp. salt
- ¼ tsp. pepper
- 1 can (15 oz.) black beans, rinsed and drained
- 3 medium tomatoes, chopped
- 1 cup fresh or frozen corn
- ⅓ cup minced fresh cilantro
  Optional ingredients: Cubed avocado, lime wedges and additional chopped cilantro

Heat oil in a Dutch oven over medium-high heat. Add the onion, garlic and jalapeno pepper; cook and stir until tender, 3-5 minutes. Add broth, quinoa, and seasonings. Bring to a boil; reduce heat. Simmer, uncovered, until quinoa is tender, about 10 minutes. Add the beans, tomatoes, corn and cilantro; heat through. Serve with optional ingredients as desired.
NOTE Wear disposable gloves when cutting hot peppers; the oils can burn skin. Avoid touching your face.
1½ CUPS 182 cal., 4g fat (1g sat. fat), 0 chol., 792mg sod., 31g carb. (5g sugars, 5g fiber), 7g pro. **DIABETIC EXCHANGES** 2 starch, ½ fat.

SCOTCH BROTH SOUP ✓

Early in winter, I prepare big pots of this hearty soup to freeze in containers. Then I can bring out one or two containers at a time. I heat the frozen soup in a saucepan on low all morning. By lunchtime, it's hot and ready to serve!
—*Ann Main, Moorefield, ON*

PREP: 3 hours 20 min. + chilling O-N
COOK: 1 hour
MAKES: 6-8 servings (2 qt.)

- 2 lbs. meaty beef soup bones (beef shanks or short ribs)
- 8 cups water
- 6 whole peppercorns
- 1½ tsp. salt
- 1 cup chopped carrots
- 1 cup chopped turnips
- 1 cup chopped celery
- ½ cup chopped onion
- ¼ cup medium pearl barley

1. In a large soup kettle, combine soup bones, water, peppercorns and salt. Cover and simmer for 2½ hours or until the meat comes easily off the bones.
2. Remove bones. Strain broth; cool and chill. Skim off fat. Remove meat from bones; dice and return to broth. Add the remaining ingredients. Bring to a boil. Reduce heat; cover and simmer 1 hour or until vegetables and barley are tender.
1 CUP 155 cal., 7g fat (3g sat. fat), 35mg chol., 499mg sod., 9g carb. (3g sugars, 2g fiber), 15g pro.

BLACK BEAN TURKEY CHILI

Beef stew capped with flaky puff pastry adds comfort and joy to your weeknight menu. Toss a salad and call your crowd to the table.
—*Daniel Anderson, Kenosha, WI*

TAKES: 30 min. • **MAKES:** 4 servings

  1   sheet frozen puff pastry, thawed
  1   pkg. (15 oz.) refrigerated beef roast au jus
  2   cans (14½ oz. each) diced tomatoes, undrained
  1   pkg. (16 oz.) frozen vegetables for stew
  ¾   tsp. pepper
  2   Tbsp. cornstarch
 1¼ cups water

1. Preheat the oven to 400°. Unfold puff pastry. Using a 4-in. round cookie cutter, cut out 4 circles. Place 2 in. apart on a greased baking sheet. Bake until golden brown, 14-16 minutes.
2. Meanwhile, shred beef with 2 forks; transfer to a large saucepan. Add the tomatoes, vegetables and pepper; bring to a boil. In a small bowl, mix cornstarch and water until smooth; stir into the beef mixture. Return to a boil, stirring constantly. Cook and stir until thickened, 1-2 minutes.
3. Ladle stew into 4 bowls; top each serving with a pastry round.
1½ CUPS WITH 1 PASTRY ROUND 604 cal., 25g fat (8g sat. fat), 73mg chol., 960mg sod., 65g carb. (10g sugars, 9g fiber), 32g pro.

🕐
BLACK BEAN TURKEY CHILI ✓
This quick chili is packed with flavor. We make it ahead and freeze some for those extra-busy days.
—*Marisela Segovia, Miami, FL*

TAKES: 30 min. • **MAKES:** 6 servings

  1   lb. lean ground turkey
  1   large green pepper, chopped
  1   medium onion, chopped
  2   Tbsp. chili powder
  ½   tsp. salt
  ¼   tsp. pepper
  ⅛   to ¼ tsp. cayenne pepper
  1   can (15 oz.) no-salt-added tomato sauce
  1   can (15 oz.) black beans, rinsed and drained
 1½ cups frozen corn (about 8 oz.), thawed
  1   large tomato, chopped
  ½   cup water
      Shredded cheddar cheese, optional

1. In a 6-qt. stockpot, cook and crumble turkey with green pepper and onion over medium-high heat until no longer pink, 5-7 minutes. Stir in the seasonings; cook 1 minute.
2. Stir in the tomato sauce, beans, corn, tomato and water; bring to a boil. Reduce heat; simmer, uncovered, to allow flavors to blend, about 10 minutes, stirring occasionally. If desired, serve with cheese.
FREEZE OPTION Freeze cooled chili in freezer containers. To use, partially thaw in refrigerator overnight. Heat through in a saucepan, stirring occasionally; add water if necessary.
1 CUP 247 cal., 7g fat (2g sat. fat), 52mg chol., 468mg sod., 27g carb. (7g sugars, 7g fiber), 21g pro. **DIABETIC EXCHANGES** 3 lean meat, 1½ starch, 1 vegetable.

READER RAVES
"Definitely a 5-star winner! We loved it. So quick; it was ready in about half an hour. This one is a keeper."

—**MARINEMOMTEXAS, TASTEOFHOME.COM**

TURKEY CABBAGE STEW

Chock-full of ground turkey, cabbage, carrots and tomatoes, this stew delivers down-home comfort food fast!
—*Susan Lasken, Woodland Hills, CA*

TAKES: 30 min. • **MAKES:** 6 servings

- 1 lb. lean ground turkey
- 1 medium onion, chopped
- 3 garlic cloves, minced
- 4 cups chopped cabbage
- 2 medium carrots, sliced
- 1 can (28 oz.) diced tomatoes, undrained
- ¾ cup water
- 1 Tbsp. brown sugar
- 1 Tbsp. white vinegar
- 1 tsp. salt
- 1 tsp. dried oregano
- ¼ tsp. dried thyme
- ¼ tsp. pepper

1. Cook the turkey, onion and garlic in a large saucepan over medium heat until meat is no longer pink, 5-7 minutes, breaking turkey into crumbles; drain.
2. Add the remaining ingredients. Bring to a boil; cover and simmer until the vegetables are tender, 12-15 minutes.
FREEZE OPTION Freeze cooled stew in freezer containers. To use, partially thaw in refrigerator overnight. Heat through in a saucepan, stirring occasionally; add broth if necessary.
1 CUP 180 cal., 6g fat (2g sat. fat), 52mg chol., 674mg sod., 16g carb. (10g sugars, 5g fiber), 17g pro. **DIABETIC EXCHANGES** 2 vegetable, 2 lean meat.

TURKEY CABBAGE STEW

BEER-CHEESE VELVET SOUP

BEER-CHEESE VELVET SOUP ✓

This soup was a big hit with a group of German exchange teachers who visited our high school. I usually serve it with soft pretzels or crusty bread, and it's also a treat with slices of cooked bratwurst or kielbasa stirred into it.
—*Paula Zsiray, Logan, UT*

TAKES: 25 min.
MAKES: 8 servings (1½ qt.)

 ¾ cup butter, cubed
 ¾ cup all-purpose flour
  1 bottle (12 oz.) light beer
  4 cups chicken or vegetable stock, divided
  2 tsp. Worcestershire sauce
  1 tsp. ground mustard
 ½ tsp. salt
 ¼ tsp. pepper
 ¼ tsp. cayenne pepper
  4 cups shredded cheddar cheese

Optional: Bread bowls, crumbled bacon and shredded cheddar cheese

1. In a large saucepan, melt butter over medium heat. Stir in flour until blended; gradually whisk in beer until smooth. Whisk in stock, Worcestershire sauce, mustard, salt, pepper and cayenne.
2. Bring to a boil, stirring constantly; cook and stir until thickened, 1-2 minutes. Reduce heat. Gradually stir in cheese until melted. If desired, serve soup in bread bowls and top with crumbled bacon and shredded cheese.
¾ CUP 450 cal., 36g fat (22g sat. fat), 102mg chol., 925mg sod., 12g carb. (1g sugars, 0 fiber), 17g pro.

EASY BUTTERNUT SQUASH SOUP

When the weather turns cold, get cozy with a bowl of this butternut squash soup. The cream adds richness, but it can be omitted if you're looking to cut calories.
—Taste of Home *Test Kitchen*

TAKES: 30 min.
MAKES: 9 servings (2¼ qt.)

  1 Tbsp. olive oil
  1 large onion, chopped
  3 garlic cloves, minced
  1 medium butternut squash (3 lbs.), peeled and cubed
  4 cups vegetable broth
 ¾ tsp. salt
 ¼ tsp. pepper
 ½ cup heavy whipping cream
      Optional: Additional heavy whipping cream and crispy sage leaves

1. In a large saucepan, heat the oil over medium heat. Add the onion; cook and stir until tender. Add the garlic; cook 1 minute longer.
2. Stir in squash, broth, salt and pepper; bring to a boil. Reduce the heat; simmer, covered, 10-15 minutes or until squash is tender. Puree soup using an immersion blender. Or cool slightly and puree soup in batches in a blender; return to pan. Add cream; cook and stir until heated through. If desired, garnish with additional heavy whipping cream and crispy sage.
1 CUP 157 cal., 7g fat (4g sat. fat), 17mg chol., 483mg sod., 23g carb. (6g sugars, 6g fiber), 3g pro.

DILL CHICKEN SOUP ✓

I could eat soup for every meal of the day, all year long. I particularly like dill and spinach—they add a brightness to this light and healthy soup.
—Robin Haas, Hyde Park, MA

TAKES: 30 min.
MAKES: 6 servings (2 qt.)

- 1 Tbsp. canola oil
- 2 medium carrots, chopped
- 1 small onion, coarsely chopped
- 2 garlic cloves, minced
- ½ cup uncooked whole wheat orzo pasta
- 1½ cups coarsely shredded rotisserie chicken
- 6 cups reduced-sodium chicken broth
- 1½ cups frozen ~~peas~~ (about 6 oz.) *GREENBEAN*
- 8 oz. fresh baby spinach (about 10 cups)
- 2 Tbsp. chopped fresh dill or 1 Tbsp. dill weed
- 2 Tbsp. lemon juice
  Coarsely ground pepper, optional

1. In a 6-qt. stockpot, heat the oil over medium heat. Add carrots, onion and garlic; saute until carrots are tender, 4-5 minutes.
2. Stir in orzo, chicken and broth; bring to a boil. Reduce heat; simmer, uncovered, 5 minutes. Stir in peas, spinach and ~~dill~~; return to a boil. Reduce heat; simmer, uncovered, until the orzo is tender, 3-4 minutes. Stir in lemon juice. If desired, top each serving with coarsely ground pepper.

1⅓ CUPS 198 cal., 6g fat (1g sat. fat), 31mg chol., 681mg sod., 20g carb. (4g sugars, 5g fiber), 18g pro. **DIABETIC EXCHANGES** 2 lean meat, 1 starch, 1 vegetable, ½ fat.

ARBORIO RICE & WHITE BEAN SOUP ✓

Soup is the ultimate comfort food. This hearty, satisfying soup with arborio rice is low in fat and comes together in about 30 minutes.
—Deanna Wolfe, Muskegon, MI

TAKES: 30 min. • **MAKES:** 4 servings

- 1 Tbsp. olive oil
- 3 garlic cloves, minced
- ¾ cup uncooked arborio rice
- 1 carton (32 oz.) vegetable broth
- ¾ tsp. dried basil
- ½ tsp. dried thyme
- ¼ tsp. dried oregano
- 1 pkg. (16 oz.) frozen broccoli-cauliflower blend
- 1 can (15 oz.) cannellini beans, rinsed and drained
- 2 cups fresh baby spinach
  Lemon wedges, optional

1. In a large saucepan, heat the oil over medium heat; saute garlic 1 minute. Add rice; cook and stir 2 minutes. Stir in broth and herbs; bring to a boil. Reduce heat; simmer, covered, until rice is al dente, about 10 minutes.
2. Stir in frozen vegetables and beans; cook, covered, over medium heat until heated through and rice is tender, 8-10 minutes, stirring occasionally. Stir in spinach until wilted. If desired, serve with lemon wedges.

1¾ CUPS 303 cal., 4g fat (1g sat. fat), 0 chol., 861mg sod., 52g carb. (2g sugars, 6g fiber), 9g pro.

TEST KITCHEN TIP

Be sure to use arborio rice in this recipe. It cooks up tender with a texture that is smoother than long grain rice.

FROGMORE STEW

FROGMORE STEW ✓

This picnic-style medley of shrimp, smoked kielbasa, corn and spuds is a specialty of South Carolina cuisine. It's commonly dubbed Frogmore Stew or Beaufort Stew in recognition of both of the Lowcountry communities that lay claim to its origin. No matter what you call it, this one-pot wonder won't disappoint!
—Taste of Home *Test Kitchen*

PREP: 10 min. • **COOK:** 35 min.
MAKES: 8 servings

16 cups water
1   large sweet onion, quartered
3   Tbsp. seafood seasoning
2   medium lemons, halved, optional
1   lb. small red potatoes
1   lb. smoked kielbasa or fully cooked hot links, cut into 1-in. pieces
4   medium ears sweet corn, cut into thirds
2   lbs. uncooked medium shrimp, peeled and deveined
    Seafood cocktail sauce
    Melted butter
    Additional seafood seasoning

1. In a stockpot, combine water, onion, seafood seasoning and, if desired, lemons; bring to a boil. Add potatoes; cook, uncovered, 10 minutes. Add kielbasa and corn; return to a boil. Reduce heat; simmer, uncovered, until the potatoes are tender, 10-12 minutes. Add the shrimp; cook until shrimp turn pink, 2-3 minutes longer.
2. Drain; transfer to a bowl. Serve with cocktail sauce, butter and additional seasoning.
1 SERVING 369 cal., 18g fat (6g sat. fat), 175mg chol., 751mg sod., 24g carb. (7g sugars, 2g fiber), 28g pro.

**PRESSURE-COOKER
SONORAN CLAM CHOWDER**

PRESSURE-COOKER SONORAN CLAM CHOWDER

Being from New England originally, I always appreciated a good, rich clam chowder. Living in the Southwest the past 35 years, I have learned to appreciate the Sonoran flavors. This recipe blends a comfort food memory with my current home flavor profiles.
—James Scott, Phoenix, AZ

PREP: 35 min. • **COOK:** 5 min.
MAKES: 10 servings (2½ qt.)

- 6 thick-sliced peppered bacon strips, chopped
- 3 Tbsp. butter
- 1 medium onion, chopped
- 1 medium sweet red pepper, chopped
- 2 cans (4 oz. each) chopped green chiles
- 4 garlic cloves, minced
- 3 cans (6½ oz. each) chopped clams, undrained
- 4 cups diced Yukon Gold potatoes (about 1½ lbs.)
- ½ cup chicken stock
- 2 cups half-and-half cream
- 1 envelope taco seasoning
- 2 Tbsp. chopped fresh cilantro, divided

1. Select saute setting on a 6-qt. electric pressure cooker. Adjust for medium heat; add bacon. Cook until crisp, stirring occasionally. Remove with a slotted spoon; drain on paper towels. Discard drippings, reserving 2 Tbsp. in pan. Add butter to drippings in pressure cooker. Add the onion, red pepper and chiles; cook and stir until tender, 7-9 minutes. Add the garlic; cook 1 minute longer. Press cancel.
2. Drain clams; pour juice into pressure cooker. Set clams aside. Stir in potatoes and stock. Lock lid; close pressure-release valve. Adjust to pressure-cook on high for 4 minutes. Allow pressure to release naturally for 4 minutes; quick-release any remaining pressure. Select saute setting and adjust for low heat. Add clams, cream, taco seasoning and 1 Tbsp. cilantro; simmer, uncovered, until the mixture is heated through, 4-5 minutes, stirring occasionally. Press cancel. Serve with bacon and remaining 1 Tbsp. cilantro.
1 CUP 271 cal., 15g fat (7g sat. fat), 61mg chol., 935mg sod., 23g carb. (4g sugars, 2g fiber), 11g pro.

SPICY CHICKEN STEW

When you're craving cozy Mexican flavors, try this slightly spicy stew that couldn't be easier to make. Round out the meal with a fresh tossed salad.
—Taste of Home *Test Kitchen*

TAKES: 30 min. • **MAKES:** 6 servings

- 2 lbs. boneless skinless chicken thighs, cut into ½-in. pieces
- 2 tsp. minced garlic
- 2 Tbsp. olive oil
- 1 can (15 oz.) garbanzo beans or chickpeas, rinsed and drained
- 1 can (14½ oz.) diced tomatoes with onions, undrained
- 1 cup lime-garlic salsa
- 1 tsp. ground cumin
- ⅓ cup minced fresh cilantro
  Sour cream, optional

In a Dutch oven, cook chicken and garlic in oil for 5 minutes. Stir in the beans, tomatoes, salsa and cumin. Cover and simmer until chicken is no longer pink, about 15 minutes. Stir in the cilantro. Top with sour cream if desired.
1½ CUPS 359 cal., 17g fat (4g sat. fat), 101mg chol., 622mg sod., 18g carb. (5g sugars, 4g fiber), 31g pro.

SPICY CHICKEN STEW

EASY CREAMY TOMATO SOUP

One spoonful of this classic will take you back your childhood, sipping warm tomato soup on a cold day. Pair it with a grilled sandwich for a hearty lunch—we suggest grilled cheese!
—Taste of Home *Test Kitchen*

PREP: 20 min. • **COOK:** 30 min.
MAKES: 4 servings

- 2 Tbsp. butter
- 1 Tbsp. olive oil
- 1 medium onion, chopped
- 2 garlic cloves, minced
- 1 can (28 oz.) whole tomatoes, undrained
- 1 cup chicken stock
- 2 Tbsp. tomato paste
- 1 tsp. dried basil
- ½ tsp. salt
- ½ tsp. sugar
- ¼ tsp. dried thyme
- ¼ tsp. pepper
- ½ cup heavy whipping cream
  Fresh basil leaves, optional

1. In a large saucepan, heat the butter and oil over medium heat until butter is melted. Add the onion; cook and stir until tender, 5-7 minutes. Add the garlic; cook 1 minute longer. Stir in tomatoes, chicken stock, tomato paste, basil, salt, sugar, thyme and pepper. Bring to a boil. Reduce heat; simmer, uncovered, to let the flavors blend, 20-25 minutes.
2. Remove the pan from heat. Using a blender, puree the soup until smooth. Return to pan. Slowly stir in the cream. Cook and stir over low heat until heated through. If desired, garnish with basil and additional cream.

1 CUP 252 cal., 20g fat (11g sat. fat), 49mg chol., 778mg sod., 15g carb. (8g sugars, 4g fiber), 5g pro.

ITALIAN CHICKEN STEW

My husband enjoys preparing this satisfying stew because it's so easy to make. With warm Italian bread, it's a winner on a cold day.
—*Jo Calizzi, Vandergrift, PA*

TAKES: 20 min. • **MAKES:** 4 servings

- 1 lb. boneless skinless chicken breasts, cubed
- 4 medium potatoes, peeled and cut into ¼-in. cubes
- 1 medium sweet red pepper, chopped
- 2 garlic cloves, minced
- 1 to 2 Tbsp. olive oil
- 1 jar (26 oz.) meatless spaghetti sauce
- 1¾ cups frozen cut green beans
- 1 tsp. dried basil
- ¼ to ½ tsp. salt
- ¼ tsp. crushed red pepper flakes
  Pepper to taste

In a Dutch oven, cook the chicken, potatoes, red pepper and garlic in oil until chicken is no longer pink and vegetables are tender. Stir in the remaining ingredients; cook and stir until heated through.

1½ CUPS 475 cal., 13g fat (3g sat. fat), 63mg chol., 995mg sod., 62g carb. (0 sugars, 11g fiber), 31g pro. **DIABETIC EXCHANGES** 4 starch, 3 lean meat, 1 fat.

EASY CREAMY TOMATO SOUP

QUICK & HEALTHY
TURKEY VEGGIE SOUP

I freeze our leftover turkey at the holidays so we can enjoy meals like this year-round. This soup is especially delicious on a chilly fall or winter day. If you're looking for a dish that's more filling, add some cooked pasta.
—*Joan Hallford, Fort Worth, TX*

TAKES: 30 min.
MAKES: 9 servings (3 qt.)

- 2   Tbsp. butter
- 1   medium onion, chopped
- 1   celery rib, chopped
- 2   garlic cloves, minced
- 5   cups reduced-sodium chicken broth
- 3   medium carrots, julienned
- ¼   tsp. pepper
- 1   lb. zucchini or yellow summer squash, julienned (about 6 cups)
- 3   medium tomatoes, chopped
- 1   can (15½ oz.) hominy, rinsed and drained
- 2½   cups frozen lima beans (about 12 oz.), thawed
- 2   cups cubed cooked turkey
- 1½   tsp. minced fresh basil or ½ tsp. dried basil
      Shredded Parmesan cheese

In a Dutch oven, heat the butter over medium-high heat. Add the onion, celery and garlic; cook and stir until tender, 5-8 minutes. Add broth, carrots and pepper. Bring to a boil; reduce heat. Simmer, uncovered, 5 minutes. Add the zucchini, tomatoes, hominy, lima beans and turkey. Cook until zucchini is tender, 5-8 minutes. Top with basil; serve with Parmesan cheese.

1⅓ CUPS 187 cal., 4g fat (2g sat. fat), 38mg chol., 614mg sod., 22g carb. (5g sugars, 5g fiber), 16g pro. **DIABETIC EXCHANGES** 2 lean meat, 1½ starch, ½ fat.

**QUICK & HEALTHY
TURKEY VEGGIE SOUP**

ITALIAN SAUSAGE & ZUCCHINI SOUP

Everyone in my family likes this soup recipe. Sometimes I add mini farfalle because my grandchildren say the noodles look like tiny butterflies. This recipe also works in a slow cooker.
—Nancy Murphy, Mount Dora, FL

TAKES: 30 min.
MAKES: 6 servings (2 qt.)

- ½ lb. bulk Italian sausage
- 1 medium onion, chopped
- 1 medium green pepper, chopped
- 3 cups beef broth
- 1 can (14½ oz.) diced tomatoes, undrained
- 1 Tbsp. minced fresh basil or 1 tsp. dried basil
- 1 Tbsp. minced fresh parsley or 1 tsp. dried parsley flakes
- 1 medium zucchini, cut into ½-in. pieces
- ½ cup uncooked orzo pasta

1. In a large saucepan, cook the sausage, onion and pepper over medium heat until sausage is no longer pink and vegetables are tender, 4-6 minutes, breaking the sausage into crumbles; drain.
2. Add broth, tomatoes, basil and parsley; bring to a boil. Stir in zucchini and orzo; return to a boil. Cook, covered, until zucchini and orzo are tender, 10-12 minutes.
1¼ CUPS 191 cal., 9g fat (3g sat. fat), 20mg chol., 789mg sod., 20g carb. (5g sugars, 2g fiber), 9g pro.

READER RAVES
"I made this soup for dinner last night, and it was delicious!"

—BICKTASW, TASTEOFHOME.COM

ITALIAN SAUSAGE & ZUCCHINI SOUP

GOES GREAT WITH ...
Pick up some dinner rolls from the bakery to serve alongside this hearty soup.

WEEKNIGHT TACO SOUP

This soup turned out delicious on the first try, when I was working without a recipe. You could also add cooked ground beef or cubed stew meat dredged in seasoned flour and browned for a heartier meal.
—*Amanda Swartz, Goderich, ON*

TAKES: 30 min.
MAKES: 6 servings (2½ qt.)

- 1 Tbsp. canola oil
- 1 large onion, chopped
- 1 medium sweet red pepper, chopped
- 1 medium green pepper, chopped
- 1 can (28 oz.) diced tomatoes, undrained
- 3 cups vegetable broth
- 1 can (15 oz.) pinto beans, rinsed and drained
- 1½ cups frozen corn
- 1 envelope taco seasoning
- ¼ tsp. salt
- ¼ tsp. pepper
- 1 pkg. (8.8 oz.) ready-to-serve long grain rice
- 1 cup sour cream
  Optional toppings: Shredded cheddar cheese, crushed tortilla chips and additional sour cream

1. In a Dutch oven, heat oil over medium heat. Add onion and peppers; cook and stir until crisp-tender, 3-5 minutes.
2. Add tomatoes, broth, beans, corn, taco seasoning, salt and pepper; bring to a boil. Reduce heat; simmer, uncovered, until the vegetables are tender, 10-15 minutes. Reduce heat. Stir in rice and sour cream; heat through. Serve with optional toppings as desired.
FREEZE OPTION Freeze cooled soup in freezer containers. To use, partially thaw in refrigerator overnight. Heat through in a saucepan, stirring occasionally; add broth if necessary.
1¾ CUPS 333 cal., 12g fat (5g sat. fat), 9mg chol., 1288mg sod., 49g carb. (10g sugars, 7g fiber), 9g pro.

ORZO SHRIMP STEW

My husband and I really enjoy seafood, so I don't skimp on shrimp in this mildly seasoned stew. We also adore the broccoli, tomatoes and pasta.
—*Lisa Stinger, Hamilton, NJ*

TAKES: 20 min. • **MAKES:** 4 servings

- 2½ cups reduced-sodium chicken broth
- 5 cups fresh broccoli florets
- 1 can (14½ oz.) diced tomatoes, undrained
- 1 cup uncooked orzo
- 1 lb. uncooked shrimp (31-40 per lb.), peeled and deveined
- ¼ tsp. salt
- ¼ tsp. pepper
- 2 tsp. dried basil
- 2 Tbsp. butter

1. Bring the broth to a boil in a Dutch oven. Add the broccoli, tomatoes and orzo. Reduce heat; simmer, uncovered, for 5 minutes, stirring occasionally.
2. Add the shrimp, salt and pepper. Cover and cook for 4-5 minutes or until shrimp turn pink and orzo is tender. Stir in basil and butter.
1¾ CUPS 387 cal., 8g fat (4g sat. fat), 153mg chol., 875mg sod., 48g carb. (7g sugars, 5g fiber), 30g pro.

CHAPTER 4

SAMMIES & WRAPS

P. 70

P. 65

P. 73

P. 78

GOES GREAT WITH ...
A hot bowl of Vegan Tortilla Soup (p. 45) is perfect with these sandwiches.

GUACAMOLE CHICKEN
SALAD SANDWICHES

GUACAMOLE CHICKEN SALAD SANDWICHES

This is inspired by a local restaurant's truly inventive guacamole studded with pomegranate seeds. It's simple to make, since rotisserie chicken is used. I serve the salad on homemade tomato bread that provides contrast in flavor and color. You can also serve it on lettuce leaves instead of bread.
—*Debra Keil, Owasso, OK*

TAKES: 20 min. • **MAKES:** 10 servings

- 1 rotisserie chicken, skin removed, cubed
- 2 medium ripe avocados, peeled and mashed
- ¾ cup pomegranate seeds
- 6 green onions, chopped
- 8 cherry tomatoes, halved
- 1 jalapeno pepper, seeded and minced
- ¼ cup fresh cilantro leaves, chopped
- 3 Tbsp. mayonnaise
- 2 Tbsp. lime juice
- 1 garlic clove, minced
- ½ tsp. salt
- ½ tsp. ground cumin
- ¼ tsp. pepper
- 20 slices multigrain bread, toasted

In a large bowl, combine all ingredients but the bread. Spread chicken salad over 10 bread slices; top each prepared slice with remaining bread.

NOTE Wear disposable gloves when cutting hot peppers; the oils can burn skin. Avoid touching your face.

1 SANDWICH 295 cal., 12g fat (2g sat. fat), 35mg chol., 370mg sod., 28g carb. (6g sugars, 6g fiber), 19g pro. **DIABETIC EXCHANGES** 2 starch, 2 lean meat, 2 fat.

DELI TURKEY LETTUCE WRAPS

DELI TURKEY LETTUCE WRAPS

I used to make these during my training days, when I worked at a restaurant in Hawaii. The wraps are low-fat, low-carb, high-protein, quick and delicious—terrific choice before or after a workout.
—*Duncan Omarzu, Astoria, NY*

TAKES: 25 min. • **MAKES:** 6 lettuce wraps

- 2 tsp. olive oil
- ½ medium red onion, thinly sliced
- 6 oz. sliced deli turkey, coarsely chopped
- 6 cherry tomatoes, halved
- 2 tsp. balsamic vinegar
- 6 Bibb or Boston lettuce leaves
- ½ medium ripe avocado, peeled and cubed
- ¼ cup shredded Swiss cheese
- ¼ cup alfalfa sprouts, optional

1. In a large skillet, heat oil over medium-high heat. Add onion; cook and stir until tender, 3-4 minutes. Add turkey; heat through. Stir in tomatoes and vinegar just until combined.
2. Serve in lettuce leaves. Top with avocado, cheese and, if desired, sprouts.

3 LETTUCE WRAPS 270 cal., 16g fat (4g sat. fat), 43mg chol., 799mg sod., 11g carb. (4g sugars, 4g fiber), 22g pro. **DIABETIC EXCHANGES** 3 lean meat, 1½ fat, 1 vegetable.

TEST KITCHEN TIP
Deli meat is typically lean, like the turkey used in these low-carb wraps, but it's also high in sodium. Switch to leftover cooked turkey or chicken to cut back on sodium.

TEX-MEX CHEESESTEAK SANDWICHES

We adore cheesesteak sandwiches and anything with Southwestern flavor so I combined the two. If you crave even more firepower, add chopped jalapenos.
—*Joan Hallford, Fort Worth, TX*

TAKES: 25 min. • **MAKES:** 4 servings

- 1   pkg. (15 oz.) refrigerated beef tips with gravy
- 1   Tbsp. canola oil
- 1   medium onion, halved and thinly sliced
- 1   banana pepper, cut into strips
- ⅛   tsp. salt
- ⅛   tsp. pepper
- 4   whole wheat hoagie buns, split
- ¼   cup mayonnaise
- ⅛   tsp. chili powder, optional
- 8   slices pepper jack cheese

1. Preheat broiler. Heat beef tips with gravy according to package directions. Meanwhile, in a small skillet, heat oil over medium-high heat. Add onion and pepper; cook and stir 4-6 minutes or until tender. Stir in salt and pepper.
2. Place buns on a baking sheet, cut side up. Mix mayonnaise and, if desired, chili powder; spread on bun bottoms. Layer with beef tips, onion mixture and cheese. Broil 3-4 in. from heat 1-2 minutes or until cheese is melted and buns are toasted.

1 SANDWICH 600 cal., 36g fat (11g sat. fat), 90mg chol., 1312mg sod., 42g carb. (9g sugars, 7g fiber), 32g pro.

TEX-MEX CHEESESTEAK SANDWICHES

SAUSAGE COBB SALAD LETTUCE WRAPS

I substituted sausage for the bacon to make a lettuce roll-up your family and friends will adore. It's flavorful, crunchy and pretty on the plate.
—*Devon Delaney, Westport, CT*

TAKES: 25 min. • **MAKES:** 6 servings

- ¾   cup ranch salad dressing
- ⅓   cup crumbled blue cheese
- ¼   cup watercress, chopped
- 1   lb. bulk pork sausage
- 2   Tbsp. minced fresh chives
- 6   large iceberg lettuce leaves, edges trimmed
- 1   medium ripe avocado, peeled and diced
- 4   hard-boiled large eggs, chopped
- 1   medium tomato, chopped

1. Mix salad dressing, blue cheese and watercress; set aside. In a large skillet, cook and crumble the sausage over medium heat until no longer pink, 5-7 minutes; drain. Stir in the chives.
2. To serve, spoon sausage into lettuce leaves. Top with the avocado, eggs and tomato. Drizzle with dressing mixture.

1 WRAP 433 cal., 38g fat (10g sat. fat), 174mg chol., 887mg sod., 7g carb. (3g sugars, 3g fiber), 15g pro.

ARTICHOKE
STEAK WRAPS

🕐 🍳 ARTICHOKE STEAK WRAPS

This simple and flavorful dish is one the whole family will love. It is surprisingly easy to make, and you can broil the steak if you don't want to venture outside.
—*Greg Fontenot, The Woodlands, TX*

TAKES: 30 min. • **MAKES:** 6 servings

- 8 oz. frozen artichoke hearts (about 2 cups), thawed and chopped
- 2 medium tomatoes, chopped
- ¼ cup chopped fresh cilantro
- ¾ tsp. salt, divided
- 1 lb. beef flat iron or top sirloin steak (1¼ lbs.)
- ¼ tsp. pepper
- 6 whole wheat tortillas (8 in.), warmed

1. Toss artichoke hearts and tomatoes with cilantro and ¼ tsp. salt.
2. Sprinkle steak with pepper and remaining salt. Grill, covered, over medium heat or broil 4 in. from heat until meat reaches desired doneness (for medium-rare, a thermometer should read 135°; medium, 140°), 5-6 minutes per side. Remove from heat; let stand 5 minutes. Cut into thin slices. Serve the steak and salsa in tortillas, folding bottoms and sides of tortillas to close.

1 WRAP 301 cal., 11g fat (4g sat. fat), 61mg chol., 506mg sod., 27g carb. (1g sugars, 5g fiber), 24g pro. **DIABETIC EXCHANGES** 3 lean meat, 1½ starch.

TEST KITCHEN TIP
Place the cilantro sprigs in a small glass container and snip with kitchen shears until chopped to desired fineness. This is a helpful way to avoid dirtying a cutting board.

COBB SALAD SUB

When we need a quick meal to share, we turn Cobb salad into a sandwich masterpiece. Sometimes I substitute tortillas for the bread and make wraps.
—*Kimberly Grusendorf, Medina, OH*

TAKES: 15 min. • **MAKES:** 12 servings

- 1 loaf (1 lb.) unsliced Italian bread
- ½ cup balsamic vinaigrette or dressing of your choice
- 5 oz. fresh baby spinach (about 6 cups)
- 1½ lbs. sliced deli ham
- 4 hard-boiled large eggs, finely chopped
- 8 bacon strips, cooked and crumbled
- ½ cup crumbled Gorgonzola cheese
- 1 cup cherry tomatoes, chopped

Cut the bread loaf in half lengthwise; hollow out top and bottom, leaving a ¾-in. shell (discard removed bread or save for another use). Brush vinaigrette over loaf halves. Layer spinach, ham, eggs, bacon, cheese and tomatoes on bread bottom. Replace top. Cut loaf in half lengthwise from top to bottom; cut crosswise 5 times to make 12 pieces.

1 PIECE 233 cal., 10g fat (3g sat. fat), 97mg chol., 982mg sod., 17g carb. (3g sugars, 1g fiber), 18g pro.

COBB SALAD SUB

BARBECUE CHICKEN SLIDERS

With rotisserie chicken, these cheesy, smoky sliders are a snap to make on a busy day. The special barbecue sauce really takes it up a notch.
—*Nancy Heishman, Las Vegas, NV*

TAKES: 25 min. • **MAKES:** 4 servings

¾ cup beer or reduced-sodium chicken broth
½ cup barbecue sauce
1 Tbsp. bourbon
1 tsp. hot pepper sauce
¼ tsp. seasoned salt
¼ tsp. ground mustard
2 cups shredded rotisserie chicken
8 slider buns, split
1½ cups shredded smoked cheddar cheese

1. Preheat broiler. In a large saucepan, mix the first 6 ingredients; bring to a boil. Reduce heat; simmer, uncovered, until slightly thickened, 8-10 minutes, stirring occasionally. Stir in chicken; heat through.
2. Place the buns on a baking sheet, cut side up. Broil 3-4 in. from heat until lightly toasted, 30-60 seconds.
3. Remove the tops of buns from baking sheet. Top bottoms with chicken mixture; sprinkle with cheese. Broil 3-4 in. from heat until cheese is melted, 1-2 minutes. Add bun tops.
FREEZE OPTION Freeze cooled chicken mixture in freezer containers. To use, partially thaw in refrigerator overnight. Heat through in a saucepan, stirring occasionally; add water if necessary.
2 SLIDERS 529 cal., 23g fat (10g sat. fat), 106mg chol., 1023mg sod., 42g carb. (15g sugars, 1g fiber), 36g pro.

ASIAN CHICKEN CRUNCH WRAPS

My kids love all kinds of wraps and Asian foods. This is an easy go-to in our house that works for everyone.
—*Mary Lou Timpson, Colorado City, AZ*

TAKES: 25 min. • **MAKES:** 4 servings

8 frozen breaded chicken tenders (about 10 oz.)
2 cups coleslaw mix
½ cup sweet chili sauce
2 green onions, chopped
2 Tbsp. chopped fresh cilantro
1 tsp. soy sauce
4 flour tortillas (8 in.), warmed
½ cup dry roasted peanuts, chopped

1. Bake chicken tenders according to the package directions. Meanwhile, in a large bowl, toss coleslaw mix with chili sauce, green onions, cilantro and soy sauce.
2. Arrange chicken down center of each tortilla; top with the coleslaw mixture and peanuts. Fold sides of tortillas over filling and roll up. Cut each diagonally in half.
1 WRAP 519 cal., 21g fat (3g sat. fat), 13mg chol., 1250mg sod., 66g carb. (19g sugars, 7g fiber), 19g pro.

TEST KITCHEN TIP

We love smoked cheddar in the sliders, but feel free to use regular cheddar or provolone.

BISTRO TURKEY SANDWICH

BISTRO TURKEY SANDWICH ✓

As a turkey lover who can't get enough during fall and winter, I was inspired to come up with a restaurant-worthy sandwich. I love it with a soft, rich cheese like Brie.
—*Grace Voltolina, Westport, CT*

TAKES: 30 min. • **MAKES:** 4 servings

- 2 Tbsp. butter, divided
- 1 large Granny Smith or Honeycrisp apple, cut into ¼-in. slices
- ½ tsp. sugar
- ¼ tsp. ground cinnamon
- ½ medium sweet onion, sliced
- ¼ cup whole-berry or jellied cranberry sauce
- 4 ciabatta rolls, split
- 1 lb. cooked turkey, sliced
- 8 slices Camembert or Brie cheese (about 8 oz.)
- 3 cups arugula (about 2 oz.)

1. Preheat broiler. In a large skillet, heat 1 Tbsp. butter over medium heat; saute the apple with sugar and cinnamon until crisp-tender, 3-4 minutes. Remove from the pan.
2. In same pan, melt remaining 1 Tbsp. butter over medium heat; saute onion until lightly browned, 3-4 minutes. Remove from heat; stir in sauteed apple.
3. Spread cranberry sauce onto cut side of roll bottoms; layer with turkey, apple mixture and cheese. Place on a baking sheet alongside roll tops, cut side up.
4. Broil 3-4 in. from heat until cheese begins to melt and roll tops are golden brown, 45-60 seconds. Add arugula; close sandwiches.
1 SANDWICH 797 cal., 28g fat (14g sat. fat), 171mg chol., 1196mg sod., 87g carb. (16g sugars, 6g fiber), 55g pro.

TEST KITCHEN TIP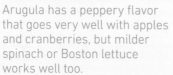

Arugula has a peppery flavor that goes very well with apples and cranberries, but milder spinach or Boston lettuce works well too.

SESAME CHICKEN VEGGIE WRAPS ✓

I'm always on the lookout for fast, nutritious recipes that will appeal to my three little kids. They happen to love edamame, so this is a smart choice for those on-the-go days.
—*Elisabeth Larsen, Pleasant Grove, UT*

TAKES: 30 min. • **MAKES:** 8 servings

- 1 cup frozen shelled edamame

DRESSING
- 2 Tbsp. orange juice
- 2 Tbsp. olive oil
- 1 tsp. sesame oil
- ½ tsp. ground ginger
- ¼ tsp. salt
- ⅛ tsp. pepper

WRAPS
- 2 cups fresh baby spinach
- 1 cup thinly sliced cucumber
- 1 cup fresh sugar snap peas, chopped
- ½ cup shredded carrots
- ½ cup thinly sliced sweet red pepper
- 1 cup chopped cooked chicken breast
- 8 whole wheat tortillas (8 in.), warmed

1. Cook edamame according to package directions. Drain; rinse with cold water and drain well. Whisk together dressing ingredients.
2. In a large bowl, combine the next 6 ingredients and edamame; toss with dressing. Place about ½ cup mixture on each tortilla. Fold bottom and sides of tortilla over filling and roll up.
1 WRAP 214 cal., 7g fat (1g sat. fat), 13mg chol., 229mg sod., 28g carb. (2g sugars, 5g fiber), 12g pro. **DIABETIC EXCHANGES** 2 starch, 1 lean meat, 1 fat.

GOES GREAT WITH ... Easy Shrimp & Scallops Ramen Soup (p. 42) turns these wraps into a fun dinner.

SESAME CHICKEN VEGGIE WRAPS

BACON & SWISS CHICKEN SANDWICHES

I created this sandwich based on one my daughter ordered at a restaurant. She likes to dip her sandwich in extra honey-mustard sauce.
—Marilyn Moberg, Papillion, NE

TAKES: 25 min. • **MAKES:** 4 servings

- ¼ cup reduced-fat mayonnaise
- 1 Tbsp. Dijon mustard
- 1 Tbsp. honey
- 4 boneless skinless chicken breast halves (4 oz. each)
- ½ tsp. Montreal steak seasoning
- 4 slices Swiss cheese
- 4 whole wheat hamburger buns, split
- 2 bacon strips, cooked and crumbled
  Lettuce leaves and tomato slices, optional

1. In a small bowl, mix mayonnaise, mustard and honey. Pound chicken with a meat mallet to ½-in. thickness. Sprinkle chicken with steak seasoning. Grill chicken, covered, over medium heat or broil 4 in. from the heat until a thermometer reads 165°, 4-6 minutes on each side. Top with cheese during the last 1 minute of cooking.
2. Grill the buns over medium heat, cut side down, until toasted, 30-60 seconds. Serve the chicken on buns with bacon, mayonnaise mixture and, if desired, lettuce and tomato.

1 SANDWICH 410 cal., 17g fat (6g sat. fat), 91mg chol., 667mg sod., 29g carb. (9g sugars, 3g fiber), 34g pro. **DIABETIC EXCHANGES** 4 lean meat, 2 starch, 2 fat.

BACON & SWISS CHICKEN SANDWICHES

GRILLED EGGPLANT SANDWICHES

GARLIC BREAD TUNA MELTS

Take this tuna melt up a few notches with garlic, cheese and tomatoes.
—*Aimee Bachmann, North Bend, WA*

TAKES: 20 min. • **MAKES:** 4 servings

- ¼ cup butter, cubed
- 3 garlic cloves, minced
- 4 French rolls or hoagie buns, split
- 2 cans (one 12 oz., one 5 oz.) albacore white tuna in water, drained and flaked
- ¼ cup reduced-fat mayonnaise
- 1¼ tsp. dill weed, divided
- 8 slices cheddar cheese
- 8 slices tomato

1. Preheat broiler. In a microwave-safe bowl, microwave butter and garlic until the butter is melted. Place the rolls on a baking sheet, cut side up; brush with butter mixture. Broil 2-3 in. from heat until lightly browned, 2-3 minutes.
2. In a small bowl, mix tuna, mayonnaise and 1 tsp. dill. Layer the roll bottoms with the tuna mixture and cheese. Broil until the cheese is melted, 1-2 minutes longer. Top with tomato; sprinkle with remaining dill. Replace tops; serve immediately.
1 SANDWICH 704 cal., 41g fat (19g sat. fat), 146mg chol., 1314mg sod., 36g carb. (3g sugars, 2g fiber), 49g pro.

GRILLED EGGPLANT SANDWICHES

Grilled to perfection, this vegetarian eggplant, tomato and goat cheese sandwich makes a simply delicious meatless meal.
—*Jennifer Jaras, Corona, CA*

TAKES: 25 min. • **MAKES:** 2 servings

- 2 Tbsp. olive oil
- 1 garlic clove, minced
- 2 ciabatta rolls, split
- 4 slices eggplant (½ in. thick)
- 1 medium heirloom tomato, cut into ½-in. slices
- ¼ tsp. salt
- ⅛ tsp. pepper
- 2 oz. fresh goat cheese, softened
- 6 fresh basil leaves

1. Mix oil and garlic; brush onto cut sides of rolls and both sides of the vegetables. Sprinkle vegetables with salt and pepper.

2. Grill eggplant, covered, over medium heat until tender, 4-5 minutes per side. Grill the tomato, covered, until lightly browned, 1-2 minutes per side. Grill rolls, cut side down, until toasted, 1-2 minutes.
3. Spread roll bottoms with goat cheese. Top with basil, eggplant and tomato; close sandwiches.
1 SANDWICH 538 cal., 21g fat (5g sat. fat), 19mg chol., 958mg sod., 81g carb. (10g sugars, 7g fiber), 15g pro.

> ## TEST KITCHEN TIP
> Make this hearty sandwich into a lower-calorie lunch or dinner by serving it open-face and using a knife and fork. You'll save more than 150 calories per serving (and bring sodium below 700mg).

COPYCAT FRIED CHICKEN SANDWICH

After trying chicken sandwiches at all the major fast food chains, I decided to come up with my own version. I know everyone says theirs is better than the original, but mine really is.

—Ralph Jones, San Diego, CA

PREP: 15 min. + marinating
COOK: 20 min./batch • **MAKES:** 6 servings

- 3 boneless skinless chicken breast halves (6 oz. each)
- ¾ cup buttermilk
- 2 tsp. hot pepper sauce
- 2 large eggs, beaten
- 2 cups all-purpose flour
- 1 Tbsp. plus 1 tsp. garlic powder
- 1 Tbsp. each onion powder and paprika
- 2 tsp. pepper
- 1 tsp. salt
- ⅓ cup canola oil
- 6 brioche hamburger buns, split
  Optional toppings: Sliced tomatoes, pickle slices, onion slices

1. Cut each chicken breast horizontally in half; place in a large bowl. Add the buttermilk and hot sauce; toss to coat. Refrigerate, covered, 8 hours or overnight.

2. Preheat air fryer to 400°. Stir the eggs into chicken mixture. In a shallow dish, whisk flour, garlic powder, onion powder, paprika, pepper and salt. Remove the chicken from buttermilk mixture. Dredge chicken in flour mixture, firmly patting to help coating adhere. Repeat, dipping chicken again into buttermilk mixture and then dredging in flour mixture.

3. Place the chicken on a wire rack over a baking sheet. Refrigerate, uncovered, for 30 minutes. Using a pastry brush, lightly dab both sides of chicken with oil until no dry breading remains.

4. In batches, arrange chicken in a single layer on greased tray in air-fryer basket. Cook until a thermometer reads 165° and coating is golden brown and crispy, 7-8 minutes on each side. Remove chicken; keep warm. Toast buns in air fryer until golden brown, 2-3 minutes. Top the bun bottoms with chicken. Top as desired; replace bun tops.

NOTE In our testing, we find cook times vary dramatically among brands of air fryers. As a result, we give wider than normal ranges on suggested cook times. Begin checking at the first time listed and adjust as needed.

1 SANDWICH 538 cal., 18g fat (3g sat. fat), 136mg chol., 778mg sod., 63g carb. (8g sugars, 4g fiber), 30g pro.

TEST KITCHEN TIP
Like it hot? Add a bit more hot pepper sauce. Spice not your thing? Simply reduce it or leave it out altogether.

GRILLED PIMIENTO CHEESE SANDWICHES

⏱ 5i

GRILLED PIMIENTO CHEESE SANDWICHES ✓

Rich and creamy pimiento cheese is a southern favorite. It makes a tasty grilled cheese sandwich, especially with sweet hot pepper jelly. Serve this with a crisp salad for a fantastic lunch.
—Amy Freeze, Avon Park, FL

TAKES: 20 min. • **MAKES:** 2 servings

- 4 slices sourdough bread
- ¼ cup butter, melted
- ½ cup refrigerated pimiento cheese
- 2 Tbsp. pepper jelly
- 6 cooked thick-sliced bacon strips

1. Brush 1 side of each bread slice with melted butter. In a large skillet, toast bread, buttered side down, over medium heat until golden brown, 3-4 minutes.
2. Remove from heat; place toasted side up. Spread cheese evenly over toasted bread slices. Top 2 slices with 1 Tbsp. jelly and 2 slices bacon each. Top with remaining bread slices, cheese facing inward. Brush outside of each sandwich with remaining melted butter. Cook until bread is golden brown and cheese is melted, 3-4 minutes on each side. If desired, serve with additional jelly.

1 SANDWICH 869 cal., 52g fat (28g sat. fat), 105mg chol., 1856mg sod., 70g carb. (19g sugars, 2g fiber), 27g pro.

CALIFORNIA ROLL WRAPS

CALIFORNIA ROLL WRAPS

I love the California rolls I get at sushi restaurants and wanted to capture those flavors in a sandwich I could take to work. I started with the standard ingredients, then added a few others to come up with this hit.
—*Mary Pax-Shipley, Bend, OR*

TAKES: 20 min. • **MAKES:** 6 wraps

- ½ cup wasabi mayonnaise
- 6 whole wheat tortillas (8 in.), warmed
- 2 pkg. (8 oz. each) imitation crabmeat
- 1 medium ripe avocado, peeled and thinly sliced
- 1½ cups julienned peeled jicama
- 1 medium sweet red pepper, julienned
- 1 small cucumber, seeded and julienned
- ¾ cup bean sprouts

Divide wasabi mayonnaise evenly among the 6 tortillas and spread to within ½ in. of edges. Layer with the crabmeat, avocado, jicama, red pepper, cucumber and bean sprouts. Roll up tightly.

1 WRAP 365 cal., 18g fat (3g sat. fat), 10mg chol., 647mg sod., 39g carb. (2g sugars, 7g fiber), 13g pro. **DIABETIC EXCHANGES** 2 starch, 2 fat, 1 vegetable, 1 lean meat.

TEST KITCHEN TIP
If you can't find wasabi mayo or don't like the spicy kick, use regular mayo instead.

MUSHROOM PASTRAMI HOAGIES

MUSHROOM PASTRAMI HOAGIES

My husband is a firefighter, so I make easy meals I can deliver to him. He likes pastrami, but ham or roast beef also work for these hoagies.
—*Deanna Eads, Kingman, AZ*

TAKES: 25 min. • **MAKES:** 6 servings

- 3 Tbsp. butter
- 1 lb. sliced fresh mushrooms
- 1 large onion, halved and sliced
- 2 medium sweet red peppers, julienned
- 2 garlic cloves, minced
- ¼ tsp. salt
- ¼ tsp. pepper
- 6 hoagie buns, split
- 1½ lbs. sliced deli pastrami
- 12 slices provolone cheese

1. Preheat broiler. In a 6-qt. stockpot, heat butter over medium heat. Add the mushrooms, onion and peppers; cook and stir until tender, 5-7 minutes. Add the garlic; cook 1 minute longer. Drain vegetable mixture; stir in salt and pepper.

2. Arrange the buns on a baking sheet. Layer bun bottoms with the pastrami and vegetable mixture; top with cheese. Broil 4-5 in. from heat 1-2 minutes or until the cheese is melted and bun tops are toasted.

1 SANDWICH 572 cal., 26g fat (14g sat. fat), 110mg chol., 1787mg sod., 43g carb. (9g sugars, 3g fiber), 43g pro.

FAJITA BURGER WRAPS

This combo gives you a tender burger, crisp veggies and a crunchy shell, plus fajita flavor. Kids love it.
—*Antonio Smith, Canal Winchester, OH*

TAKES: 30 min. • **MAKES:** 4 servings

1	lb. lean ground beef (90% lean)
2	Tbsp. fajita seasoning mix
2	tsp. canola oil
1	medium onion, halved and sliced
1	medium green pepper, cut into thin strips
1	medium red sweet pepper, cut into thin strips
4	flour tortillas (10 in.), warmed
¾	cup shredded cheddar cheese

1. In a large bowl, combine the beef and seasoning mix, mixing lightly but thoroughly. Shape into four ½-in.-thick patties.

2. In a large skillet, heat oil over medium heat. Add the burgers; cook 4 minutes on each side. Remove from the pan. In same skillet, add the onion and peppers; cook and stir until lightly browned and tender, 5-7 minutes.

3. On center of each tortilla, place ½ cup pepper mixture, 1 burger and 3 Tbsp. cheese. Fold sides of tortilla over burger; fold top and bottom to close, forming a square.

4. Wipe the skillet clean. Place wraps in skillet, seam side down. Cook over medium heat until golden brown and a thermometer inserted in the beef reads 160°, 1-2 minutes on each side.

1 WRAP 533 cal., 23g fat (9g sat. fat), 92mg chol., 1190mg sod., 45g carb. (5g sugars, 3g fiber), 34g pro.

GRILLED GOAT CHEESE & ARUGULA SANDWICHES

To create a more grown-up grilled cheese, I threw in tangy goat cheese and peppery arugula. I enjoy a similar combination on pizza.
—*Jess Apfe, Berkeley, CA*

TAKES: 30 min. • **MAKES:** 4 servings

½	cup sun-dried tomato pesto
8	slices sourdough bread
1½	cups roasted sweet red peppers, drained and patted dry
8	slices part-skim mozzarella cheese
½	cup crumbled goat cheese
1	cup fresh arugula
¼	cup butter, softened

1. Spread pesto over 4 slices of bread. Layer with peppers, mozzarella cheese, goat cheese and arugula; top with remaining bread. Spread outsides of sandwiches with butter.

2. In a large skillet, toast sandwiches over medium heat for 3-4 minutes on each side or until golden brown and cheese is melted.

1 SANDWICH 499 cal., 30g fat (17g sat. fat), 84mg chol., 1438mg sod., 33g carb. (9g sugars, 2g fiber), 22g pro.

FAJITA BURGER WRAPS

BUFFALO TOFU WRAP

BUFFALO TOFU WRAP

My family loves the tofu filling in these wraps. For parties, we often serve it as a dip with tortilla chips or pita bread. It's easy to double the recipe if needed.
—*Deanna Wolfe, Muskegon, MI*

TAKES: 20 min. • **MAKES:** 6 servings

- 1 cup shredded dairy-free cheddar-flavored cheese
- ½ cup vegan mayonnaise
- ¼ cup finely chopped onion
- ¼ cup finely chopped celery
- 3 Tbsp. Louisiana-style hot sauce
- 1 Tbsp. lemon juice
- ½ tsp. garlic powder
- ¼ tsp. salt
- ¼ tsp. pepper
- 1 pkg. (16 oz.) extra-firm tofu, drained
- 1½ cups fresh baby spinach
- 6 spinach tortillas (8 in.), warmed

In a large bowl, combine the first 9 ingredients. Crumble tofu into the bowl; mix well. Spoon about ½ cup tofu mixture down the center of each tortilla; top with spinach. Fold bottom and side of tortilla over filling; roll up.
1 WRAP 452 cal., 29g fat (7g sat. fat), 0 chol., 1066mg sod., 38g carb. (1g sugars, 2g fiber), 11g pro.

TEST KITCHEN TIPS

For a vegan option, use non-dairy cheese and vegan mayo. The tofu portion can be prepared ahead and chilled for a few hours or overnight.

VIETNAMESE CHICKEN BANH MI SANDWICHES

My version of the classic Vietnamese sandwich combines the satisfying flavor of chicken sausage with tangy vegetables pickled in rice vinegar. Stuff the ingredients in a hoagie bun and dinner is ready to go!
—*Angela Spengler, Niceville, FL*

TAKES: 25 min. • **MAKES:** 4 servings

- 1 pkg. (12 oz.) fully cooked spicy chicken sausage links
- 2 tsp. olive oil, divided
- ⅓ cup hoisin sauce
- 1 Tbsp. honey
- 2 tsp. reduced-sodium soy sauce
- 1 garlic clove, minced
- ¼ tsp. Chinese five-spice powder
- 1 medium onion, thinly sliced
- ½ cup shredded cabbage
- ½ cup shredded carrots
- 2 tsp. rice vinegar
- 4 hoagie buns, split
- 4 lettuce leaves

1. Cut each sausage in half lengthwise. In a large skillet, brown the sausage in 1 tsp. oil. Remove and keep warm.
2. Add hoisin, honey, soy sauce, garlic and five-spice powder to the skillet. Bring to a boil. Cook and stir until the garlic is tender and sauce is thickened. Return sausages to pan; toss to coat.
3. In a small skillet, saute the onion, cabbage and carrots in remaining oil until crisp-tender. Stir in vinegar. Serve sausage in buns with lettuce and onion mixture.

NOTE Hoisin sauce can be found in the Asian section of the grocery store.

1 SANDWICH EQUALS 452cal., 15g fat (3g sat. fat), 66mg chol., 1,331mg sod., 57g carb., 3g fiber, 25g pro.

VIETNAMESE CHICKEN BANH MI SANDWICHES

GOES GREAT WITH ...

A simple side like potato chips is ideal for this for full-flavored sandwich.

HEARTY BREADED FISH SANDWICHES

Fishing for a burger alternative? Consider it caught. A hint of cayenne is cooled by a creamy yogurt and mayo sauce in this fish sandwich that will put your local drive-thru to shame.
—Taste of Home *Test Kitchen*

TAKES: 30 min. • **MAKES:** 4 servings

- ½ cup dry bread crumbs
- ½ tsp. garlic powder
- ½ tsp. cayenne pepper
- ½ tsp. dried parsley flakes
- 4 cod fillets (6 oz. each)
- 4 whole wheat hamburger buns, split
- ¼ cup plain yogurt
- ¼ cup fat-free mayonnaise
- 2 tsp. lemon juice
- 2 tsp. sweet pickle relish
- ¼ tsp. dried minced onion
- 4 lettuce leaves
- 4 slices tomato
- 4 slices sweet onion

1. In a shallow bowl, combine bread crumbs, garlic powder, cayenne and parsley. Coat fillets with bread crumb mixture.
2. On a lightly oiled grill rack, grill cod, covered, over medium heat or broil 4 in. from heat for 4-5 minutes on each side or until the fish flakes easily with a fork. Grill buns over medium heat for 30-60 seconds or until toasted.
3. Meanwhile, in a small bowl, combine the yogurt, mayonnaise, lemon juice, relish and minced onion; spread over bun bottoms. Top with cod, lettuce, tomato and onion; replace bun tops.
1 SANDWICH 292 cal., 4g fat (1g sat. fat), 68mg chol., 483mg sod., 32g carb. (7g sugars, 4g fiber), 32g pro. **DIABETIC EXCHANGES** 5 lean meat, 2 starch.

GRILLED PESTO, HAM & PROVOLONE SANDWICHES

These Italian-style sandwiches are loaded with zesty flavors. To lighten them a little, use fat-free mayo. We serve them with minestrone or a crisp salad.
—Priscilla Yee, Concord, CA

TAKES: 20 min. • **MAKES:** 4 servings

- 2 Tbsp. mayonnaise
- 4 tsp. prepared pesto
- 8 slices sourdough bread
- 8 oz. thinly sliced deli ham
- ½ cup loosely packed basil leaves
- 4 pickled sweet cherry peppers, chopped
- 1 plum tomato, thinly sliced
- ¾ cup shredded provolone cheese
- 2 Tbsp. butter, softened

1. In a small bowl, mix mayonnaise and pesto; spread over 4 slices of bread. Layer with ham, basil, peppers, tomato and cheese. Top with the remaining bread. Spread outsides of sandwiches with butter.
2. Using a large cast-iron skillet or electric griddle, toast sandwiches over medium heat until golden brown and the cheese is melted, 2-3 minutes on each side.
1 PANINI 464 cal., 26g fat (10g sat. fat), 64mg chol., 1701mg sod., 35g carb. (4g sugars, 2g fiber), 24g pro.

PEPPERED PORK PITAS

LOADED AVOCADO BLT

My husband invented this twist on bacon, lettuce and tomato sandwich. I like to make it with eight slices of bacon, and I sometimes add Gorgonzola cheese to the avocado spread.
—*Lori Grant, Kingsport, TN*

TAKES: 15 min. • **MAKES:** 2 servings

- ½ small ripe avocado, peeled
- 2 Tbsp. mayonnaise
- ½ tsp. lemon juice
- 2 Tbsp. crumbled Gorgonzola cheese
- 4 slices Italian bread, toasted
- 1½ cups fresh baby spinach
- 4 tomato slices
- 4 thick-sliced applewood smoked bacon strips, cooked

1. Mash avocado with a fork; stir in the mayonnaise and lemon juice. Gently stir in cheese. Spread over all toast slices.
2. Top 2 slices of toast with spinach, tomato, bacon and remaining pieces of toast, avocado spread side down.
1 SANDWICH 420 cal., 29g fat (7g sat. fat), 27mg chol., 921mg sod., 27g carb. (3g sugars, 5g fiber), 15g pro.

READER RAVES
"Yum! This was a good Friday-night dinner."

—**LAURIE7627, TASTEOFHOME.COM**

PEPPERED PORK PITAS

Believe it: Cracked black pepper is all it takes to give my pork pitas some pop. With these, any weeknight meal is awesome. I like to fill the pitas with caramelized onions and garlic mayo.
—*Katherine White, Henderson, NV*

TAKES: 20 min. • **MAKES:** 4 servings

- 1 lb. boneless pork loin chops, cut into thin strips
- 1 Tbsp. olive oil
- 2 tsp. coarsely ground pepper
- 2 garlic cloves, minced
- 1 jar (12 oz.) roasted sweet red peppers, drained and julienned
- 4 whole pita breads, warmed
  Optional: Garlic mayonnaise and torn leaf lettuce

In a small bowl, combine the pork, oil, pepper and garlic; toss to coat. Place a large skillet over medium-high heat. Add pork mixture; cook and stir until no longer pink. Stir in the red peppers; heat through. Serve on pita breads. Top with mayonnaise and lettuce if desired.
1 SANDWICH 380 cal., 11g fat (3g sat. fat), 55mg chol., 665mg sod., 37g carb. (4g sugars, 2g fiber), 27g pro. **DIABETIC EXCHANGES** 3 lean meat, 2 starch, 1 fat.

GOES GREAT WITH ...
Toss a handful of waffle fries into the air fryer to serve with these tasty BLTs.

LOADED AVOCADO BLT

TURKEY SANDWICH WITH RASPBERRY-MUSTARD SPREAD

My hearty sandwich has different yet complementary flavors and textures. It's filled with flavor and nutrients, without all the unhealthy fats, sodium and added sugar that many other sandwiches have. And it's absolutely delicious!
—*Sarah Savage, Buena Vista, VA*

TAKES: 25 min. • **MAKES:** 2 servings

- 1 Tbsp. honey
- 1 Tbsp. spicy brown mustard
- 1 tsp. red raspberry preserves
- ¼ tsp. mustard seed
- 1 Tbsp. olive oil
- 4 oz. fresh mushrooms, thinly sliced
- 1 cup fresh baby spinach, coarsely chopped
- 1 garlic clove, minced
- ½ tsp. chili powder
- 4 slices multigrain bread, toasted
- 6 oz. sliced cooked turkey breast
- ½ medium ripe avocado, sliced

1. Combine honey, mustard, preserves and mustard seed. In a large skillet, heat oil over medium-high heat. Add mushrooms; cook and stir until tender, 4-5 minutes. Add the spinach, garlic and chili powder; cook and stir until spinach is wilted, 3-4 minutes.
2. Spread half the mustard mixture over 2 slices of toast. Layer with the turkey, mushroom mixture and avocado. Spread remaining mustard mixture over the remaining toast slices; place over top.

1 SANDWICH 449 cal., 16g fat (3g sat. fat), 68mg chol., 392mg sod., 40g carb. (14g sugars, 7g fiber), 35g pro.

TEST KITCHEN TIP
If you don't have mustard seed handy, substitute stone-ground mustard for the spicy brown mustard.

TURKEY SANDWICH WITH RASPBERRY-MUSTARD SPREAD

SMOKED GOUDA VEGGIE MELT

CUBAN PORK WRAPS

Hot and juicy pork in tortillas may remind you of a Cuban sandwich with ham and cheese. We always include the pickles, of course.
—*Aimee Bachmann, North Bend, WA*

TAKES: 20 min. • **MAKES:** 4 servings

- ¾ lb. thin boneless pork loin chops, cut into strips
- 1 Tbsp. canola oil
- ⅛ tsp. pepper
- 1 Tbsp. Dijon mustard
- 4 multigrain tortillas (10 in.), warmed
- 8 oz. sliced deli ham
- 8 slices Swiss cheese
- 4 thin sandwich pickle slices
- ¼ cup thinly sliced red onion

1. Preheat oven to 350°. In a bowl, toss pork with oil and pepper. Place a large skillet over medium-high heat. Add the pork; cook and stir 2-3 minutes or until browned. Remove from heat.
2. To assemble, spread mustard onto the center of tortillas; layer with ham, cheese, pickle, onion and pork. Fold the bottom and sides of tortillas over filling and roll up. Place on an ungreased baking sheet; bake 4-6 minutes or until heated through.
1 WRAP 501 cal., 22g fat (8g sat. fat), 86mg chol., 1230mg sod., 37g carb. (5g sugars, 7g fiber), 39g pro.

SMOKED GOUDA VEGGIE MELT

After a long day of teaching, I like to make these cheesy open-faced sandwiches. My 8-year-old daughter is a big fan too.
—*Charlie Herzog, West Brookfield, VT*

TAKES: 25 min. • **MAKES:** 4 servings

- 1 cup chopped fresh mushrooms
- 1 cup chopped fresh broccoli
- 1 medium sweet red pepper, chopped
- 1 small onion, chopped
- 2 Tbsp. olive oil
- 8 slices Italian bread (½ in. thick)
- ½ cup mayonnaise
- 1 garlic clove, minced
- 1 cup shredded smoked Gouda cheese

1. Preheat the oven to 425°. Place the mushrooms, broccoli, pepper and onion in a greased 15x10x1-in. baking pan. Drizzle with oil; toss to coat. Roast 10-12 minutes or until tender.
2. Meanwhile, place bread slices on a baking sheet. Mix mayonnaise and garlic; spread over bread.
3. Change oven setting to broil. Spoon vegetables over bread slices; sprinkle with cheese. Broil 3-4 in. from the heat 2-3 minutes or until cheese is melted.
2 OPEN-FACED SANDWICHES 523 cal., 37g fat (9g sat. fat), 34mg chol., 695mg sod., 35g carb. (5g sugars, 3g fiber), 14g pro.

CHAPTER 5

BEEF & GROUND BEEF

P. 98

P. 95

P. 90

P. 88

GOES GREAT WITH ...
Top off this meal-in-one with scoops of Quick Mango Sorbet (p. 306).

TAKEOUT BEEF FRIED RICE

TAKEOUT BEEF FRIED RICE

Transform leftover cooked beef into a quick dinner for six. You can use chuck roast or flank steak.
—Taste of Home *Test Kitchen*

TAKES: 30 min. • **MAKES:** 6 servings

- 1 Tbsp. plus 1 tsp. canola oil, divided
- 3 large eggs
- 1 can (11 oz.) mandarin oranges
- 2 medium sweet red peppers, chopped
- 1 cup fresh sugar snap peas, trimmed
- 1 small onion, thinly sliced
- 3 garlic cloves, minced
- ½ tsp. crushed red pepper flakes
- 4 cups cold cooked rice
- 2 cups cooked beef, sliced across grain into bite-sized pieces
- 1 cup beef broth
- ¼ cup reduced-sodium soy sauce
- ½ tsp. salt
- ¼ tsp. ground ginger

1. In a large skillet, heat 1 Tbsp. oil over medium-high heat. Whisk the eggs until blended; pour into skillet. Mixture should set immediately at its edge. As eggs set, push cooked egg toward center, letting uncooked portions flow underneath. When eggs are thickened and no liquid egg remains, remove to a cutting board and chop. Meanwhile, drain oranges, reserving 2 Tbsp. juice.
2. In same skillet, heat remaining 1 tsp. oil over medium-high heat. Add peppers, sugar snap peas and onion; cook and stir until crisp-tender, 1-2 minutes. Add garlic and pepper flakes; cook 1 minute longer. Add remaining ingredients and reserved juice; heat through. Gently stir in eggs and drained oranges.
1⅓ CUPS 367 cal., 9g fat (2g sat. fat), 136mg chol., 793mg sod., 45g carb. (11g sugars, 3g fiber), 26g pro. **DIABETIC EXCHANGES** 3 starch, 3 lean meat, 1 fat.

CHEESEBURGER QUESADILLAS

CHEESEBURGER QUESADILLAS

I created these fun cheeseburger quesadilla mashups in honor of my family's two favorite foods. They're so yummy and easy to make!
—*Jennifer Stowell, Deep River, IA*

TAKES: 25 min. • **MAKES:** 4 servings

- 1 lb. ground beef
- 1 cup ketchup
- ⅓ cup prepared mustard
- 4 bacon strips, cooked and crumbled
- 2 Tbsp. Worcestershire sauce
- ⅔ cup mayonnaise
- 2 Tbsp. 2% milk
- 2 Tbsp. dill pickle relish
- ¼ tsp. pepper
- 8 flour tortillas (8 in.)
- 1 cup shredded cheddar cheese
   Optional: Shredded lettuce and chopped tomatoes

1. In a large skillet, cook beef over medium heat, until no longer pink, 6-8 minutes, crumbling beef; drain. Stir in the ketchup, mustard, bacon and Worcestershire sauce; bring to a boil. Reduce heat; simmer, uncovered, 5-7 minutes or until slightly thickened, stirring occasionally.
2. Meanwhile, in a small bowl, combine mayonnaise, milk, relish and pepper.
3. Preheat the griddle over medium heat. Sprinkle 4 tortillas with cheese; top with the beef mixture and remaining tortillas. Place on griddle; cook until tortillas are golden brown and cheese is melted, 1-2 minutes on each side. Serve with sauce and, if desired, lettuce and tomatoes.
1 QUESADILLA WITH ABOUT ¼ CUP SAUCE 1002 cal., 60g fat (17g sat. fat), 110mg chol., 2115mg sod., 75g carb. (18g sugars, 4g fiber), 39g pro.

TEST KITCHEN TIP

Spice up your cheeseburger quesadillas by mixing cayenne pepper into the beef mixture.

HASH BROWN-TOPPED STEAK

My husband and I enjoy cooking together. One night we were craving grilled steak and cheese-stuffed baked potatoes but were feeling a little impatient. Here's the quicker meal-in-one idea we invented.
—*Judy Armstrong, Prairieville, LA*

TAKES: 30 min. • **MAKES:** 4 servings

- 2 Tbsp. butter
- 1 small onion, chopped
- 3 garlic cloves, minced
- 2 cups frozen shredded hash brown potatoes, thawed
- ¾ tsp. salt, divided
- 1 cup shredded Jarlsberg cheese
- 1 beef top sirloin steak (1 in. thick and 1½ lbs.), cut into 4 portions
- ½ tsp. pepper
- 2 Tbsp. minced fresh chives

1. In a large skillet, heat the butter over medium-high heat. Add onion; cook and stir for 2-3 minutes or until tender. Add the garlic; cook 2 minutes longer.
2. Stir in hash browns and ¼ tsp. salt; spread in an even layer. Reduce heat to medium; cook 5 minutes. Turn hash browns over; cook, covered, 5-6 minutes longer or until heated through and the bottom is lightly browned. Sprinkle with the cheese; cover and remove from heat. Keep warm.
3. Sprinkle the beef with the pepper and remaining salt. Grill beef, covered, over medium heat 5-7 minutes on each side or until meat reaches desired doneness (for medium-rare, a thermometer should read 135°; medium, 140°; medium-well, 145°).
4. Remove steaks from heat; top each with a fourth of the potato mixture. Sprinkle with chives.
1 SERVING 403 cal., 20g fat (10g sat. fat), 102mg chol., 703mg sod., 10g carb. (1g sugars, 1g fiber), 45g pro.

SMOTHERED BURRITOS

My brother-in-law teased that I knew how to make only five things using ground beef. I had to prove him wrong, and came back with these burritos.
—*Kim Kenyon, Greenwood, MO*

TAKES: 30 min. • **MAKES:** 4 servings

- 1 can (10 oz.) green enchilada sauce
- ¾ cup salsa verde
- 1 lb. ground beef
- 4 flour tortillas (10 in.), warmed
- 1½ cups shredded cheddar cheese, divided

1. Preheat oven to 375°. In a small bowl, mix enchilada sauce and salsa verde.
2. In a large skillet, cook the beef over medium heat until no longer pink, 8-10 minutes, breaking into crumbles; drain. Stir in ½ cup sauce mixture.
3. Spoon ⅔ cup beef mixture across center of each tortilla; top each with 3 Tbsp. cheese. Fold the bottom and sides of tortilla over filling and roll up.
4. Place in a greased 11x7-in. baking dish. Pour remaining sauce mixture over top; sprinkle with remaining ¾ cup cheese. Bake, uncovered, until the cheese is melted, 10-15 minutes.
1 BURRITO 624 cal., 33g fat (15g sat. fat), 115mg chol., 1470mg sod., 44g carb. (6g sugars, 2g fiber), 36g pro.

HASH BROWN-TOPPED STEAK

INDIAN-SPICED BEEFY LETTUCE WRAPS

INDIAN-SPICED BEEFY LETTUCE WRAPS

Since I love the flavors of Indian food, I almost always have coconut milk, a jar of mango chutney and garam masala seasoning in my pantry. This is one of my go-to recipes when I am short on time but want something that tastes spectacular. If you'd like to give this a different style of Asian flair, use hoisin sauce in place of chutney and Chinese five-spice powder instead of the garam masala.
—*Noelle Myers, Grand Forks, ND*

TAKES: 30 min. • **MAKES:** 4 servings

- 1 lb. ground beef
- 1 medium onion, finely chopped
- 2 garlic cloves, minced
- ⅓ cup mango chutney
- 2 Tbsp. soy sauce
- 1 tsp. garam masala
- 1 pkg. (12.70 oz.) Asian crunch salad mix
- ¼ cup canned coconut milk
- 12 Bibb or Boston lettuce leaves
- 1 medium mango, peeled and sliced

1. In a large skillet, cook the beef, onion and garlic over medium heat until beef is no longer pink and onion is tender, 6-8 minutes, breaking up the beef into crumbles; drain. Stir in the chutney, soy sauce and garam masala; heat through. Add salad mix (reserve packets); cook and stir until slightly wilted, about 5 minutes.
2. Combine coconut milk and reserved dressing packet until smooth. Spoon the beef mixture into lettuce leaves; sprinkle with contents from reserved toppings packet. Drizzle with coconut milk mixture and top with mango.
3 FILLED LETTUCE WRAPS 493 cal., 22g fat (8g sat. fat), 74mg chol., 957mg sod., 48g carb. (33g sugars, 5g fiber), 24g pro.

PAPA BURGER ✓

When whipping up something for Father's Day or the Fourth of July, I go big and tall with this fully loaded, juicy burger.
—*Chase Bailey, Costa Mesa, CA*

TAKES: 30 min. • **MAKES:** 4 servings

- 1 lb. ground beef or ground bison
- ⅓ cup finely chopped onion
- 1 slice whole wheat or white bread, broken into small pieces
- 2 Tbsp. red wine vinegar
- 1 Tbsp. liquid smoke
- 2 tsp. Worcestershire sauce
- 1 tsp. hamburger or steak seasoning
- ¼ to ½ tsp. garlic salt
- ¼ to ½ tsp. pepper
- ¼ cup all-purpose flour
- 4 onion hamburger buns, split
- 4 Bibb or Boston lettuce leaves
- ⅓ cup prepared Thousand Island salad dressing
- 4 slices process American cheese
- 4 slices red onion
- 1 large heirloom tomato, sliced

1. Combine first the 9 ingredients; mix lightly but thoroughly. Shape into four ¾-in.-thick patties. Press patties into flour to lightly coat both sides.
2. In a large cast-iron or other heavy skillet, cook burgers over medium heat until a thermometer reads 160°, 4-5 minutes per side. Layer bun bottoms with salad dressing, lettuce, burgers, cheese, onion and tomato slices. Replace bun tops.
1 BURGER 546 cal., 28g fat (10g sat. fat), 77mg chol., 976mg sod., 39g carb. (10g sugars, 2g fiber), 31g pro.

PAPA BURGER

EASY MEATBALL STROGANOFF

This recipe has fed not only my family, but many neighborhood kids!
—*Julie May, Hattiesburg, MS*

TAKES: 30 min. • **MAKES:** 4 servings

3 cups uncooked egg noodles
1 Tbsp. olive oil
1 pkg. (12 oz.) frozen fully cooked Italian meatballs, thawed
1½ cups beef broth
1 tsp. dried parsley flakes
¾ tsp. dried basil
½ tsp. salt
½ tsp. dried oregano
¼ tsp. pepper
1 cup heavy whipping cream
¾ cup sour cream

1. Cook egg noodles according to the package directions for al dente; drain.
2. Meanwhile, in a large skillet, heat oil over medium-high heat. Brown the meatballs; remove from pan. Add broth, stirring to loosen browned bits from the pan. Add the seasonings. Bring to a boil; cook until liquid is reduced to ½ cup, 5-7 minutes.
3. Add meatballs, noodles and cream. Bring to a boil. Reduce heat; simmer, covered, until slightly thickened, 3-5 minutes. Stir in sour cream; heat through.

1 SERVING 717 cal., 57g fat (30g sat. fat), 172mg chol., 1291mg sod., 31g carb. (5g sugars, 2g fiber), 20g pro.

READER RAVES

"The best stroganoff I've made. We had it for dinner, and everyone thought it was a keeper."

—PHYTZ38, TASTEOFHOME.COM

SKILLET BBQ BEEF POTPIE

Beef potpie is a classic comfort food, but who's got time to see it through? This speedy crowd-pleaser is also an excellent way to use leftover stuffing.
—*Priscilla Yee, Concord, CA*

TAKES: 25 min. • **MAKES:** 4 servings

1 lb. lean ground beef (90% lean)
⅓ cup thinly sliced green onions, divided
2 cups frozen mixed vegetables, thawed
½ cup salsa
½ cup barbecue sauce
3 cups cooked cornbread stuffing
½ cup shredded cheddar cheese
¼ cup chopped sweet red pepper

1. In a large skillet, cook beef and ¼ cup green onion over medium heat until beef is no longer pink, 6-8 minutes; crumble beef; drain. Stir in mixed vegetables, salsa and barbecue sauce; cook, covered, over medium-low heat for 4-5 minutes or until heated through.
2. Layer stuffing over beef; sprinkle with cheese, red pepper and remaining green onion. Cook, covered, 3-5 minutes longer or until heated through and the cheese is melted.

1½ CUPS 634 cal., 27g fat (9g sat. fat), 85mg chol., 1372mg sod., 62g carb. (19g sugars, 9g fiber), 33g pro.

BAKED BEEF TACOS

BAKED BEEF TACOS ✓

We give tacos a fresh approach by baking the shells upright in refried beans and tomatoes. The bottom gets soft, and the top stays crisp and crunchy.
—*Patricia Stagich, Elizabeth, NJ*

PREP: 15 min. • **BAKE:** 20 min.
MAKES: 12 servings

1½ lbs. ground beef
1 envelope taco seasoning
2 cans (10 oz. each) diced tomatoes and green chiles, divided
1 can (16 oz.) refried beans
2 cups shredded Mexican cheese blend, divided
¼ cup chopped fresh cilantro
1 tsp. hot pepper sauce, optional
12 taco shells
Chopped green onions

1. Preheat the oven to 425°. In a large skillet, cook beef over medium heat, 6-8 minutes or until no longer pink, crumble meat; drain. Stir in seasoning and 1 can undrained tomatoes; heat through.
2. Mix beans, ½ cup cheese, cilantro, remaining can of undrained tomatoes and, if desired, pepper sauce. Spread onto the bottom of a greased 13x9-in. baking dish.
3. Stand taco shells upright on bean mixture. Fill each with 1 Tbsp. cheese and about ⅓ cup beef mixture. Bake, covered, 15 minutes.
4. Uncover; sprinkle with remaining cheese. Bake, uncovered, 5-7 minutes or until cheese is melted and shells are lightly browned. Sprinkle with green onion.
1 TACO WITH ¼ CUP BEAN MIXTURE
277 cal., 15g fat (7g sat. fat), 52mg chol., 836mg sod., 17g carb. (0 sugars, 3g fiber), 17g pro.

BASIL-BUTTER STEAKS WITH ROASTED POTATOES

A few ingredients and 30 minutes are all you'll need for this incredibly satisfying meal. A simple basil butter gives these steaks a very special taste.
—*Taste of Home Test Kitchen*

TAKES: 30 min. • **MAKES:** 4 servings

1 pkg. (15 oz.) frozen Parmesan and roasted garlic red potato wedges
4 beef tenderloin steaks (1¼ in. thick and 6 oz. each)
½ tsp. salt
½ tsp. pepper
5 Tbsp. butter, divided
2 cups grape tomatoes
1 Tbsp. minced fresh basil

1. Bake the potato wedges according to package directions.
2. Meanwhile, sprinkle steaks with salt and pepper. In a 10-in. cast-iron or other ovenproof skillet, brown the steaks in 2 Tbsp. butter. Add tomatoes to skillet. Bake, uncovered, at 425° until the meat reaches desired doneness, 15-20 minutes (for medium-rare, a thermometer should read 135°; medium, 140°; medium-well, 145°).
3. In a small bowl, combine basil and remaining butter. Spoon over steaks and serve with potatoes.
1 SERVING 538 cal., 29g fat (13g sat. fat), 112mg chol., 740mg sod., 27g carb. (2g sugars, 3g fiber), 41g pro.

READER RAVES
"The steaks were very tender. This is a great busy-weeknight dinner!"

—NEWCOUNTRYWIFE, TASTEOFHOME.COM

BASIL-BUTTER STEAKS WITH
ROASTED POTATOES

SHEET-PAN STEAK DINNER

Asparagus and steak form a classic combination for a delicious dinner. Cooking them together makes for easy prep and cleanup. In our house, any meal that can be put in the oven while we get a few more things done for the day is a win!
—*Pamela Forrest, Springfield, OR*

PREP: 15 min. • **BAKE:** 25 min.
MAKES: 4 servings

1 tsp. minced fresh rosemary
½ tsp. each salt, pepper, paprika and garlic powder
1½ lbs. beef flank steak
1 lb. fresh asparagus, trimmed
2 Tbsp. avocado oil
2 Tbsp. butter, melted
1 garlic clove, minced

1. Preheat oven to 400°. In a small bowl, combine the rosemary and seasonings; set aside.
2. Place steak on 1 side of a 15x10x1-in. baking pan; place the asparagus on the other side in a single layer. Brush steak with oil and sprinkle with seasoning mix. Combine butter and garlic; pour over the asparagus.
3. Cover with foil; bake until the meat reaches desired doneness (for medium-rare, a thermometer should read 135°; medium, 140°; medium-well, 145°), 25-30 minutes. Let steak stand 5-10 minutes before slicing. Serve with asparagus.
5 OZ. COOKED BEEF WITH 8 ASPARAGUS SPEARS 380 cal., 25g fat (10g sat. fat), 96mg chol., 448mg sod., 3g carb. (1g sugars, 1g fiber), 34g pro.

TEST KITCHEN TIP

You can swap out the flank steak for any cut that requires low-and-slow cooking or one that's perfect for high-heat grilling. Try skirt steak, flap steak, bavette or flat iron steak.

SHEET-PAN STEAK DINNER

LOUISIANA MEAT PIES

LOUISIANA MEAT PIES ✓

I always found the food of Louisiana so full of flavor. These meat pies are my version of the region's cuisine. I promise you won't just have one!
—*Kristyne Mcdougle Walter, Lorain, OH*

PREP: 30 min. + chilling
COOK: 10 min./batch • **MAKES:** 9 servings

- 1 Tbsp. canola oil
- ½ lb. ground beef
- ½ lb. uncooked breakfast sausage links, casings removed
- 2 celery ribs, chopped
- 1 large sweet red pepper, chopped
- 1 medium onion, chopped
- 2 Tbsp. all-purpose flour
- ½ tsp. seasoned salt
- ¼ tsp. garlic powder
- ¼ tsp. cayenne pepper
- ½ cup vegetable broth
- 3 sheets frozen puff pastry, thawed
- 1 large egg, beaten

1. In a large skillet, heat oil over medium heat. Add beef, sausage, celery, sweet red pepper and onion. Cook until meat is no longer pink and the vegetables are tender, 6-8 minutes, breaking up meat into crumbles; drain. Return to pan. Stir in flour, salt, garlic powder and cayenne until blended; gradually whisk in the broth. Cook and stir until thickened, 3-5 minutes. Transfer to a large bowl; refrigerate for 30 minutes.
2. Preheat air fryer to 360°. On a lightly floured surface, unfold the puff pastry sheets. Cut each sheet into six 4½x3-in.

rectangles. Divide filling among centers of 9 pastry rectangles. Brush edges of pastry with beaten egg. Top with the remaining pastry rectangles; press edges with a fork to seal. Prick tops with a fork and brush with beaten egg.
3. In batches, place pies in a single layer on a greased tray in air-fryer basket. Cook until golden brown, 10-12 minutes.
FREEZE OPTION Freeze unbaked pastries on a parchment-lined baking sheet until firm. Transfer to an airtight container; return to freezer. To use, cook frozen pastries as directed until golden brown and heated through, increasing time to 15-20 minutes.
1 MEAT PIE 551 cal., 33g fat (8g sat. fat), 50mg chol., 717mg sod., 51g carb. (1g sugars, 7g fiber), 15g pro.

MOCK FILET MIGNON ✓

This always gets rave reviews—and plenty of requests for the recipe!
—*Cheri Legaard, Fortuna, ND*

TAKES: 30 min. • **MAKES:** 6 servings

- 1½ lbs. lean ground beef
- 2 cups cooked rice
- 1 cup finely chopped onion
- 1 Tbsp. Worcestershire sauce
- 1½ tsp. salt
- ¼ tsp. garlic powder
- ¼ tsp. pepper
- 6 bacon strips

1. In a large bowl, combine the beef, rice, onion, Worcestershire sauce, salt, garlic powder and pepper. Shape into 6 round patties. Wrap 1 strip of bacon around each patty; fasten with a wooden toothpick.
2. Place in an ungreased shallow baking dish. Bake at 450° for 20 minutes or until meat is no longer pink.
1 SERVING 379 cal., 22g fat (8g sat. fat), 84mg chol., 834mg sod., 18g carb. (2g sugars, 1g fiber), 25g pro.

BROCCOLI-CHEDDAR BEEF ROLLS

My grandmother's recipe for beef rolls is easy to change up. Load them with ham, veggies, or even olives, as you like!
—*Kent Call, Riverside, UT*

TAKES: 30 min. • **MAKES:** 6 servings

- ½ lb. lean ground beef (90% lean)
- 2 cups chopped fresh broccoli
- 1 small onion, chopped
- ½ tsp. salt
- ¼ tsp. pepper
- 6 hard rolls
- 2 cups shredded cheddar cheese, divided

1. Preheat oven to 325°. In a large skillet, cook beef with broccoli and onion over medium heat until no longer pink, 4-6 minutes. Crumble beef and stir in salt and pepper.
2. Cut one-third off the top of each roll; discard or save for another use. Hollow out bottoms, leaving ½-in.-thick shells; place on a baking sheet.
3. Tear bread removed from centers into ½-in. pieces and place in a bowl. Stir 1½ cups cheese into beef mixture. Spoon into bread shells. Sprinkle with remaining ½ cup cheese. Bake until heated through and cheese is melted, 10-15 minutes.
1 STUFFED ROLL 394 cal., 18g fat (9g sat. fat), 61mg chol., 783mg sod., 34g carb. (2g sugars, 2g fiber), 23g pro.

EASY ZITI BAKE
(PICTURED ON COVER)
I enjoy making this baked ziti recipe for family and friends. It's easy to prepare, and I like to get creative with the sauce. Sometimes I might add my home-canned tomatoes, mushrooms or vegetables.
—*Elaine Anderson, New Galilee, PA*

PREP: 20 min. • **BAKE:** 45 min. + standing
MAKES: 6-8 servings.

- 12 ounces uncooked ziti or small tube pasta
- 2 pounds ground beef
- 1 jar (24 ounces) spaghetti sauce
- 2 large eggs, beaten
- 1 carton (15 ounces) ricotta cheese
- 2 ½ cups shredded mozzarella cheese, divided
- ½ cup grated Parmesan cheese
  Cook pasta according to package directions.

1. Meanwhile, preheat oven to 350°. In a large skillet, cook beef over medium heat until no longer pink; drain. Stir in the spaghetti sauce.
2. In a large bowl, combine eggs, ricotta cheese, 1-½ cups mozzarella cheese and the Parmesan cheese. Drain pasta; add to cheese mixture and stir until blended.
3. Spoon a third of the meat sauce into a greased 13x9-in. baking dish; top with half of the pasta mixture. Repeat layers. Top with remaining meat sauce.
4. Cover and bake 40 minutes or until a thermometer reads 160°. Uncover; sprinkle with remaining mozzarella cheese. Bake 5-10 minutes longer or until cheese is melted. Let stand 15 minutes before serving.
1 PIECE 630 cal., 30g fat (15g sat. fat), 164mg chol., 878mg sod., 45g carb. (11g sugars, 3g fiber), 45g pro.

BEEF & PEPPER SKILLET

BEEF & PEPPER SKILLET

I love Mexican-inspired food. I also enjoy experimenting with recipes like this one and making them as healthy as possible—and downright good!
—Jenny Dubinsky, Inwood, WV

TAKES: 30 min. • **MAKES:** 6 servings

- 1 lb. lean ground beef (90% lean)
- 1 can (14½ oz.) diced tomatoes with mild green chiles, undrained
- 1 can (14½ oz.) beef broth
- 1 Tbsp. chili powder
- ¼ tsp. salt
- ⅛ tsp. garlic powder
- 2 cups instant brown rice
- 1 medium sweet red pepper, sliced
- 1 medium green pepper, sliced
- 1 cup shredded Colby-Monterey Jack cheese

1. In a large cast-iron or other heavy skillet, cook beef over medium heat until no longer pink, 6-8 minutes, breaking into crumbles; drain.
2. Add tomatoes, broth, chili powder, salt and garlic powder; bring to a boil. Stir in rice and peppers. Reduce heat; simmer, covered, until the liquid is absorbed, 8-10 minutes. Remove from heat; sprinkle with cheese. Let stand, covered, until cheese is melted.
FREEZE OPTION Before adding cheese, cool beef mixture. Freeze beef mixture and cheese separately in freezer containers. To use, partially thaw in refrigerator overnight. Heat through in a saucepan, stirring occasionally; add broth if necessary. Sprinkle with the cheese.
1⅓ CUPS 340 cal., 13g fat (7g sat. fat), 64mg chol., 807mg sod., 31g carb. (5g sugars, 4g fiber), 23g pro.

SOUTHWESTERN
BEEF & RICE SKILLET

GOES GREAT WITH …
A simple green salad makes a tasty addition to this savory dinner.

SOUTHWESTERN BEEF & RICE SKILLET

I like to serve this kicked-up skillet dish with warm flour tortillas and a side of guacamole. If you like things a little spicier, simply add more jalapeno and enjoy the heat!
—*Pat Hockett, Ocala, FL*

TAKES: 30 min. • **MAKES:** 4 servings

- 1 lb. lean ground beef (90% lean)
- 1 medium onion, chopped
- 1 medium green pepper, chopped
- 1 jalapeno pepper, seeded and finely chopped
- 1½ cups uncooked instant rice
- 1 can (14½ oz.) diced tomatoes with mild green chiles
- 1½ cups beef broth
- 1 tsp. ground cumin
- ¼ tsp. salt
- ¼ tsp. pepper
- 1 cup shredded Mexican cheese blend

1. In a large skillet, cook the beef, onion, green pepper and jalapeno over medium heat until meat is no longer pink and vegetables are tender, 8-10 minutes, breaking beef into crumbles; drain.
2. Add the rice, tomatoes and chiles, broth and seasonings. Bring to a boil, then reduce heat. Simmer, covered, until liquid is absorbed, about 5 minutes. Fluff with a fork. Remove from heat; sprinkle with the cheese. Let stand, covered, until cheese is melted.
1½ CUPS 482 cal., 19g fat (8g sat. fat), 96mg chol., 962mg sod., 41g carb. (5g sugars, 4g fiber), 33g pro.

TEST KITCHEN TIP
Leave some jalapeno pepper seeds in the dish if you like spicy foods; they'll add an extra kick.

GRILLED RIBEYES WITH GREEK RELISH

GRILLED RIBEYES WITH GREEK RELISH

The classic Grecian flavors of olives, feta cheese and tomatoes are a surefire hit. Combine them to complement a perfectly grilled steak, and it's magic.
—*Mary Lou Cook, Welches, OR*

TAKES: 30 min. • **MAKES:** 4 servings

- 4 plum tomatoes, seeded and chopped
- 1 cup chopped red onion
- ⅔ cup pitted Greek olives
- ¼ cup minced fresh cilantro
- ¼ cup lemon juice, divided
- 2 Tbsp. olive oil
- 2 garlic cloves, minced
- 2 beef ribeye steaks (¾ lb. each)
- 1 cup crumbled feta cheese

1. For relish, combine the tomatoes, onion, olives, cilantro, 2 Tbsp. lemon juice, oil and garlic.
2. Drizzle remaining lemon juice over steaks. Grill the steaks, covered, over medium heat or broil 4 in. from heat 5-7 minutes on each side, until meat reaches desired doneness (for medium-rare, a thermometer should read 135°; medium, 140°; medium-well, 145°). Let stand 5 minutes before cutting steaks in half. Serve with relish and cheese.
4 OZ. COOKED BEEF WITH ⅔ CUP RELISH AND ¼ CUP CHEESE 597 cal., 44g fat (16g sat. fat), 115mg chol., 723mg sod., 11g carb. (4g sugars, 3g fiber), 37g pro.

ITALIAN JOES ON TEXAS TOAST

This is toasty-good for busy nights. If you double the crushed tomatoes, meat and wine, you'll have enough sauce to freeze.
—Ashley Armstrong, Kingsland, GA

TAKES: 30 min. • **MAKES:** 8 servings

1   lb. ground beef
1   small green pepper, finely chopped
1   medium onion, finely chopped
3   garlic cloves, minced
½   cup dry red wine or beef broth
1   can (14½ oz.) diced tomatoes, undrained
¼   cup tomato paste
¼   tsp. salt
⅛   tsp. pepper
1   pkg. (11¼ oz.) frozen garlic Texas toast
8   slices part-skim mozzarella cheese

1. Preheat the oven to 425°. In a large skillet, cook beef with green pepper, onion and garlic over medium-high heat until meat is no longer pink, 5-7 minutes; crumble the beef; drain. Stir in wine and bring to a boil; cook until wine is reduced by half, about 2 minutes. Stir in tomatoes, tomato paste, salt and pepper; return to a boil. Reduce heat; simmer, uncovered, until mixture is thickened, 2-3 minutes, stirring occasionally.
2. Meanwhile, place Texas toasts on a foil-lined 15x10x1-in. pan; bake until lightly browned, 8-10 minutes.
3. Spoon beef mixture onto toasts; top with the cheese. Bake until the cheese is melted, 3-4 minutes. Serve immediately.
1 OPEN-FACED SANDWICH 353 cal., 19g fat (7g sat. fat), 58mg chol., 626mg sod., 25g carb. (5g sugars, 2g fiber), 22g pro.

LEMONY GREEK BEEF & VEGETABLES
(PICTURED ON PAGE 83)

I love the lemon in this recipe—the latest addition to my collection of quick, healthy dinners. I am sensitive to cow's milk, so I use goat cheese crumbles on my portion instead of Parmesan.
—Alice Neff, Lake Worth, FL

TAKES: 30 min. • **MAKES:** 4 servings

1   bunch baby bok choy
1   lb. ground beef
1   Tbsp. olive oil
5   medium carrots, sliced
3   garlic cloves, minced
¼   cup plus 2 Tbsp. white wine, divided
1   can (15 to 16 oz.) navy beans, rinsed and drained
2   Tbsp. minced fresh oregano or 2 tsp. dried oregano
¼   tsp. salt
2   Tbsp. lemon juice
½   cup shredded Parmesan cheese

1. Trim and discard root end of bok choy. Coarsely chop leaves. Cut stalks into 1-in. pieces. Set aside.
2. In a large skillet, cook the beef over medium-high heat until no longer pink, 5-7 minutes, breaking it into crumbles; drain. Remove from skillet and set aside.
3. In same skillet, heat oil over medium-high heat. Add carrots and bok choy stalks; cook and stir until crisp-tender, 5-7 minutes. Stir in garlic, bok choy leaves and ¼ cup wine. Cook, stirring to loosen browned bits from the pan, until greens wilt, 3-5 minutes.
4. Stir in ground beef, beans, oregano, salt and enough remaining wine to keep mixture moist. Reduce heat; simmer for 3 minutes. Stir in lemon juice; sprinkle with Parmesan cheese.
1½ CUPS 478 cal., 21g fat (7g sat. fat), 77mg chol., 856mg sod., 36g carb. (7g sugars, 10g fiber), 36g pro.

ITALIAN JOES ON TEXAS TOAST

AIR-FRYER STEAK FAJITAS

Zesty salsa and tender strips of steak make these traditional fajitas extra special.
—*Rebecca Baird, Salt Lake City, UT*

TAKES: 30 min. • **MAKES:** 6 servings

- 2   large tomatoes, seeded and chopped
- ½   cup diced red onion
- ¼   cup lime juice
- 1   jalapeno pepper, seeded and minced
- 3   Tbsp. minced fresh cilantro
- 2   tsp. ground cumin, divided
- ¾   tsp. salt, divided
- 1   beef flank steak (about 1½ lbs.)
- 1   large onion, halved and sliced
- 6   whole wheat tortillas (8 in.), warmed
      Optional: Sliced avocado and lime wedges

1. For salsa, place first 5 ingredients in a small bowl; stir in 1 tsp. cumin and ¼ tsp. salt. Let stand until serving.
2. Preheat the air fryer to 400°. Sprinkle the steak with the remaining cumin and salt. Place on a greased tray in air-fryer basket. Cook until the meat reaches desired doneness (for medium-rare, a thermometer should read 135°; medium, 140°; medium-well, 145°), 6-8 minutes per side. Remove from basket and let stand 5 minutes.
3. Meanwhile, place the onion on tray in air-fryer basket. Cook until crisp-tender, 2-3 minutes, stirring once. Slice steak thinly across the grain; serve in tortillas with onion and salsa. If desired, serve with avocado and lime wedges.
1 FAJITA 309 cal., 9g fat (4g sat. fat), 54mg chol., 498mg sod., 29g carb. (3g sugars, 5g fiber), 27g pro. **DIABETIC EXCHANGES** 4 lean meat, 2 starch.

AIR-FRYER STEAK FAJITAS

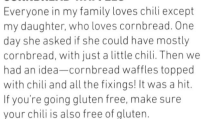

CHILI-TOPPED CORNBREAD WAFFLES

Everyone in my family loves chili except my daughter, who loves cornbread. One day she asked if she could have mostly cornbread, with just a little chili. Then we had an idea—cornbread waffles topped with chili and all the fixings! It was a hit. If you're going gluten free, make sure your chili is also free of gluten.
—*Courtney Stultz, Weir, KS*

TAKES: 20 min. • **MAKES:** 8 servings

- 1½ cups gluten-free all-purpose baking flour (without xanthan gum)
- 1½ cups cornmeal
- 2 tsp. baking powder
- 1 tsp. sea salt
- 2 large eggs, room temperature
- 2 cups 2% milk
- ½ cup olive oil
- 2 cans (15 oz.) chili with beans or 4 cups leftover chili, warmed
  Optional toppings: Jalapeno slices, shredded cheddar cheese, sour cream, cubed avocado and minced fresh cilantro

1. Preheat waffle maker. In a large bowl, whisk flour, cornmeal, baking powder and salt. In another bowl, whisk eggs, milk and oil until blended. Add to dry ingredients; stir just until moistened. Bake the waffles according to the manufacturer's directions until golden brown.
2. Serve with chili and your choice of optional toppings.
1 SERVING 464 cal., 20g fat (4g sat. fat), 64mg chol., 796mg sod., 57g carb. (6g sugars, 6g fiber), 15g pro.

GOES GREAT WITH ...
Toss together BBLT Chopped Salad (p. 297) while the waffles are baking.

CHILI-TOPPED CORNBREAD WAFFLES

ONE-POT MEATY SPAGHETTI

I used to help my mom make this when I was growing up, and the recipe stuck with me. It was a beloved comfort food at college and is now a weeknight staple for my fiance and me.
—Kristin Michalenko, Seattle, WA

TAKES: 30 min. • **MAKES:** 6 servings

- 1 lb. extra-lean ground beef (95% lean)
- 2 garlic cloves, minced
- 1 tsp. sugar
- 1 tsp. dried basil
- ½ tsp. dried oregano
- ¼ tsp. salt
- ¼ tsp. paprika
- ¼ tsp. pepper
- 1 can (28 oz.) diced tomatoes, undrained
- 1 can (15 oz.) tomato sauce
- 2 cups water
- ¼ cup chopped fresh parsley
- 8 oz. uncooked whole wheat spaghetti, broken in half
- ¼ cup grated Parmesan cheese
  Additional chopped parsley

1. In a 6-qt. stockpot, cook the beef with garlic over medium heat until no longer pink, 5-7 minutes, breaking up beef into crumbles. Stir in sugar and seasonings. Add tomatoes, tomato sauce, water and ¼ cup parsley; bring to a boil. Reduce heat; simmer, covered, 5 minutes.
2. Stir in spaghetti, a little at a time; return to a boil. Reduce heat to medium-low; cook, uncovered, until spaghetti is al dente, 8-10 minutes, stirring occasionally. Stir in cheese. Sprinkle with additional parsley.
1⅓ CUPS 292 cal., 6g fat (2g sat. fat), 46mg chol., 737mg sod., 40g carb. (6g sugars, 8g fiber), 24g pro. **DIABETIC EXCHANGES** 3 starch, 2 lean meat.

SLOPPY JOE BISCUIT CUPS

I'm a busy teacher and mom, so weekday meals with shortcuts are a huge help. I always have to share the recipe when I take these to school.
—Julie Ahern, Waukegan, IL

TAKES: 30 min. • **MAKES:** 10 biscuit cups

- 1 lb. lean ground beef (90% lean)
- ¼ cup each finely chopped celery, onion and green pepper
- ½ cup barbecue sauce
- 1 tube (12 oz.) refrigerated flaky biscuits (10 count)
- ½ cup shredded cheddar cheese

1. Preheat oven to 400°. In a large skillet, cook beef and vegetables over medium heat until the beef is no longer pink, 5-7 minutes, breaking up beef into crumbles; drain. Stir in the barbecue sauce; bring to a boil. Reduce heat; simmer, uncovered, 2 minutes, stirring occasionally.
2. Separate the dough into 10 biscuits; flatten into 5-in. circles. Press onto bottoms and up sides of 10 greased muffin cups. Fill with beef mixture.
3. Bake until the biscuits are golden brown, 9-11 minutes. Sprinkle with cheese; bake until cheese is melted, 1-2 minutes longer.
2 BISCUIT CUPS 463 cal., 22g fat (8g sat. fat), 68mg chol., 1050mg sod., 41g carb. (16g sugars, 1g fiber), 25g pro.

SPICY LASAGNA DINNER

4. Drain pasta. Add to tomato mixture; toss to coat. Sprinkle with cheese; let stand, covered, until cheese is melted.

FREEZE OPTION Freeze cooled pasta mixture and cheese in separate freezer containers. To use, partially thaw in refrigerator overnight. Heat through in a skillet, stirring occasionally; add water if necessary. Remove from heat. Sprinkle with cheese; let stand, covered, until the cheese is melted.

1 CUP 319 cal., 11g fat (5g sat. fat), 60mg chol., 1403mg sod., 31g carb. (7g sugars, 3g fiber), 24g pro.8

BLACK BEAN & BEEF TOSTADAS

You only need a handful of ingredients to make one of our family's favorites. Also easy to double for company!
—Susan Brown, Kansas City, KS

TAKES: 30 min. • **MAKES:** 4 servings

- ½ lb. lean ground beef (90% lean)
- 1 can (10 oz.) diced tomatoes and green chiles, undrained
- 1 can (15 oz.) black beans, rinsed and drained
- 1 can (16 oz.) refried beans, warmed
- 8 tostada shells
  Optional: Shredded reduced-fat Mexican cheese blend, shredded lettuce, salsa and sour cream

1. In a large skillet, cook the beef over medium-high heat until no longer pink, 4-6 minutes; breaking up the beef into crumbles. Stir in tomatoes; bring to a boil. Reduce heat; simmer, uncovered, until liquid is almost evaporated, 6-8 minutes. Stir in the black beans; heat through.

2. To serve, spread refried beans over tostada shells. Top with beef mixture; add toppings as desired.

2 TOSTADAS 392 cal., 14g fat (4g sat. fat), 35mg chol., 1011mg sod., 46g carb. (2g sugars, 10g fiber), 23g pro.

SPICY LASAGNA DINNER

Shortcut lasagna bails me out when I'm in a frenzy to serve dinner. A leafy salad and buttery garlic toast round out the easy meal.
—Donna Booth, Tomahawk, KY

TAKES: 30 min. • **MAKES:** 6 servings

- 1 pkg. (6.4 oz.) lasagna dinner mix
- 1 lb. lean ground beef (90% lean)
- 1 large onion, chopped
- 1 medium green pepper, chopped
- 1 garlic clove, minced
- 1 jar (14 oz.) meatless spaghetti sauce
- ½ cup chunky salsa
- 1 tsp. garlic powder
- 1 tsp. Italian seasoning
- ½ tsp. dried thyme
- ½ tsp. ground cumin
- ¼ tsp. salt
- ¼ tsp. crushed red pepper flakes
- 1 cup shredded mozzarella and provolone cheese blend

1. Fill a large saucepan three-fourths full with water; bring to a boil. Add the pasta from lasagna dinner mix; cook, uncovered, 10-12 minutes or until tender.
2. Meanwhile, in a large skillet, cook the beef, onion, green pepper and garlic over medium heat 6-8 minutes or until beef is no longer pink and vegetables are tender, breaking up beef into crumbles; drain.
3. Stir in the spaghetti sauce, salsa, seasonings and contents of seasoning packet from lasagna dinner mix. Bring to a boil. Reduce heat; simmer, uncovered, 5 minutes. Remove from heat.

BLACK BEAN & BEEF TOSTADAS

GOES GREAT WITH ...
Zap a packet of Spanish rice in the microwave for a fast and easy side dish.

EASY STUFFED POBLANOS

My partner adores these saucy stuffed peppers—and I love how quickly they come together. Top with low-fat sour cream and your favorite salsa.
—*Jean Erhardt, Portland, OR*

TAKES: 25 min. • **MAKES:** 4 servings

- ½ lb. Italian turkey sausage links, casings removed
- ½ lb. lean ground beef (90% lean)
- 1 pkg. (8.8 oz.) ready-to-serve Spanish rice
- 4 large poblano peppers
- 1 cup enchilada sauce
- ½ cup shredded Mexican cheese blend
  Minced fresh cilantro, optional

1. Preheat broiler. In a large skillet, cook turkey and beef over medium heat until no longer pink, 5-7 minutes, breaking up meat into crumbles; drain.
2. Prepare rice according to package directions. Add rice to meat mixture.
3. Cut peppers lengthwise in half; remove seeds. Place on a foil-lined 15x10x1-in. baking pan, cut side down. Broil 4 in. from heat until skins blister, about 5 minutes. With tongs, carefully turn peppers.
4. Fill with turkey mixture; top with enchilada sauce and sprinkle with cheese. Broil until cheese is melted, 1-2 minutes longer. If desired, top with cilantro.

NOTE Wear disposable gloves when cutting hot peppers; the oils can burn skin. Avoid touching your face.

2 STUFFED PEPPER HALVES 312 cal., 13g fat (4g sat. fat), 63mg chol., 1039mg sod., 27g carb. (5g sugars, 2g fiber), 22g pro.

TEST KITCHEN TIP

Don't have poblanos? Bell peppers also work well for this family-favorite recipe.

EASY STUFFED POBLANOS

STEAK & BLUE CHEESE PIZZA

STEAK & BLUE CHEESE PIZZA

Even my hubby who doesn't normally like blue cheese adores this heavenly pizza! If time allows, cook the onion until it's rich and caramelized for an unbeatable flavor.
—*Kadija Bridgewater, Boca Raton, FL*

TAKES: 30 min. • **MAKES:** 6 servings

- ½ lb. beef top sirloin steak, thinly sliced
- ¼ tsp. salt
- ¼ tsp. pepper
- 2 Tbsp. olive oil, divided
- 2 cups sliced baby portobello mushrooms
- 1 large onion, sliced
- ½ cup heavy whipping cream
- ¼ cup crumbled blue cheese
- 1 prebaked 12-in. pizza crust
- 2 tsp. minced fresh parsley

1. Preheat oven to 450°. Sprinkle beef with salt and pepper. In a large skillet, heat 1 Tbsp. oil over medium heat. Add beef and mushrooms; cook until beef is no longer pink, 3-4 minutes. Remove from pan.
2. Cook onion in the remaining oil until tender, 2-3 minutes. Add the cream and blue cheese; cook until slightly thickened, 3-5 minutes longer.
3. Place the crust on a 12-in. pizza pan or baking sheet. Spread with the cream mixture; top with beef mixture. Sprinkle with parsley. Bake until the sauce is bubbly and crust is lightly browned, 10-12 minutes.
1 PIECE 365 cal., 19g fat (8g sat. fat), 47mg chol., 535mg sod., 33g carb. (3g sugars, 2g fiber), 18g pro.

CHEESEBURGER CUPS
(PICTURED ON COVER)

This is a terrific recipe for moms with young kids and busy lives. The simple, inexpensive dish is made with handy ingredients and takes just a short time. Best of all, kids will go crazy for these darling dinner bites!
—*Jeri Millhouse, Ashland, OH*

TAKES: 30 min. • **MAKES:** 5 servings.

- 1 pound ground beef
- ½ cup ketchup
- 2 tablespoons brown sugar
- 1 tablespoon prepared mustard
- 1½ teaspoons Worcestershire sauce
- 1 tube (12 ounces) refrigerated buttermilk biscuits
- ½ cup cubed Velveeta

1. In a large skillet, cook beef over medium heat until no longer pink, breaking it into crumbles; drain. Stir in the ketchup, brown sugar, mustard and Worcestershire sauce. Remove from the heat; set aside.
2. Press each biscuit onto the bottom and up the sides of a greased muffin cup. Spoon beef mixture into cups; top with cheese cubes. Bake at 400° until cups are golden brown, 14-16 minutes.
FREEZE OPTION Freeze cooled pastries in a freezer container, separating layers with waxed paper. To use, thaw pastries in the refrigerator for 8 hours. Reheat on a baking sheet in a preheated 375° oven until heated through.
2 CHEESEBURGER CUPS 440 cal., 16g fat (7g sat. fat), 78mg chol., 1142mg sod., 45g carb. (13g sugars, 0 fiber), 27g pro.

KUNG PAO SLOPPY JOES

What happens when you combine two favorites into one easy dish? Clean plates, that's what! My family loves Chinese food, but takeout can be expensive and not always the healthiest. This stovetop kung pao sloppy joe recipe will please everyone at dinnertime, including the kids. My husband prefers to skip the bun and eat it over brown rice or rolled in lettuce leaves.
—Julie Peterson, Crofton, MD

TAKES: 30 min. • **MAKES:** 6 servings

1 lb. lean ground beef (90% lean)
1 small sweet red pepper, chopped
4 green onions, chopped, divided
2 garlic cloves, minced
2 tsp. minced fresh gingerroot
1 to 1½ tsp. Sriracha chili sauce
½ cup reduced-sodium soy sauce
6 Tbsp. rice vinegar, divided
¼ cup water
3 Tbsp. sesame oil, divided
2 Tbsp. cornstarch
2 Tbsp. brown sugar
1 pkg. (12 oz.) broccoli coleslaw mix
6 hamburger buns, split, or flour
   tortillas (8 in.)
½ cup chopped unsalted peanuts
   Fresh cilantro leaves, optional

1. In a large cast-iron or other heavy skillet, cook beef, red pepper and half the green onion over medium-high heat until beef is no longer pink and vegetables are tender, 6-8 minutes; crumble meat; drain. Add garlic, ginger and chili sauce; cook 1 minute longer.
2. In a small bowl, mix soy sauce, 4 Tbsp. vinegar, water, 1 Tbsp. oil, cornstarch and brown sugar until smooth; stir into the beef mixture. Bring to a boil, stirring constantly; cook and stir until thickened, 1-2 minutes.
3. For the slaw, in a large bowl, combine coleslaw mix and the remaining green onion, 2 Tbsp. vinegar and 2 Tbsp. oil; toss to coat. Spoon ½ cup beef mixture onto bun bottoms. Top with ½ cup slaw and peanuts. If desired, top with cilantro leaves. Serve the remaining slaw on the side.

FREEZE OPTION Freeze cooled meat mixture in freezer containers. To use, partially thaw in refrigerator overnight. Heat through in a saucepan, stirring occasionally; add water if necessary.

1 SANDWICH 461 cal., 21g fat (5g sat. fat), 47mg chol., 1299mg sod., 44g carb. (16g sugars, 4g fiber), 25g pro.

READER RAVES

"Loved these! Great weeknight dinner. Some spice but not too much, and the slaw topping is a great extra crunch."

—CURLYLIS85, TASTEOFHOME.COM

ONE-SKILLET LASAGNA

ONE-SKILLET LASAGNA

This is hands-down one of the best skillet lasagna recipes our testing panel has ever tasted. And with classic flavors and cheesy layers, it's definitely kid-friendly.
—Taste of Home *Test Kitchen*

TAKES: 30 min. • **MAKES:** 6 servings

¾ lb. ground beef
2 garlic cloves, minced
1 can (14½ oz.) diced tomatoes with basil, oregano and garlic, undrained
2 jars (14 oz. each) spaghetti sauce
⅔ cup condensed cream of onion soup, undiluted
2 large eggs, lightly beaten
1¼ cups 1% cottage cheese
¾ tsp. Italian seasoning
9 no-cook lasagna noodles
½ cup shredded Colby-Monterey Jack cheese
½ cup shredded part-skim mozzarella cheese

1. In a large skillet, cook beef and garlic over medium heat until meat is no longer pink, breaking up beef into crumbles; drain. Stir in tomatoes and spaghetti sauce; heat through. Transfer to a large bowl.
2. In a small bowl, combine soup, eggs, cottage cheese and Italian seasoning.
3. Return 1 cup meat sauce to the skillet; spread evenly. Layer with 1 cup cottage cheese mixture, 1½ cups meat sauce and half the noodles, breaking to fit. Repeat layers of cottage cheese mixture, meat sauce and noodles. Top with remaining meat sauce. Bring to a boil. Reduce heat; cover and simmer for 15-17 minutes or until noodles are tender.
4. Remove from the heat. Sprinkle with shredded cheeses; cover and let stand for 2 minutes or until cheese is melted.
1 SERVING 478 cal., 20g fat (8g sat. fat), 128mg chol., 1552mg sod., 43g carb. (15g sugars, 4g fiber), 31g pro.

CHAPTER 6
CHICKEN CLASSICS

P. 115

P. 128

P. 116

P. 120

MIGHTY NICE CURRIED CHICKEN WITH RICE

MIGHTY NICE CURRIED CHICKEN WITH RICE ✓

This was one of the first chicken recipes I prepared for my husband more than 54 years ago. His exclamation? Mighty nice! That's how it got its name. At times I add some more broth to make more of the yummy sauce.
—*Kay Stansberry, Athens, TN*

PREP: 15 min. • **COOK:** 45 min.
MAKES: 4 servings

- 1   broiler/fryer chicken (3 to 4 lbs.), cut up
- 1   tsp. salt
- ½   tsp. pepper
- ¼   cup butter
- 2   medium tart apples, peeled and sliced
- 1   large onion, finely chopped
- 2   Tbsp. all-purpose flour
- 2   Tbsp. curry powder
- 1   can (14½ oz.) chicken broth
- 3   Tbsp. golden raisins
- ½   tsp. grated orange zest
- 2   Tbsp. slivered almonds, toasted
     Hot cooked rice

1. Sprinkle the chicken with salt and pepper. In a large skillet, heat the butter over medium heat. Brown the chicken on both sides; remove from the pan.
2. In the same pan, add apples and onion; cook and stir until softened, 2-3 minutes. Stir in the flour and curry powder until blended; cook an additional 2 minutes. Gradually stir in chicken broth. Add the chicken back to pan along with raisins and orange zest. Reduce heat; simmer, covered, until a thermometer reads 165°, 30-35 minutes. Sprinkle with almonds; serve with hot cooked rice.

7 OZ. COOKED CHICKEN WITH 1½ CUPS SAUCE 657 cal., 39g fat (15g sat. fat), 187mg chol., 1210mg sod., 23g carb. (13g sugars, 4g fiber), 52g pro.

JALAPENO POPPER STUFFED CHICKEN BREASTS

JALAPENO POPPER STUFFED CHICKEN BREASTS ✓

My husband is not crazy about chicken, but one of his favorite snacks is jalapeno poppers. So I created this fast dinnertime recipe to give our chicken plenty of flavor. He loves it cooked this way, and best of all is the quick cooking with little cleanup!
—*Donna Gribbins, Shelbyville, KY*

PREP: 15 min. • **COOK:** 15 min./batch
MAKES: 4 servings

- 4   oz. cream cheese, softened
- 1   cup shredded cheddar cheese
- 1   jalapeno pepper, seeded and finely chopped
- 4   boneless skinless chicken breast halves (6 oz. each)
- ½   tsp. salt
- ½   tsp. pepper
- 8   thick-sliced bacon strips

1. Preheat the air fryer to 375°. In a small bowl, mix cream cheese, cheddar cheese and jalapeno. Cut a pocket horizontally in the thickest part of each chicken breast. Fill with the cheese mixture. Sprinkle the chicken with salt and pepper. Wrap 2 bacon strips around each chicken breast; secure with toothpicks.
2. In batches, place chicken seam side down on a greased tray in air-fryer basket. Cook until a thermometer inserted into the chicken reads 165°, 14-16 minutes, turning once. Let stand for 5 minutes. Discard the toothpicks before serving.

NOTE In our testing, we find cook times vary dramatically among brands of air fryers. As a result, we give wider than normal ranges on suggested cook times. Begin checking at the first time listed and adjust as needed.

1 STUFFED CHICKEN BREAST 518 cal., 33g fat (15g sat. fat), 171mg chol., 1150mg sod., 3g carb. (1g sugars, 0 fiber), 51g pro.

TWICE-COOKED FRIED CHICKEN

Fried chicken is my favorite food, so it's no surprise that I've tried dozens of recipes looking for the perfect one. This recipe is the result of my mission to create my own foolproof rendition.
—Audrey Alfaro, Rapid City, SD

PREP: 25 min. + chilling.
COOK: 3½ hours • **MAKES:** 6 servings

- 1 broiler/fryer chicken (3 to 4 lbs.), cut up
- 3 cups chicken broth
- 1 tsp. crushed red pepper flakes
- 1 tsp. garlic powder
- 1 tsp. paprika
- 1 tsp. lemon-pepper seasoning
- 2 cups buttermilk
- ½ cup Louisiana-style hot sauce

COATING
- 1½ cups all-purpose flour
- 2 tsp. paprika
- 2 tsp. seasoned salt
- 1 tsp. garlic powder
- 1 tsp. lemon-pepper seasoning
- 1 tsp. onion powder
- 1 tsp. ground cumin
- 1 tsp. kosher salt
- ½ tsp. pepper
- Oil for deep-fat frying

1. In a 5- or 6-qt. slow cooker, combine the first 6 ingredients. Cook, covered, on low until meat is tender, 3-4 hours. Remove chicken from the slow cooker; discard liquid.

2. In a small bowl, whisk the buttermilk and hot sauce until blended. Pour into a shallow dish. Add the chicken; turn to coat. Refrigerate 1 hour. Drain chicken, discarding buttermilk mixture.

3. In a bowl or shallow dish, mix flour and seasonings. Add chicken, a few pieces at a time; turn to coat. Shake off excess.

4. In a deep skillet, heat 2 in. oil to 375°. Fry chicken, a few pieces at a time, until the chicken is golden brown and juices run clear, 4-6 minutes on each side. Drain on paper towels.

5 OZ. COOKED CHICKEN 571 cal., 44g fat (7g sat. fat), 105mg chol., 524mg sod., 9g carb. (1g sugars, 0 fiber), 35g pro.

AIR-FRYER DIRECTIONS

Preheat air fryer to 350°. In batches, arrange coated chicken pieces in a single layer on a greased tray in air-fryer basket; spritz with cooking spray. Cook 5 minutes. Flip, spritz with cooking spray. Cook until browned, 5-6 minutes longer.

TWICE-COOKED FRIED CHICKEN

**CHUNKY CHICKEN
CACCIATORE**

 ✓

CHUNKY CHICKEN CACCIATORE

This recipe is so versatile! Look in your
fridge for anything else you want to
throw in. And if you're a vegetarian,
go ahead and leave out the chicken.
—*Stephanie Loaiza, Layton, UT*

PREP: 10 min. • **COOK:** 4 hours
MAKES: 6 servings

- 6 boneless skinless chicken thighs
  (about 1½ lbs.)
- 2 medium zucchini, cut into 1-in. slices
- 1 medium green pepper, cut into 1-in.
  pieces
- 1 large sweet onion, coarsely chopped
- ½ tsp. dried oregano
- 1 jar (24 oz.) garden-style spaghetti
  sauce
  Hot cooked spaghetti
  Optional: Sliced ripe olives and
  shredded Parmesan cheese

1. Place chicken and vegetables in
a 3-qt. slow cooker; sprinkle with the
oregano. Pour sauce over top. Cook,
covered, on low 4-5 hours or until
chicken is tender.
2. Remove chicken; break up slightly
with 2 forks. Return to slow cooker.
Serve with spaghetti. If desired, top
with olives and cheese.
FREEZE OPTION Place first 6 ingredients
in a freezer container and freeze. To use,
place container in refrigerator 48 hours
or until contents are completely thawed.
Cook and serve as directed.
1 SERVING 285 cal., 11g fat (2g sat. fat),
76mg chol., 507mg sod., 21g carb. (14g
sugars, 3g fiber), 24g pro. **DIABETIC
EXCHANGES** 3 lean meat, 1½ starch.

SOUTHERN FRIED CHICKEN STRIPS

What's not to love with these golden fried chicken strips? A hint of garlic makes them irresistible.
—*Genise Krause, Sturgeon Bay, WI*

PREP: 30 min. • **COOK:** 5 min./batch
MAKES: 6 servings

- 1 large egg
- ½ cup buttermilk
- 1 cup all-purpose flour
- 1½ tsp. garlic powder
- 1½ tsp. pepper
- ½ tsp. salt
- ½ tsp. paprika
- 2 lbs. chicken tenderloins
  Oil for deep-fat frying
- 2 Tbsp. grated Parmesan cheese
  Ranch salad dressing, optional

1. In a shallow bowl, whisk the egg and buttermilk. In a separate shallow bowl, combine flour, garlic powder, pepper, salt and paprika. Dip chicken into egg mixture, then into flour mixture.
2. In an electric skillet or Dutch oven, heat the oil to 375°. Fry chicken, a few pieces at a time, 2-3 minutes on each side or until no longer pink. Drain on paper towels. Sprinkle with cheese, and serve with ranch salad dressing if desired.

5 OZ. COOKED CHICKEN 327 cal., 11g fat (2g sat. fat), 126mg chol., 320mg sod., 18g carb. (2g sugars, 1g fiber), 39g pro.

TEST KITCHEN TIP
Instead of buying buttermilk, place 1 Tbsp. white vinegar or lemon juice in a liquid measuring cup and add enough milk to measure 1 cup. Stir, then let stand for 5 minutes. Or you can substitute 1 cup plain yogurt for the buttermilk.

SOUTHERN FRIED
CHICKEN STRIPS

CHICKEN SAUSAGE & GNOCCHI SKILLET

I had a bunch of fresh vegetables and combined them with sausage, gnocchi and goat cheese when I needed a quick dinner. Mix and match ingredients you have on hand to give it your own spin.
—*Dahlia Abrams, Detroit, MI*

TAKES: 30 min. • **MAKES:** 4 servings

- 1 pkg. (16 oz.) potato gnocchi
- 1 Tbsp. butter
- 1 Tbsp. olive oil
- 2 fully cooked Italian chicken sausage links (3 oz. each), sliced
- ½ lb. sliced baby portobello mushrooms
- 1 medium onion, finely chopped
- 1 lb. fresh asparagus, trimmed and cut into ½-in. pieces
- 2 garlic cloves, minced
- 2 Tbsp. white wine or chicken broth
- 2 oz. herbed fresh goat cheese
- 2 Tbsp. minced fresh basil or 2 tsp. dried basil
- 1 Tbsp. lemon juice
- ¼ tsp. salt
- ⅛ tsp. pepper
  Grated Parmesan cheese

1. Cook gnocchi according to package directions; drain. Meanwhile, in a large skillet, heat butter and oil over medium-high heat. Add sausage, mushrooms and onion; cook and stir until the sausage is browned and vegetables are tender. Add asparagus and garlic; cook and stir 2-3 minutes longer.
2. Stir in wine. Bring to a boil; cook until liquid is almost evaporated. Add goat cheese, basil, lemon juice, salt and pepper. Stir in gnocchi; heat through. Sprinkle with Parmesan cheese.
1½ CUPS 454 cal., 15g fat (6g sat. fat), 58mg chol., 995mg sod., 56g carb. (11g sugars, 5g fiber), 21g pro.

EASY CHICKEN PESTO STUFFED PEPPERS

On busy weeknights, I neither want to spend more than 30 minutes preparing dinner nor do I want to wash a towering pile of dishes. This recipe delivers on both counts without sacrificing flavor!
—*Olivia Cruz, Greenville, SC*

TAKES: 25 min. • **MAKES:** 4 servings

- 4 medium sweet yellow or orange peppers
- 1½ cups shredded rotisserie chicken
- 1½ cups cooked brown rice
- 1 cup prepared pesto
- ½ cup shredded Havarti cheese
  Fresh basil leaves, optional

1. Preheat the broiler. Cut the peppers lengthwise in half; remove stems and seeds. Place peppers skin side up on a baking sheet. Broil 4 in. from heat until skins blister, about 5 minutes. Reduce oven temperature to 350°.
2. Meanwhile, in a large bowl, combine chicken, rice and pesto. When peppers are cool enough to handle, fill with the chicken mixture; return to baking sheet. Bake until heated through, about 5 minutes. Sprinkle with the cheese; bake until cheese is melted, 3-5 minutes longer. If desired, sprinkle with basil before serving.
2 STUFFED PEPPER HALVES 521 cal., 31g fat (7g sat. fat), 62mg chol., 865mg sod., 33g carb. (7g sugars, 5g fiber), 25g pro.

GOES GREAT WITH ...
Ladle out bowls of Beer-Cheese Velvet Soup (p. 49) to complete this menu.

**MEDITERRANEAN
BRAISED CHICKEN THIGHS**

**1 CHICKEN THIGH WITH ⅓ CUP ARTICHOKE
MIXTURE** 378 cal., 26g fat (7g sat. fat),
91mg chol., 551mg sod., 10g carb. (1g
sugars, 0 fiber), 25g pro.

PRESSURE-COOKER
TEQUILA SALSA CHICKEN

I had this dish at a Mexican restaurant
when celebrating a friend's birthday. I
fell in love with the spicy, smoky flavor
from the tequila and decided to try it
at home in my Instant Pot. Boy, was it
a success! It's also fabulous stuffed
into flour tortillas or for making nachos.
This can be made with frozen chicken
breasts; just increase the cooking time
to 15 minutes.
—Trisha Kruse, Eagle, ID

TAKES: 15 min. • **MAKES:** 3 cups

- 1   envelope taco seasoning
- 1   lb. boneless skinless chicken
      breasts
- 1   cup chunky salsa
- ¼   cup tequila
      Hot cooked rice
      Optional toppings: Avocado slices,
      chopped fresh cilantro and lime
      wedges

1. Sprinkle taco seasoning over chicken
breasts; place in a 6-qt. electric pressure
cooker. Combine salsa and tequila; pour
over chicken. Lock lid; close pressure-
release valve. Adjust to pressure-cook
on high for 6 minutes. Quick-release
pressure. A thermometer inserted
into chicken should read at least 165°.
2. Remove chicken. When cool enough
to handle, shred meat with 2 forks;
return to pressure cooker. Serve with
rice, and optional toppings as desired.
¾ CUP 187 cal., 3g fat (1g sat. fat), 63mg
chol., 1107mg sod., 11g carb. (2g sugars,
0 fiber), 23g pro.

MEDITERRANEAN
BRAISED CHICKEN THIGHS

This chicken and artichoke dish was
inspired by a once-in-a-lifetime trip
to Santorini for my parents' 40th
anniversary. It's cooked in a big skillet
until the chicken basically falls off the
bone and all the flavors meld together
into a sauce that will have you spooning
mouthfuls. It's really a showstopper!
—Grace Vallo, Salem, NH

PREP: 15 min. • **COOK:** 30 min.
MAKES: 6 servings

- 2   Tbsp. butter
- 2   Tbsp. olive oil
- 6   bone-in chicken thighs (about 2 lbs.)
- 1   can (14 oz.) water-packed small
      artichoke hearts, drained
- 3   shallots, halved
- ⅓   cup dry white wine
- ½   cup pitted Greek olives
- ⅓   cup reduced-sodium chicken broth
- 1   Tbsp. lemon juice
- 1   garlic clove, thinly sliced
- 1   Tbsp. drained capers
- 1   tsp. ground sumac or za'atar
      seasoning

1. Preheat the oven to 375°. In a 12-in.
cast-iron or other ovenproof skillet, heat
butter and oil over medium-high heat.
Brown chicken, skin side down. Turn
thighs over; arrange artichokes and
shallots around chicken. Cook 1 minute.
Add wine to pan; cook 1 minute longer,
stirring to loosen browned bits from pan.
2. Add the remaining ingredients to
the pan. Bake 15-20 minutes or until
a thermometer inserted into the
chicken reads 170°-175°.

PRESSURE-COOKER
TEQUILA SALSA CHICKEN

CHICKEN PARMESAN STROMBOLI

I love chicken Parmesan and my family loves stromboli so one day I decided to combine the two using a few convenience products. It turned out far better than I could have hoped for. It's now a staple in our house.
—*Cyndy Gerken, Naples, FL*

PREP: 20 min. • **BAKE:** 20 min.
MAKES: 6 servings

- 4 frozen breaded chicken tenders (about 1½ oz. each)
- 1 tube (13.8 oz.) refrigerated pizza crust
- 8 slices part-skim mozzarella cheese
- ⅓ cup shredded Parmesan cheese
- 1 Tbsp. olive oil
- ½ tsp. garlic powder
- ¼ tsp. dried oregano
- ¼ tsp. pepper
- Marinara sauce, warmed

1. Prepare the chicken tenders according to package directions. Preheat the oven to 400°. Unroll dough onto a parchment-lined baking sheet. Layer crust with the mozzarella, chicken tenders and Parmesan to within ½ in. of edges. Roll up jelly-roll style, starting with a short side; pinch seam to seal and tuck ends under. Combine olive oil, garlic powder, oregano and pepper; brush over top.
2. Bake for 18-22 minutes or until crust is dark golden brown. Let stand 5 minutes before slicing. Serve with the marinara sauce for dipping.

1 PIECE 408 cal., 18g fat (7g sat. fat), 34mg chol., 859mg sod., 42g carb. (5g sugars, 2g fiber), 21g pro.

CHICKEN PARMESAN
STROMBOLI

GOES GREAT WITH ...
Cap off the stromboli with Contest-Winning Easy Tiramisu (p. 311).

**CHIPOTLE-ORANGE
CHICKEN**

1 CHICKEN BREAST HALF 324 cal., 8g fat
(1g sat. fat), 95mg chol., 414mg sod., 29g
carb. (24g sugars, 1g fiber), 35g pro.

BARBECUE CHICKEN QUESADILLAS

When my kids were small, I'd stuff
leftover chicken into these oven-baked
quesadillas. I often grab rotisserie
chicken instead.
—*Pam Martin, Canandaigua, NY*

TAKES: 25 min. • **MAKES:** 6 servings

- 3 cups shredded cooked chicken
- 1 can (4 oz.) chopped green chiles
- ½ cup salsa
- ⅓ cup barbecue sauce
- ¼ cup taco sauce
- 8 flour tortillas (8 in.)
- ¾ cup shredded sharp cheddar cheese
  Optional: Sour cream and additional
  salsa

1. Preheat oven to 450°. In a large bowl,
toss together the first 5 ingredients.
2. Divide 4 tortillas between 2 baking
sheets; spread with chicken mixture.
Sprinkle with the cheese and top with
remaining tortillas.
3. Bake 6-8 minutes or until lightly
browned and cheese is melted. Cut
each quesadilla into 6 wedges. Serve
with sour cream and additional salsa
if desired.

4 WEDGES 446 cal., 15g fat (5g sat. fat),
76mg chol., 815mg sod., 46g carb. (6g
sugars, 3g fiber), 29g pro.

CHIPOTLE-ORANGE CHICKEN

Big on flavor and easy on time, this recipe
is appealing. The sweet-hot sauce gets
its heat from the chipotle pepper. I like
to serve this slow-cooker chicken dish
with a side of rice.
—*Susan Hein, Burlington, WI*

PREP: 15 min. • **COOK:** 3 hours
MAKES: 2 servings

- 2 boneless skinless chicken breast
  halves (6 oz. each)
- ⅛ tsp. salt
  Dash pepper
- ¼ cup chicken broth
- 3 Tbsp. orange marmalade
- 1½ tsp. canola oil
- 1½ tsp. balsamic vinegar
- 1½ tsp. minced chipotle pepper in adobo
  sauce
- 1½ tsp. honey
- ½ tsp. chili powder
- ⅛ tsp. garlic powder

- 2 tsp. cornstarch
- 1 Tbsp. cold water

1. Sprinkle the chicken with salt and
pepper. Transfer to a 1½-qt. slow cooker.
In a small bowl, combine the broth,
marmalade, oil, vinegar, chipotle pepper,
honey, chili powder and garlic powder;
pour over chicken. Cover; cook on low
for 3-4 hours or until a thermometer
reads 165°.
2. Remove chicken to a serving platter
and keep warm. Place cooking juices
in a small saucepan; bring to a boil.
Combine cornstarch and water until
smooth. Gradually stir into pan. Bring
to a boil; cook and stir for 2 minutes
or until thickened. Serve with chicken.
FREEZE OPTION Cool chicken mixture.
Freeze in freezer containers. To use,
partially thaw in refrigerator overnight.
Heat through slowly in a covered skillet
until a thermometer inserted into the
chicken reads 165°, stirring occasionally;
add broth or water if necessary.

SWEET & HOT CHICKEN WITH DILL PICKLE SAUCE ✓

This is my low-carb version of Nashville hot chicken. We try to cut down on carbs as much as possible, so the breaded and fried version and the sandwich version of this dish are out. Instead, I make a baked version with the same delicious flavors. This is also wonderful made with chicken tenders and served as wraps.
—Fay Moreland, Wichita Falls, TX

PREP: 25 min. + marinating *2-3 hours*
BAKE: 40 min. • **MAKES:** 8 servings

1 cup sweet pickle juice
2 Tbsp. hot pepper sauce
1 tsp. granulated garlic
½ tsp. pepper
8 bone-in chicken thighs (about 3 lbs.)

PICKLE SAUCE
½ cup sour cream
½ cup chopped sliced sweet pickles
¼ cup sweet pickle juice
2 tsp. dill weed
½ tsp. salt
½ tsp. onion powder
¼ tsp. granulated garlic
¼ tsp. pepper

SPICE RUB
1 Tbsp. sweet smoked paprika
½ tsp. granulated garlic
¼ tsp. salt
¼ tsp. pepper

HOT SAUCE DIP
1 cup hot sauce
½ cup unsalted butter
½ cup brown sugar substitute blend equivalent to 1 cup brown sugar

1. In a bowl or shallow dish, combine the sweet pickle juice, hot sauce, granulated garlic and pepper. Add chicken and turn to coat. Refrigerate, covered, 2-3 hours.
2. Preheat oven to 375°. In a small bowl, combine pickle sauce ingredients until well blended. Refrigerate until serving.
3. In another small bowl, combine the spice rub ingredients. Remove chicken from marinade, discarding marinade. Place chicken on a greased, foil-lined baking sheet. Sprinkle with spice rub. Bake 30 minutes.
4. Meanwhile, in a small saucepan, heat the hot sauce and butter until the butter is melted. Whisk in brown sugar blend; simmer until the sauce thickens slightly, 1-2 minutes. Remove chicken from oven. Using tongs, dunk cooked pieces into the sauce; return to baking sheet. Increase the oven temperature to 400°; bake until a thermometer reads 170°-175°, about 10 minutes. Serve the chicken with dipping sauces, and additional pickle slices if desired.

1 CHICKEN THIGH WITH 2 TBSP. PICKLE SAUCE 350 cal., 23g fat (9g sat. fat), 106mg chol., 484mg sod., 12g carb. (10g sugars, 1g fiber), 23g pro.

AIR-FRYER CHICKEN PARMESAN

AIR-FRYER CHICKEN PARMESAN

Quick, simple and oh-so-tasty, this air-fryer chicken Parmesan recipe is the perfect weeknight dish to have. It's just as crispy as the classic, if not crispier!
—Taste of Home *Test Kitchen*

TAKES: 20 min. • **MAKES:** 4 servings

2 large eggs
½ cup seasoned bread crumbs
⅓ cup grated Parmesan cheese
¼ tsp. pepper
4 boneless skinless chicken breast halves (6 oz. each)
1 cup pasta sauce
1 cup shredded mozzarella cheese
  Optional: Chopped fresh basil and hot cooked pasta

1. Preheat air fryer to 375°. In a shallow bowl, lightly beat the eggs. In another shallow bowl, combine bread crumbs, Parmesan cheese and pepper. Dip the chicken into egg, then coat with crumb mixture.
2. Place chicken in a single layer on a greased tray in air-fryer basket. Cook until a thermometer reads 165°, 10-12 minutes, turning halfway through. Top the chicken with sauce and mozzarella. Cook until cheese is melted, 3-4 minutes longer. If desired, sprinkle with chopped basil and additional Parmesan cheese and serve with pasta.

NOTE In our testing, we find cook times vary dramatically among brands of air fryers. As a result, we give wider than normal ranges on suggested cook times. Begin checking at the first time listed and adjust as needed.

1 CHICKEN BREAST HALF 416 cal., 16g fat (7g sat. fat), 215mg chol., 863mg sod., 18g carb. (6g sugars, 2g fiber), 49g pro.

**MISO BUTTER
ROASTED CHICKEN**

MISO BUTTER ROASTED CHICKEN

I love this recipe because the prep work is done in the beginning. Look for a prepared spatchcock chicken in your grocery store. However if you can't find it, get your butcher to spatchcock the chicken and then the only work left to do is to chop the veggies.
—*Stefanie Schaldenbrand, Los Angeles, CA*

PREP: 25 min.
BAKE: 1½ hours + standing
MAKES: 6 servings

- 1 lb. medium fresh mushrooms
- 1 lb. baby red potatoes
- 1 lb. fresh Brussels sprouts, halved
- 6 garlic cloves, minced
- 1 Tbsp. olive oil
- 1½ tsp. minced fresh thyme or ½ tsp. dried thyme
- ½ tsp. salt
- ½ tsp. pepper
- 1 roasting chicken (5 to 6 lbs.)
- ¼ cup butter, softened
- ¼ cup white miso paste

1. Preheat oven to 425°. Mix mushrooms, potatoes, Brussels sprouts and garlic; drizzle with oil. Sprinkle with thyme, salt and pepper; toss to coat. Place in a shallow roasting pan.
2. Place the chicken on a work surface, breast side down and tail end facing you. Using kitchen shears, cut along each side of backbone; discard backbone. Turn the chicken over so breast side is up; flatten by pressing down firmly on breastbone until it cracks. Place chicken on a rack over vegetables. Twist and tuck wings under to secure in place. Combine the butter and miso paste; spread over the skin (mixture will be thick).
3. Roast until a thermometer inserted into the thickest part of chicken thigh reads 170°-175°, 1½-1¾ hours, covering loosely with foil after 45 minutes of cooking. (The miso mixture on chicken will appear very dark while roasting.)
4. Remove chicken from oven; tent with foil. Let stand 15 minutes before carving.

AIR-FRYER CHICKEN TACO POCKETS

If desired, skim fat and thicken pan drippings for gravy and serve with the chicken. Top chicken with additional fresh thyme if desired.
1 SERVING 653 cal., 37g fat (13g sat. fat), 170mg chol., 912mg sod., 25g carb. (3g sugars, 4g fiber), 54g pro.

AIR-FRYER CHICKEN TACO POCKETS

We love these easy taco-flavored sandwiches made with crescent dough. They make a quick and easy lunch or supper with a bowl of soup or a crisp salad. I also like to cut them into smaller servings for parties.
—*Donna Gribbins, Shelbyville, KY*

TAKES: 25 min. • **MAKES:** 8 servings

- 2 tubes (8 oz. each) refrigerated crescent rolls
- ½ cup salsa, plus more for serving
- ½ cup sour cream
- 2 Tbsp. taco seasoning
- 1 cup shredded rotisserie chicken
- 1 cup shredded cheddar cheese
  Optional toppings: Shredded lettuce, guacamole and additional sour cream

1. Preheat the air fryer to 375°. Unroll 1 tube crescent dough and separate into 2 rectangles; press perforations to seal. Repeat with the second tube. In a bowl, combine salsa, sour cream and taco seasoning. Spoon chicken onto the left side of each rectangle; top with salsa mixture. Sprinkle with cheese. Fold dough over filling; pinch edges to seal.
2. In batches if necessary, place pockets on tray in air-fryer basket. Cook until golden brown, 13-15 minutes. Cut in half. Serve with salsa, and optional toppings as desired.
½ POCKET 393 cal., 24g fat (7g sat. fat), 47mg chol., 896mg sod., 29g carb. (7g sugars, 0 fiber), 16g pro.

THREE-CUP BUTTERMILK FRIED CHICKEN

This recipe combines my Chinese roots with the southern-style fried chicken I've eaten over the past few years in Oklahoma. Three-cup chicken gets its name from the quintessential ingredients: soy sauce, wine and sesame oil.
—Edward Chiu, Broken Arrow, OK

PREP: 20 min. + marinating
COOK: 30 min. • **MAKES:** 6 servings

1½ lbs. boneless skinless chicken thighs, cut into 1-in. cubes
1 cup buttermilk
2 green onions
1 Tbsp. sesame oil
15 garlic cloves
1 piece fresh gingerroot (2 in.), peeled and sliced
1 cup Chinese cooking wine or sherry
6 Tbsp. brown sugar
6 Tbsp. reduced-sodium soy sauce
 Oil for deep-fat frying
2 cups all-purpose flour
1 Tbsp. cornstarch
1 Tbsp. water
1 cup fresh Thai basil leaves
 Hot cooked rice

1. Place chicken and buttermilk in a shallow dish, turning once to coat. Refrigerate 1 hour or overnight. Drain the chicken, discarding buttermilk. Meanwhile, thinly slice green part of onions; reserve for the garnish. Slice white part into ¼-in. pieces.
2. In a large skillet, heat sesame oil over medium-high heat. Add white part of green onion, garlic and ginger; stir-fry until fragrant and slightly browned, 3-4 minutes. Add wine, brown sugar and soy sauce, stirring until the sugar dissolves. Reduce heat; simmer for 10-15 minutes, stirring occasionally.
3. In a deep fryer or electric skillet, heat 2 in. oil to 375°. Place flour in a shallow dish. Add the chicken, several pieces at a time, and toss to coat; shake off excess. Fry chicken, several at a time, until golden brown, 3-4 minutes. Drain on paper towels.
4. In a small bowl, combine cornstarch and water. Remove the ginger slices and garlic cloves from the sauce; slowly stir in cornstarch mixture. Simmer, stirring constantly, until thickened, 1-2 minutes.
5. Add the chicken and basil; stir to coat. Remove from heat; garnish with green onions. Serve with rice.

1 CUP 456 cal., 22g fat (4g sat. fat), 76mg chol., 775mg sod., 33g carb. (14g sugars, 1g fiber), 25g pro.

READER RAVES
"Definitely a great recipe—easy and flavorful. Mmmm."

—COURTNEY876, TASTEOFHOME.COM

THREE-CUP BUTTERMILK FRIED CHICKEN

HERBY CHICKEN WITH APRICOTS & FETA

HERBY CHICKEN WITH APRICOTS & FETA

Mix up your weeknight menu with an herby braised chicken dish with Middle Eastern flair. I love to serve it with a side of couscous.
—*Sally Sibthorpe, Shelby Township, MI*

PREP: 20 min. • **COOK:** 25 min.
MAKES: 8 servings

1½ tsp. salt
1 tsp. dill weed
½ tsp. dried oregano
½ tsp. dried thyme
½ tsp. pepper
8 boneless skinless chicken thighs (about 2 lbs.)
3 Tbsp. canola oil
1 small onion, chopped
8 dried apricots
8 pitted dates
½ cup chicken stock
¼ cup lemon juice
1 cup crumbled feta cheese
2 green onions, thinly sliced
Hot cooked couscous, optional

1. Combine first 5 ingredients; sprinkle over chicken. In a large skillet, heat oil over medium heat. Brown chicken in batches; return all to skillet. Add the onion, apricots and dates; cook 5 minutes longer.
2. Stir in stock and lemon juice; bring to a boil. Reduce heat; simmer, covered, until a thermometer reads 170°, 5-7 minutes. Uncover and top with the feta and green onion. If desired, serve with couscous.
1 CHICKEN THIGH WITH ¼ CUP APRICOT MIXTURE 282 cal., 16g fat (4g sat. fat), 83mg chol., 674mg sod., 10g carb. (7g sugars, 2g fiber), 24g pro. **DIABETIC EXCHANGES** 3 lean meat, 2 fat, ½ starch.

GREEK CHICKEN SHEET-PAN DINNER

I love roasted vegetables and keeping things simple. One bowl and one sheet pan, that's it. You could use boneless chicken and add other veggies. Serve it with cucumber salad.
—*Sara Martin, Whitefish, MT*

PREP: 10 min. • **BAKE:** 40 min.
MAKES: 4 servings

- 4 bone-in chicken thighs, skin removed
- ½ cup Greek vinaigrette
- 8 small red potatoes, quartered
- 1 medium sweet red pepper, cut into ½-in. strips
- 1 can (14 oz.) water-packed artichoke hearts, drained and halved
- ¾ cup pitted ripe olives, drained
- 1 small red onion, cut into 8 wedges
- ¼ tsp. pepper
- ⅓ cup crumbled feta cheese

1. Preheat the oven to 375°. Spray a 15x10x1-in. baking pan with cooking spray; set aside.
2. In a large bowl, combine the first 7 ingredients; toss to coat. Place the chicken and vegetables in a single layer on baking pan; sprinkle with the pepper. Bake until a thermometer inserted into chicken reads 170°-175° and vegetables are tender, 30-35 minutes.
3. If desired, preheat broiler. Broil the chicken and vegetables 3-4 in. from the heat until lightly browned, 2-3 minutes. Remove from the oven, cool slightly. Sprinkle with feta cheese.

1 SERVING 481 cal., 24g fat (5g sat. fat), 92mg chol., 924mg sod., 31g carb. (3g sugars, 4g fiber), 31g pro.

TEST KITCHEN TIP
Be sure to use a sheet pan that has a lip so the juices don't run over and burn on the bottom of your oven.

GREEK CHICKEN SHEET-PAN DINNER

GOES GREAT WITH ...
Quick Garlic Toast (p. 299) makes a fast yet tasty addition to this meal-in-one entree.

HONEY CHICKEN STIR-FRY
(PICTURED ON COVER)

I am a new mom, and my schedule depends upon our young son, so I like meals that can be ready in little time. This all-in-one chicken stir-fry recipe with a hint of sweetness from honey is a big timesaver.
—*Caroline Sperry, Allentown, MI*

TAKES: 30 min. • **MAKES:** 4 servings.

- 2 tsp. cornstarch
- 1 Tbsp. cold water
- 3 tsp. olive oil, divided
- 1 lb. boneless skinless chicken breasts, cut into 1-in. pieces
- 1 garlic clove, minced
- 3 Tbsp. honey
- 2 Tbsp. reduced-sodium soy sauce
- ⅛ tsp. salt
- ⅛ tsp. pepper
- 1 pkg (16 oz.) frozen broccoli stir-fry vegetable blend
  Hot cooked rice, optional

1. Mix the cornstarch and water until smooth. In a large nonstick skillet, heat 2 tsp. oil over medium-high heat; stir-fry chicken and garlic 1 minute. Add honey, soy sauce, salt and pepper; cook and stir until chicken is no longer pink, 2-3 minutes. Remove from pan.
2. In same pan, stir-fry vegetable blend in the remaining oil just until tender, 4-5 minutes. Return the chicken to pan. Stir cornstarch mixture and add to pan; bring to a boil. Cook and stir until thickened, about 1 minute. Serve with rice if desired.
1 CUP STIR-FRY 249 cal., 6g fat (1g sat. fat), 63mg chol., 455mg sod., 21g carb. (15g sugars, 3g fiber), 25g pro. **DIABETIC EXCHANGES** 3 lean meat, 2 vegetable, ½ starch.

WEEKNIGHT CHICKEN CORDON BLEU

Ever cut a recipe from a magazine and see too late that you missed part of it? I figured out this one on my own, and now my son says it's his favorite.
—*Mary Ann Turk, Diamond, MO*

TAKES: 30 min. • **MAKES:** 4 servings

- 4 boneless skinless chicken breast halves (6 oz. each)
- ½ tsp. salt
- ¼ tsp. pepper
- 1 Tbsp. plus 2 tsp. canola oil, divided
- 3 cups cut fresh green beans (2-in. pieces)
- 1 cup sliced fresh mushrooms
- 4 thin slices deli ham
- 4 slices part-skim mozzarella cheese

1. Sprinkle the chicken with salt and pepper. In a large skillet, heat 1 Tbsp. oil over medium heat. Add chicken; cook for 4-6 minutes on each side or until a thermometer reads 165°. Remove from pan.
2. Heat remaining oil in same pan. Add the green beans and mushrooms; cook and stir 3-4 minutes or until beans are crisp-tender. Return the chicken to pan; top each with 1 slice each of ham and cheese. Cook, covered, 1-2 minutes or just until cheese is melted.
1 CHICKEN BREAST HALF WITH ½ CUP VEGETABLES 367 cal., 16g fat (5g sat. fat), 119mg chol., 763mg sod., 7g carb. (3g sugars, 2g fiber), 47g pro.

BUFFALO CHICKEN CRUNCH WRAPS

CHICKEN WITH PUMPKIN ALFREDO

I love pumpkin and my kids love pasta, so this was a match made in heaven. Plus, it is a terrific way to get some veggies into their diet. Use dairy- or gluten-free ingredients if needed.
—*Courtney Stultz, Weir, KS*

PREP: 15 min. • **COOK:** 30 min.
MAKES: 4 servings

- 1   Tbsp. olive oil
- 2   boneless skinless chicken breast halves (6 oz. each)
- 1   Tbsp. Italian seasoning
- ¾   tsp. salt
- ½   tsp. pepper
- 8   oz. uncooked spiral pasta
- 2   cups fresh broccoli florets
- ¼   cup butter, cubed
- 3   garlic cloves, minced
- 1   cup half-and-half cream
- 1   cup canned pumpkin
- ½   cup shredded Parmesan cheese
- ⅛   tsp. ground nutmeg
- 4   bacon strips, cooked and crumbled
       Minced fresh parsley

1. In a large skillet, heat oil over medium heat. Sprinkle the chicken with Italian seasoning, salt and pepper. Add to the skillet; cook until a thermometer reads 165°, 6-8 minutes on each side. Remove and keep warm.
2. Meanwhile, in a large saucepan, cook pasta according to package directions, adding broccoli during the last 5 minutes of cooking. In the same skillet used to cook chicken, heat butter over medium heat. Add garlic; cook 1 minute. Stir in the half-and-half, pumpkin, Parmesan cheese and nutmeg until combined.
3. Drain pasta and broccoli; stir into sauce. Slice chicken; serve with the pasta mixture. Sprinkle with bacon, parsley and, if desired, additional Parmesan cheese.
1 SERVING 631 cal., 30g fat (15g sat. fat), 123mg chol., 936mg sod., 53g carb. (6g sugars, 5g fiber), 35g pro.

BUFFALO CHICKEN CRUNCH WRAPS

My daughter-in-law loves Buffalo chicken, so I came up with this easy-to-make crunch wrap using the same flavors and grilled it in a panini press. In less than 30 minutes, you'll have a hot, crunchy pocket of spicy, cheesy chicken ready for a weeknight dinner or weekend lunch. They are also wonderful served with extra blue cheese dressing or sour cream for dipping.
—*Theresa Ravencraft, Marysville, OH*

PREP: 15 min. • **COOK:** 10 min./batch
MAKES: 6 servings

- 4   cups cubed or shredded rotisserie chicken
- 1   cup shredded Colby-Monterey Jack cheese
- 1   cup shredded cheddar cheese
- ⅔   cup chopped celery
- ⅔   cup blue cheese salad dressing
- ⅓   cup Buffalo wing sauce
- 6   flour tortillas (10 in.), warmed

1. Preheat the panini maker or indoor electric grill. In a large bowl, combine the first 6 ingredients. On center of each tortilla, divide chicken mixture.
2. Fold 1 side of the tortilla over filling. Continue to bring the edges of tortilla toward the center, pleating them on top of each other and covering filling.
3. In batches, place wraps on panini maker, seam side down. Cook wraps, covered, until tortilla is browned and cheese is melted, 6-8 minutes.
1 WRAP 676 cal., 38g fat (14g sat. fat), 127mg chol., 1428mg sod., 39g carb. (4g sugars, 3g fiber), 42g pro

CHICKEN WITH
PUMPKIN ALFREDO

AIR-FRYER ROSEMARY-LEMON CHICKEN THIGHS

These air-fryer chicken thighs remind me of Sunday dinner. The lemon and herb butter really makes the chicken flavorful and juicy! If you don't have an air fryer the chicken can be baked in the oven at 400° for about 45 minutes.
—*Alyssa Lang, North Scituate, RI*

PREP: 10 min. • **COOK:** 25 min.
MAKES: 4 servings

- ¼ cup butter, softened
- 3 garlic cloves, minced
- 2 tsp. minced fresh rosemary or ½ tsp. dried rosemary, crushed
- 1 tsp. minced fresh thyme or ¼ tsp. dried thyme
- 1 tsp. grated lemon zest
- 1 Tbsp. lemon juice
- 4 bone-in chicken thighs (about 1½ lbs.)
- ⅛ tsp. salt
- ⅛ tsp. pepper

1. Preheat air fryer to 400°. In a small bowl, combine butter, garlic, rosemary, thyme, lemon zest and lemon juice. Spread 1 tsp. butter mixture under the skin of each chicken thigh. Spread remaining butter over the skin of each thigh. Sprinkle with salt and pepper.
2. Place chicken skin side up on greased tray in air-fryer basket. Cook 20 minutes, turning once. Turn chicken again (skin side up) and cook until a thermometer reads 170°-175°, about 5 minutes.

1 CHICKEN THIGH 329 cal., 26g fat (11g sat. fat), 111mg chol., 234mg sod., 1g carb. (0 sugars, 0 fiber), 23g pro.

AIR-FRYER ROSEMARY-LEMON CHICKEN THIGHS

PAPRIKA CHICKEN STROGANOFF

PAPRIKA CHICKEN STROGANOFF

Stroganoff is such a comfort food. While traditionally a beef dish, it can easily be adapted for other proteins and is just as delicious. With this creamy chicken stroganoff, I get to enjoy all the lovely sauciness with the benefits of the lighter white meat.
—*Leo Lo, Albuquerque, NM*

PREP: 20 min. • **COOK:** 30 min.
MAKES: 6 servings

- 8 oz. uncooked wide egg noodles
- 1½ lbs. boneless skinless chicken breasts, cut into ½-in.-thick strips
- 2 tsp. paprika
- 1½ tsp. salt, divided
- ¾ tsp. pepper, divided
- 1 Tbsp. olive oil
- 1 lb. sliced baby portobello mushrooms
- 1 Tbsp. butter
- 1 large red onion, halved and sliced
- 3 garlic cloves, minced
- 1 cup dry white wine or chicken stock
- 1 cup chicken stock
- 1 Tbsp. Worcestershire sauce
- 1 Tbsp. Dijon mustard
- 1 cup creme fraiche or sour cream
- 1 Tbsp. minced fresh Italian parsley

1. Cook noodles according to package directions; drain.
2. Meanwhile, toss chicken with paprika, ½ tsp. salt and ¼ tsp. pepper. In a Dutch oven, heat oil over medium-high heat. In batches, saute chicken until browned, 2-3 minutes. Remove from pan.
3. In same pan, saute the mushrooms in butter until lightly browned, 4-5 minutes. Add onion; cook and stir until softened, 3-4 minutes. Add garlic; cook and stir 1 minute.
4. Add wine, stirring to loosen browned bits from pan. Add stock, Worcestershire sauce and mustard; bring to a boil. Cook, uncovered, until liquid is reduced by half, 10-12 minutes. Stir in the chicken; cook, uncovered, over medium-low until the chicken is no longer pink, 3-5 minutes.
5. Stir in creme fraiche, parsley and the remaining salt and pepper; remove from heat. Stir in noodles.

1⅔ CUPS 505 cal., 24g fat (12g sat. fat), 133mg chol., 874mg sod., 35g carb. (4g sugars, 3g fiber), 33g pro.

TEST KITCHEN TIP

Creme fraiche is similar to sour cream but thinner and richer.

LEMONY CHICKEN & RICE

I couldn't say who loves this recipe the most because it gets raves every time I serve it! Occasionally I even get a phone call or an email from a friend requesting the recipe. It's certainly a favorite for my grown children and 15 grandchildren.
—*Maryalice Wood, Langley, BC*

PREP: 15 min. + marinating
BAKE: 55 min.
MAKES: 2 casseroles (4 servings each)

- 2 cups water
- ½ cup reduced-sodium soy sauce
- ¼ cup lemon juice
- ¼ cup olive oil
- 2 garlic cloves, minced
- 2 tsp. ground ginger
- 2 tsp. pepper
- 16 bone-in chicken thighs, skin removed (about 6 lbs.)
- 2 cups uncooked long grain rice
- 4 Tbsp. grated lemon zest, divided
- 2 medium lemons, sliced

1. In a large shallow dish, combine the first 7 ingredients. Add chicken; turn to coat and cover. Refrigerate 4 hours or overnight.
2. Preheat oven to 325°. Spread 1 cup rice into each of 2 greased 13x9-in. baking dishes. Top the dishes with 1 Tbsp. lemon zest each, 8 chicken thighs and half the marinade. Top with the sliced lemons.
3. Bake, covered, 40 minutes. Bake, uncovered, until a thermometer inserted into chicken reads 170°-175°, 15-20 minutes longer. Sprinkle with remaining lemon zest.

2 CHICKEN THIGHS WITH ¾ CUP RICE MIXTURE 624 cal., 26g fat (6g sat. fat), 173mg chol., 754mg sod., 41g carb. (1g sugars, 1g fiber), 53g pro.

SHEET-PAN HONEY MUSTARD CHICKEN

This sheet-pan dinner is an easy gluten-free, low-carb meal ideal for busy weekdays. The chicken is tender, juicy and so delicious! It made the list of our favorite meals. You can substitute any low-carb vegetable for green beans.
—Denise Browning, San Antonio, TX

PREP: 20 min. • **BAKE:** 40 min.
MAKES: 6 servings

- 6 bone-in chicken thighs (about 2¼ lbs.)
- ¾ tsp. salt, divided
- ½ tsp. pepper, divided
- 2 medium lemons
- ⅓ cup olive oil
- ⅓ cup honey
- 3 Tbsp. Dijon mustard
- 4 garlic cloves, minced
- 1 tsp. paprika
- ½ cup water
- ½ lb. fresh green beans, trimmed
- 6 miniature sweet peppers, sliced into rings
- ¼ cup pomegranate seeds, optional

1. Preheat the oven to 425°. Place the chicken in a greased 15x10x1-in. baking pan. Sprinkle with ½ tsp. salt and ¼ tsp. pepper. Thinly slice 1 lemon; place over chicken. Cut remaining lemon crosswise in half; squeeze juice into a small bowl. Whisk in oil, honey, mustard, garlic and paprika. Pour half the sauce over the chicken; reserve remaining sauce for beans. Pour water into the pan. Bake 25 minutes.

2. Meanwhile, combine beans, sweet peppers and the remaining sauce, ¼ tsp. salt and ¼ tsp. pepper; toss to coat. Arrange vegetables around chicken in pan. Bake until a thermometer inserted into chicken reads 170°-175° and beans are tender, 15-20 minutes. If desired, sprinkle with pomegranate seeds.

1 SERVING 419 cal., 26g fat (6g sat. fat), 81mg chol., 548mg sod., 22g carb. (17g sugars, 2g fiber), 24g pro.

TEST KITCHEN TIP

This recipe was tested with Dijon mustard, but feel free to experiment with spicy brown, honey or gourmet varieties.

CHICKEN CORDON BLEU SKILLET

CHICKEN CORDON BLEU SKILLET

Here's a good and hearty supper. If I have fresh mushrooms on hand, I slice them and toss them in the skillet. You could even add cooked vegetables such as broccoli or cauliflower too.
—*Sandy Harz, Spring Lake, MI*

TAKES: 25 min. • **MAKES:** 4 servings

    8 oz. uncooked medium egg noodles
       (about 5 cups)
    1 lb. boneless skinless chicken
       breasts, cut in 1-in. pieces
  ½ tsp. pepper
    1 Tbsp. butter
    1 can (10¾ oz.) condensed cream of
       chicken soup, undiluted
  ½ cup shredded Swiss cheese
  ½ cup cubed fully cooked ham
  ¼ cup water
       Minced fresh parsley

1. Cook noodles according to package directions; drain.
2. Meanwhile, sprinkle chicken with pepper. In a large cast-iron or other heavy skillet, heat butter over medium-high heat; saute chicken just until browned, 3-5 minutes. Stir in soup, cheese, ham and water; cook, covered, over medium heat until the cheese is melted and chicken is no longer pink, 6-8 minutes, stirring occasionally. Stir in noodles. Sprinkle with parsley.
1½ CUPS 516 cal., 18g fat (8g sat. fat), 147mg chol., 878mg sod., 47g carb. (2g sugars, 3g fiber), 40g pro.

CHAPTER 7

PORK, HAM & SAUSAGE

P. 151

P. 149

P. 139

P. 146

GOES GREAT WITH ...

Bright and tasty, Dill & Chive Peas (p. 298) round out this entree nicely.

SKILLET PORK CHOPS IN PINEAPPLE-SOY SAUCE

SKILLET PORK CHOPS IN PINEAPPLE-SOY SAUCE

Although we like pork, it really has very little flavor. One night I was fixing some beautiful boneless pork loin chops and decided to add a fruity sauce. The chops were moist and juicy, and the sauce was delicious. They were perfect served over hot cooked rice. This dinner takes less than 30 minutes, so it is wonderful for weeknight meals and nice enough for company as well.
—Donna Gribbins, Shelbyville, KY

TAKES: 30 min. • **MAKES:** 6 servings

- 6 boneless pork loin chops (5 oz. each)
- ½ tsp. salt
- ½ tsp. pepper
- 3 Tbsp. olive oil
- 2 shallots, minced
- 1 cup pineapple preserves
- ¼ cup soy sauce
- 1 Tbsp. Dijon mustard
- 1 bunch green onions, thinly sliced

1. Season the pork chops with salt and pepper. In a large nonstick skillet, heat olive oil over medium heat. Cook pork chops until a thermometer reads 145°, 6-8 minutes on each side; remove from pan, reserving drippings.
2. In same pan, saute the shallots in drippings until lightly browned. Whisk together pineapple preserves, soy sauce and Dijon; add to the pan. Bring to a boil. Reduce heat; simmer, until thickened slightly, about 5 minutes.
3. Add the chops back to pan, turning to coat. Sprinkle with sliced green onion.
1 PORK CHOP WITH 2 TBSP. SAUCE
407 cal., 15g fat (4g sat. fat), 68mg chol., 914mg sod., 38g carb. (33g sugars, 1g fiber), 29g pro.

PORK QUESADILLAS WITH FRESH SALSA

PORK QUESADILLAS WITH FRESH SALSA

I threw this together one night when I was in the mood for quesadillas but didn't feel like going out. The homemade salsa is so tasty and versatile that you may want to double the recipe.
—Adam Gaylord, Natick, MA

TAKES: 30 min.
MAKES: 4 servings (¾ cup salsa)

- 1 Tbsp. olive oil
- 1 each small green, sweet red and orange peppers, sliced
- 1 medium red onion, sliced
- ¾ lb. thinly sliced cooked pork (about 3 cups)
- ¼ tsp. salt
- ⅛ tsp. pepper

SALSA
- 2 medium tomatoes, seeded and chopped
- 1 Tbsp. chopped red onion
- 1 Tbsp. minced fresh cilantro
- 2 tsp. olive oil
- 1 to 2 tsp. chopped seeded jalapeno pepper
- 1 tsp. cider vinegar
- ⅛ tsp. salt
- Dash pepper

QUESADILLAS
- 4 flour tortillas (10 in.)
- 1½ cups shredded part-skim mozzarella cheese

1. In a large skillet, heat oil over medium-high heat. Add peppers and onion; cook for 4-5 minutes or until tender, stirring occasionally. Stir in the pork, salt and pepper; heat through. Meanwhile, in a small bowl, combine salsa ingredients.
2. Place tortillas on a griddle. Layer half of each tortilla with ¼ cup cheese, 1 cup pork mixture and 2 Tbsp. cheese; fold other half over filling.
3. Cook over medium heat 1-2 minutes on each side or until golden brown and the cheese is melted. Cut into wedges. Serve with salsa.
NOTE Wear disposable gloves when cutting hot peppers; the oils can burn skin. Avoid touching your face.
1 QUESADILLA WITH 3 TBSP. SALSA
589 cal., 25g fat (9g sat. fat), 104mg chol., 873mg sod., 41g carb. (6g sugars, 9g fiber), 43g pro.

SOUTHERN PORK & RICE ✓

At our house, we're big on healthy eating. These tender chops with colorful rice and black-eyed peas are a meal fancy enough for a dinner party.
—Annie Holmes, Murfreesboro, TN

TAKES: 25 min. • **MAKES:** 4 servings

- 4 boneless pork loin chops (6 oz. each)
- 1 tsp. seafood seasoning, divided
- 1 Tbsp. olive oil
- 1 medium sweet red pepper, chopped
- 1 medium onion, chopped
- 2 tsp. Worcestershire sauce
- 1 can (15½ oz.) black-eyed peas, rinsed and drained
- 1 can (14½ oz.) diced tomatoes with mild green chiles
- 1 cup uncooked instant rice
- 1 cup reduced-sodium chicken broth

1. Sprinkle the pork with ¾ tsp. seafood seasoning. In a large skillet, heat oil over medium heat; brown the chops on both sides. Remove from pan.
2. Add pepper and onion to skillet; cook and stir until tender, 4-5 minutes. Stir in the remaining seafood seasoning, Worcestershire sauce, peas, tomatoes, rice and broth. Bring to a boil. Place the chops over top. Reduce heat; simmer, covered, until a thermometer inserted into the pork reads 145°, 2-3 minutes. Let stand, covered, 5 minutes before serving.

1 PORK CHOP WITH 1¼ CUPS RICE MIXTURE 484 cal., 13g fat (4g sat. fat), 82mg chol., 764mg sod., 45g carb. (7g sugars, 6g fiber), 42g pro. **DIABETIC EXCHANGES** 5 lean meat, 3 starch, ½ fat.

> ### TEST KITCHEN TIP
> Make this meal gluten free by using gluten-free broth and Worcestershire sauce.

SOUTHERN PORK & RICE

HAM & SCALLOPED POTATOES ✓

I often fix this saucy skillet dish when I'm running late because it is easy and takes so little time to prepare. The recipe won the first prize in our local paper some years back.
—Emma Magielda, Amsterdam, NY

TAKES: 30 min. • **MAKES:** 4 servings

- 4 medium potatoes, peeled and thinly sliced
- 2 Tbsp. butter
- ⅓ cup water
- ½ cup 2% milk
- 2 to 3 Tbsp. onion soup mix
- 3 Tbsp. minced fresh parsley
- 1 cup cubed Velveeta
- 1 cup cubed fully cooked ham

1. In a large skillet, cook the potatoes in butter until potatoes are lightly browned. Add water; bring to a boil. Reduce heat; cover and simmer for 14-15 minutes or until potatoes are tender.
2. Meanwhile in a small bowl, combine the milk, soup mix and parsley; stir in cheese. Pour over potatoes. Add ham; cook and stir gently over medium heat until the cheese is melted and the sauce is bubbly.

1 SERVING 353 cal., 17g fat (10g sat. fat), 56mg chol., 1170mg sod., 36g carb. (6g sugars, 2g fiber), 16g pro.

BANH MI SKEWERS

I love banh mi sandwiches but wanted to make them a little easier to serve for a party. These unique skewers are a really fun twist!
—*Elisabeth Larsen, Pleasant Grove, UT*

PREP: 45 min. + chilling
COOK: 10 min./batch
MAKES: 12 servings

- 1   cup white vinegar or rice vinegar
- ¼   cup sugar
- ½   tsp. salt
- 1   English cucumber, thinly sliced
- 2   medium carrots, thinly sliced
- 4   radishes, thinly sliced
- 1   cup mayonnaise
- 1   Tbsp. Sriracha chili sauce
- 2   Tbsp. minced fresh cilantro
- 2   green onions, thinly sliced
- 1   Tbsp. soy sauce
- 1   garlic clove, minced
- ¼   tsp. cayenne pepper
- 1½ lbs. ground pork
- 2   Tbsp. canola oil
- 1   French bread baguette (10½ oz.), cut into 24 slices

1. In a large bowl, combine vinegar, sugar and salt; whisk until sugar is dissolved. Add the cucumber, carrots and radishes; set aside. Combine the mayonnaise and chili sauce; refrigerate until serving.
2. In another large bowl, combine the cilantro, green onion, soy sauce, garlic and cayenne. Add pork; mix lightly but thoroughly. Shape into 36 balls.
3. In a large skillet, heat oil over medium heat. Cook meatballs in batches until cooked through, turning occasionally.
4. Drain vegetable mixture. On 12 metal or wooden skewers, alternately thread vegetables and meatballs; start and end each skewer with a baguette slice. Serve with Sriracha mayonnaise.
1 SKEWER WITH ABOUT 1 TBSP. SAUCE
336 cal., 24g fat (5g sat. fat), 39mg chol., 416mg sod., 16g carb. (2g sugars, 1g fiber), 13g pro.

BANH MI SKEWERS

COPYCAT HONEY BAKED HAM

For holidays and special occasions my family loves a good old-fashioned baked ham. This one is really easy.
—Donna Gribbins, Shelbyville, KY

PREP: 10 min.
COOK: 4 hours 5 min. + standing
MAKES: 16 servings

- 1 spiral-sliced fully cooked bone-in ham (8 to 10 lbs.)
- 1 cup water
- ¾ cup honey, divided

GLAZE
- 1 cup sugar
- ½ tsp. ground cinnamon
- ½ tsp. ground allspice
- ½ tsp. pepper
- ½ tsp. paprika
- ¼ tsp. ground ginger
- ¼ tsp. ground nutmeg
- ¼ tsp. ground mustard
- ¼ tsp. Chinese five-spice powder
- ⅛ tsp. ground cloves

1. In a 7-qt. slow cooker, place the ham and water. Brush the ham with ½ cup honey. Cook, covered, on low until a thermometer reads 140°, 4-5 hours.
2. Preheat broiler. Combine the glaze ingredients. Transfer ham to a rack in a shallow roasting pan, cut side down. Brush with the remaining ¼ cup honey; sprinkle with the glaze mixture, pressing to adhere. Broil 6-8 in. from the heat until lightly browned and the sugar is melted, 3-5 minutes, rotating as needed. Cover with foil; let stand until glaze hardens, about 30 minutes.

5 OZ. COOKED HAM 288 cal., 6g fat (2g sat. fat), 100mg chol., 1192mg sod., 26g carb. (26g sugars, 0 fiber), 33g pro.

COPYCAT HONEY BAKED HAM

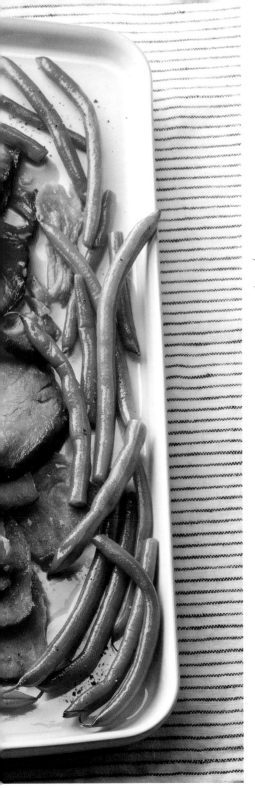

PORK & ASPARAGUS SHEET-PAN DINNER ✓

When time is of the essence, it's nice to have a quick and easy meal idea in your back pocket. This recipe is delicious, and you can clean up in a flash.
—Joan Hallford, Fort Worth, TX

PREP: 20 min. • **BAKE:** 20 min.
MAKES: 4 servings

- ¼ cup olive oil, divided
- 3 cups diced new potatoes
- 3 cups cut fresh asparagus (1-in. pieces)
- ¼ tsp. salt
- ¼ tsp. pepper
- 1 large gala or Honeycrisp apple, peeled and cut into 1-in. wedges
- 2 tsp. brown sugar
- 1 tsp. ground cinnamon
- ¼ tsp. ground ginger
- 4 boneless pork loin chops (1 in. thick and about 6 oz. each)
- 2 tsp. Southwest seasoning

1. Preheat oven to 425°. Line a 15x10x1-in. baking pan with foil; brush with 2 tsp. olive oil.
2. In a large bowl, toss the potatoes with 1 Tbsp. olive oil. Place in 1 section of the prepared baking pan. In same bowl, toss asparagus with 1 Tbsp. olive oil; place in another section of pan. Sprinkle salt and pepper over potatoes and asparagus.
3. In same bowl, toss apple with 1 tsp. olive oil. In a small bowl, mix brown sugar, cinnamon and ginger; sprinkle over apples and toss to coat. Transfer to a different section of pan.
4. Brush pork chops with the remaining 1 Tbsp. olive oil; sprinkle both sides with Southwest seasoning. Place chops in remaining section of pan. Bake until a thermometer inserted into pork reads 145° and potatoes and apples are tender, 20-25 minutes. Let stand for 5 minutes before serving.
1 SERVING 486 cal., 23g fat (5g sat. fat), 82mg chol., 447mg sod., 32g carb. (10g sugars, 5g fiber), 37g pro.

CREAMY PAPRIKA PORK

When I was little, I would often ask my mom to make favorite meat. She knew I was requesting this homey pork recipe. It has been in my family for more than 30 years, and it's still a favorite!
—Alexandra Barnett, Forest, VA

TAKES: 30 min. • **MAKES:** 4 servings

- 1 pork tenderloin (1 lb.), cut into 1-in. cubes
- 1 tsp. all-purpose flour
- 4 tsp. paprika
- ¾ tsp. salt
- ¼ tsp. pepper
- 1 Tbsp. butter
- ¾ cup heavy whipping cream
  Hot cooked egg noodles or rice
  Minced fresh parsley, optional

1. Toss pork with flour and seasonings. In a large skillet, heat the butter over medium heat; saute pork until lightly browned, 4-5 minutes.
2. Add cream; bring to a boil, stirring to loosen browned bits from the pan. Cook, uncovered, until the cream is slightly thickened, 5-7 minutes.
3. Serve with the noodles. Sprinkle with parsley if desired.
¾ CUP PORK MIXTURE 320 cal., 23g fat (14g sat. fat), 122mg chol., 524mg sod., 3g carb. (1g sugars, 1g fiber), 24g pro.

TEST KITCHEN TIP
Always store paprika in the refrigerator to keep its flavor as fresh as possible.

HAM STEAKS WITH GRUYERE, BACON & MUSHROOMS

ONE-POT RED BEANS & RICE

This one-pot meal is ready in about 30 minutes. It uses simple ingredients and is one of my husband's favorites, so it's been a go-to recipe in our house for many years.
—*Janice Conklin, Stevensville, MT*

TAKES: 30 min. • **MAKES:** 6 servings

- 1 Tbsp. olive oil
- 2 celery ribs, sliced
- 1 medium onion, chopped
- 1 medium green pepper, chopped
- 1 pkg. (14 oz.) smoked turkey sausage, sliced
- 1 carton (32 oz.) reduced-sodium chicken broth
- 1 can (16 oz.) kidney beans, rinsed and drained
- 1¼ cups uncooked converted rice
- ⅓ cup tomato paste
- 1 bay leaf
- 1½ tsp. Cajun seasoning
- ¼ tsp. cayenne pepper
  Hot pepper sauce, optional

1. In a Dutch oven, heat oil over medium-high heat. Add celery, onion and green pepper; cook and stir until crisp-tender, 3-4 minutes. Add sausage; cook until browned, 2-3 minutes.
2. Stir in broth, beans, rice, tomato paste, bay leaf, Cajun seasoning and cayenne pepper. Bring to a boil; reduce the heat. Simmer, uncovered, until rice is tender and liquid is absorbed, 15-20 minutes, stirring occasionally. Discard bay leaf. If desired, serve with pepper sauce.
1⅓ CUPS 347 cal., 6g fat (2g sat. fat), 41mg chol., 1272mg sod., 50g carb. (6g sugars, 5g fiber), 22g pro.

> ## TEST KITCHEN TIP
> Converted rice is sometimes labeled parboiled rice in grocery stores.

HAM STEAKS WITH GRUYERE, BACON & MUSHROOMS

This hearty dish has a big wow factor. The Gruyere cheese, bacon and fresh mushroom is an amazing combo.
—*Lisa Speer, Palm Beach, FL*

TAKES: 25 min. • **MAKES:** 4 servings

- 2 Tbsp. butter
- ½ lb. sliced fresh mushrooms
- 1 shallot, finely chopped
- 2 garlic cloves, minced
- ⅛ tsp. coarsely ground pepper
- 1 fully cooked boneless ham steak (about 1 lb.), cut into 4 pieces
- 1 cup shredded Gruyere cheese
- 4 bacon strips, cooked and crumbled
- 1 Tbsp. minced fresh parsley, optional

1. In a large nonstick skillet, heat butter over medium-high heat. Add mushrooms and shallot; cook and stir 4-6 minutes or until tender. Add garlic and pepper; cook 1 minute longer. Remove from pan; keep warm. Wipe skillet clean.
2. In same skillet, cook ham over medium heat for 3 minutes. Turn; sprinkle with cheese and bacon. Cook, covered, 2-4 minutes longer or until cheese is melted and ham is heated through. Serve with mushroom mixture, and sprinkle with parsley if desired.
1 SERVING 352 cal., 22g fat (11g sat. fat), 113mg chol., 1576mg sod., 5g carb. (2g sugars, 1g fiber), 34g pro.

ONE-POT RED BEANS & RICE

GOES GREAT WITH ... ✕
Pick up a few dinner rolls from the bakery to serve with this tasty dinner.

QUICK HAWAIIAN PIZZA

Our family never quite liked the taste of canned pizza sauce, so I tried mixing BBQ sauce into spaghetti sauce to add some sweetness. I have made my pizzas with this special and easy sauce ever since, and my family loves it.
—Tonya Schieler, Carmel, IN

TAKES: 25 min. • **MAKES:** 6 pieces

- 1   prebaked 12-in. thin whole wheat pizza crust
- ½   cup marinara sauce
- ¼   cup barbecue sauce
- 1   medium sweet yellow or red pepper, chopped
- 1   cup cubed fresh pineapple
- ½   cup chopped fully cooked ham
- 1   cup shredded part-skim mozzarella cheese
- ½   cup shredded cheddar cheese

1. Preheat oven to 425°. Place the dough on a baking sheet. Mix the marinara and barbecue sauces; spread over crust.
2. Top with remaining ingredients. Bake until crust is browned and cheeses are melted, 10-15 minutes.
1 PIECE 290 cal., 10g fat (5g sat. fat), 29mg chol., 792mg sod., 36g carb. (11g sugars, 5g fiber), 16g pro. **DIABETIC EXCHANGES** 2 starch, 2 lean meat, ½ fat.

QUICK HAWAIIAN PIZZA

30 seconds. Make a well in the center of the shallot mixture; add egg. Stir-fry for 1-2 minutes or until egg is completely set. **3.** Add the coleslaw mix, green onion, vinegar, sugar, soy sauce, fish sauce, chili garlic sauce, lime juice and peanuts; heat through. Return pork to pan and heat through. Drain noodles; toss with pork mixture. Garnish with cilantro, additional peanuts, lime wedges and bean sprouts.

1¼ CUPS 361 cal., 8g fat (2g sat. fat), 78mg chol., 1669mg sod., 53g carb. (23g sugars, 2g fiber), 19g pro.

TEST KITCHEN TIP

As pad thai is a quick stir-fry at high heat, a wok works best because of its high-sided design. However, if you don't own a wok, any kind of large skillet—be it nonstick, stainless steel or a nicely-seasoned cast iron skillet—should do the trick!

EASY PAD THAI

EASY PAD THAI

Skip the takeout restaurant and give this pad thai recipe a try if you need an easy and quick meal.
—Taste of Home *Test Kitchen*

TAKES: 30 min. • **MAKES:** 4 servings

- 4 oz. uncooked thick rice noodles
- ½ lb. pork tenderloin, cut into thin strips
- 2 tsp. canola oil
- 2 shallots, thinly sliced
- 2 garlic cloves, minced
- 1 large egg, lightly beaten
- 3 cups coleslaw mix
- 4 green onions, thinly sliced
- ⅓ cup rice vinegar
- ¼ cup sugar
- 3 Tbsp. reduced-sodium soy sauce
- 2 Tbsp. fish sauce or additional reduced-sodium soy sauce
- 1 Tbsp. chili garlic sauce
- 1 Tbsp. lime juice
- 2 Tbsp. chopped salted peanuts Chopped fresh cilantro leaves, lime wedges and fresh bean sprouts

1. Cook noodles according to package directions.
2. In a large nonstick skillet or wok, stir-fry pork in oil over high heat until lightly browned; remove and set aside. Add shallot to pan and cook until tender, about 1 minute; add garlic and cook

GRILLED PORK CHOPS WITH SMOKIN' SAUCE

While growing up, my husband always had pork chops that were pan-fried or baked, but he knew they could be better. So he combined his love of grilling with the desire to create his own signature sauce, and the result was this recipe.
—*Vicky Drnek, Rome, GA*

TAKES: 25 min. • **MAKES:** 4 servings

- ¼ cup water
- ¼ cup ketchup
- 1 Tbsp. Dijon mustard
- 1 Tbsp. molasses
- 1½ tsp. brown sugar
- 1 tsp. Worcestershire sauce
- ¼ tsp. kosher salt
- ¼ tsp. chipotle hot pepper sauce
- ⅛ tsp. pepper

PORK CHOPS

- 1¼ tsp. mustard seed
- 1¼ tsp. smoked paprika
- 1¼ tsp. whole peppercorns
- 1 tsp. onion powder
- 1 tsp. garlic powder
- ½ tsp. kosher salt
- ¼ tsp. cayenne pepper
- 1½ tsp. brown sugar
- 4 bone-in pork loin chops (7 oz. each)

1. In a small saucepan, mix the first 9 ingredients; bring to a boil over medium heat. Reduce heat; simmer, uncovered, until slightly thickened, about 10 minutes, stirring occasionally. Reserve ¼ cup sauce for serving.
2. Using a mortar and pestle or spice grinder, crush seasonings with brown sugar. Rub mixture over chops.
3. Place chops on an oiled grill over medium heat. Grill, covered, until a thermometer reads 145°, 5-6 minutes per side, brushing top with remaining sauce after turning. Let stand for 5 minutes before serving. Serve pork with the reserved sauce.

1 PORK CHOP WITH 1 TBSP. SAUCE 263 cal., 9g fat (3g sat. fat), 86mg chol., 721mg sod., 13g carb. (11g sugars, 1g fiber), 31g pro.
DIABETIC EXCHANGES 4 lean meat, 1 starch.

SAUSAGE-TOMATO COCONUT CURRY

GOES GREAT WITH ...
For dessert, serve 10-minute Coconut-Layered Pound Cake (p. 308).

SAUSAGE-TOMATO COCONUT CURRY

Made in one pan, this recipe is delicious and satisfying and can easily be altered for vegetarian diets by using a different protein, such as chickpeas, instead of the sausage.
—*Jess Apfe, Berkeley, CA*

TAKES: 30 minutes • **MAKES:** 4 servings

- 2 Tbsp. olive oil
- 1 pkg. (12 oz.) fully cooked roasted garlic chicken sausage links or flavor of your choice, cut into ½-in. slices
- 1 medium onion, chopped
- 2 Tbsp. red curry paste
- 1 garlic clove, minced
- 1 can (14½ oz.) fire-roasted diced tomatoes, undrained
- 1 can (13.66 oz.) coconut milk
- 2 cups chopped fresh spinach
- ¼ tsp. salt
- ⅛ tsp. pepper
- 3 cups hot cooked rice

1. In a large skillet, heat oil over medium-high heat. Add sausage and onion; cook and stir until onion is tender and sausage is browned, 3-5 minutes. Add curry paste and garlic; cook 1 minute longer.

2. Stir in the tomatoes and coconut milk. Bring to a boil; reduce the heat. Simmer, uncovered, until sauce starts to thicken, 7-10 minutes. Add the spinach, salt and pepper; cook and stir until the spinach begins to wilt. Serve with rice.

1¼ CUPS CURRY WITH ¾ CUP RICE
560 cal., 30g fat (18g sat. fat), 70mg chol., 1139mg sod., 49g carb. (7g sugars, 2g fiber), 22g pro.

TEST KITCHEN TIP
Fire-roasted diced tomatoes add a subtle smokiness that helps build flavor.

ASPARAGUS
HAM DINNER

ASPARAGUS HAM DINNER

I've been making this light meal for my family for years now, and it's always well received. With asparagus, tomato, pasta and chunks of ham, it's a tempting blend of tastes and textures.
—*Rhonda Zavodny, David City, NE*

TAKES: 25 min. • **MAKES:** 6 servings

- 2 cups uncooked corkscrew or spiral pasta
- ¾ lb. fresh asparagus, cut into 1-in. pieces
- 1 medium sweet yellow pepper, julienned
- 1 Tbsp. olive oil
- 6 medium tomatoes, diced
- 6 oz. boneless fully cooked ham, cubed
- ¼ cup minced fresh parsley
- ½ tsp. salt
- ½ tsp. dried oregano
- ½ tsp. dried basil
- ⅛ to ¼ tsp. cayenne pepper
- ¼ cup shredded Parmesan cheese

Cook pasta according to package directions. Meanwhile, in a large cast-iron or other heavy skillet, saute asparagus and yellow pepper in oil until crisp-tender. Add tomatoes and ham; heat through. Drain pasta; add to mixture. Stir in parsley and seasonings. Sprinkle with cheese.

1⅓ CUPS 204 cal., 5g fat (1g sat. fat), 17mg chol., 561mg sod., 29g carb. (5g sugars, 3g fiber), 12g pro. **DIABETIC EXCHANGES** 1½ starch, 1 vegetable, 1 lean meat, ½ fat.

PIZZA RING

PIZZA RING

My 7-year-old, Sarah, loves pizza. This is a recipe she came up with, and it was a huge success! Other pizza toppings can be added.
—*Tricia Richardson, Springdale, AR*

TAKES: 30 min. • **MAKES:** 8 servings

- 1 lb. bulk Italian sausage
- 1 can (15 oz.) pizza sauce, divided
- 1½ cups shredded part-skim mozzarella cheese, divided
- 4 oz. Canadian bacon, chopped
- 2 tubes (8 oz. each) refrigerated crescent rolls

1. Cook the sausage in a large skillet over medium heat until no longer pink, breaking it into crumbles; drain. Stir in ½ cup pizza sauce, 1 cup cheese and Canadian bacon.

2. Unroll crescent dough and separate into triangles. On an ungreased 14-in. pizza pan, arrange triangles in a ring with points toward outside and wide ends overlapping at the center, leaving a 4-in. opening. Press the overlapping dough to seal.

3. Spoon the filling onto wide end of the triangles. Fold pointed end of triangles over filling, tucking points under to form a ring (filling will be visible).

4. Bake at 375° for 12-15 minutes or until golden brown and heated through. Sprinkle with remaining cheese. Bake 5 minutes longer or until the cheese is melted. Serve with the remaining pizza sauce.

2 PIECES WITH 2 TBSP. PIZZA SAUCE
214 cal., 13g fat (4g sat. fat), 22mg chol., 593mg sod., 13g carb. (4g sugars, 0 fiber), 10g pro.

RAMONA'S CHILAQUILES

A dear neighbor shared this recipe, which she used to make from scratch. My version takes a few shortcuts.
—*Marina Castle Kelley, Canyon Country, CA*

TAKES: 30 min. • **MAKES:** 4 servings

- ½ lb. lean ground beef (90% lean)
- ½ lb. fresh chorizo or bulk spicy pork sausage
- 1 medium onion, finely chopped
- 1 garlic clove, minced
- 1 can (14½ oz.) diced tomatoes with mild green chiles, undrained
- 1 can (10 oz.) diced tomatoes and green chiles, undrained
- 4 cups tortilla chips (about 6 oz.)
- 1 cup shredded Monterey Jack cheese
  Chopped fresh cilantro
  Optional toppings: Sour cream, diced avocado and sliced red onion

1. Preheat the oven to 350°. In a large skillet, cook the beef and chorizo with the onion and garlic over medium heat until beef is no longer pink, 5-7 minutes, crumble meat; drain. Stir in both cans of tomatoes; bring to a boil. In a greased 1½-qt. or 8-in.-square baking dish, layer 2 cups chips, half the meat mixture and ½ cup cheese; repeat layers.
2. Bake, uncovered, until the cheese is melted, 12-15 minutes. Sprinkle with cilantro. If desired, serve with toppings.
1 SERVING 573 cal., 35g fat (14g sat. fat), 110mg chol., 1509mg sod., 28g carb. (5g sugars, 4g fiber), 33g pro.

TEST KITCHEN TIP
Chilaquiles are indulgent any way you fix them, but they can be lightened up. Use chorizo chicken sausage and baked chips to lop off 15g fat.

RAMONA'S CHILAQUILES

HAM & SWISS STROMBOLI

This is an excellent dish to take to someone for dinner. It's also easy to change up the recipe with your favorite meats or cheeses.
—*Tricia Bibb, Hartselle, AL*

TAKES: 30 min. • **MAKES:** 6 servings

- 1 tube (11 oz.) refrigerated crusty French loaf
- 6 oz. sliced deli ham
- ¼ cup finely chopped onion
- 8 bacon strips, cooked and crumbled
- 6 oz. sliced Swiss cheese
  Honey mustard, optional

1. Preheat oven to 375°. Unroll dough on a baking sheet. Place ham down center third of dough to within 1 in. of edges; top with onion, bacon and cheese. Fold long sides of dough over the filling, pinching seam and ends to seal; tuck ends under. Cut several slits in top.
2. Bake until golden brown, 20-25 minutes. Cut into slices. If desired, serve with honey mustard.
FREEZE OPTION Securely wrap and freeze the cooled unsliced stromboli in heavy-duty foil. To use, reheat the stromboli on an ungreased baking sheet in a preheated 375° oven until heated through and a thermometer inserted in the center reads 165°.
1 PIECE 272 cal., 11g fat (5g sat. fat), 40mg chol., 795mg sod., 26g carb. (3g sugars, 1g fiber), 18g pro.

PRESSURE-COOKER SPICY PORK & SQUASH RAGU

This marvelously spicy combo is perfect for fall weather—so satisfying after a day spent outdoors.
—Monica Osterhaus, Paducah, KY

PREP: 20 min. • **COOK:** 15 min. + releasing
MAKES: 10 servings

- 2 cans (14½ oz. each) stewed tomatoes, undrained
- 1 pkg. (12 oz.) frozen cooked winter squash, thawed
- 1 large sweet onion, cut into ½-in. pieces
- 1 medium sweet red pepper, cut into ½-in. pieces
- ¾ cup reduced-sodium chicken broth
- 1½ tsp. crushed red pepper flakes
- 2 lbs. boneless country-style pork ribs
- 1 tsp. salt
- ¼ tsp. garlic powder
- ¼ tsp. pepper
  Hot cooked pasta
  Shaved Parmesan cheese, optional

1. Combine the first 6 ingredients in a 6-qt. electric pressure cooker. Sprinkle ribs with salt, garlic powder and pepper; place in the pressure cooker. Lock lid; close pressure-release valve. Adjust to pressure-cook on high 15 minutes. Let the pressure release naturally for 10 minutes; quick-release any remaining pressure.
2. Remove cover; stir to break the pork into smaller pieces. Serve with pasta. If desired, top with Parmesan cheese.
FREEZE OPTION Freeze cooled ragu in freezer containers. To use, partially thaw in refrigerator overnight. Heat through in a saucepan, stirring occasionally.
1 CUP RAGU 196 cal., 8g fat (3g sat. fat), 52mg chol., 469mg sod., 13g carb. (6g sugars, 2g fiber), 18g pro. **DIABETIC EXCHANGES** 2 lean meat, 1 starch.

PRESSURE-COOKER SPICY PORK & SQUASH RAGU

PEPPERED PORK WITH MUSHROOM SAUCE

Using preseasoned pork tenderloin gives us flavorful, quick and satisfying meals without a big mess or leftovers. I have used all flavors of pork tenderloin for this recipe. Making the sauce doesn't take much extra time and results are well worth it.

—*Jolene Roszel, Helena, MT*

TAKES: 30 min. • **MAKES:** 4 servings

- 2 Tbsp. olive oil, divided
- 1 peppercorn pork tenderloin (1 lb.) or flavor of your choice, cut into ¾-in. slices
- ½ cup sliced fresh mushrooms
- ¼ cup chopped onion
- 2 Tbsp. all-purpose flour
- 1 cup reduced-sodium beef broth

1. In a large skillet, heat 1 Tbsp. oil over medium heat. Brown the pork on both sides. Remove from pan.

2. In same pan, heat remaining oil over medium-high heat. Add mushrooms and onion; cook and stir until tender, 4-5 minutes.

3. In a small bowl, mix flour and broth until smooth. Stir into the mushroom mixture. Bring to a boil; cook and stir until sauce is thickened. Return pork to the pan. Cook until a thermometer inserted into pork reads 145°.

3 OZ. COOKED PORK WITH ¼ CUP SAUCE 208 cal., 11g fat (2g sat. fat), 55mg chol., 785mg sod., 7g carb. (1g sugars, 0 fiber), 21g pro.

TEST KITCHEN TIP

Pre-marinated pork tenderloin makes easy work of weeknight dinners. Flavors vary per store, but this versatile sauce will complement most varieties.

PEPPERED PORK WITH MUSHROOM SAUCE

AIR-FRYER THIN PORK CHOPS

Instant mashed potatoes and bread crumbs have a similar texture, so I wondered how the combination would be as a breading for pork chops. This is now the only way we make pork chops!
—*Carrie Farias, Oak Ridge, NJ*

PREP: 15 min. • **COOK:** 5 min./batch
MAKES: 4 servings

- 1 large egg
- 2 Tbsp. fat-free milk
- 2 Tbsp. Dijon mustard
- ¾ cup panko bread crumbs
- ¾ cup mashed potato flakes
- 2 tsp. ground mustard
- 2 tsp. minced fresh sage
- ⅓ cup all-purpose flour
- 8 thin boneless pork loin chops (2 oz. each)
- ½ tsp. salt
  Cooking spray

1. In a shallow bowl, whisk egg, milk and Dijon mustard. In another shallow bowl, mix bread crumbs, potato flakes, ground mustard and sage. Place flour in another shallow bowl. Sprinkle pork with salt.
2. Preheat air fryer to 400°. Dip the pork into flour to coat both sides; shake off excess. Dip into egg mixture, then into bread crumb mixture, patting to help coating adhere.
3. In batches, place chops on greased tray in air-fryer basket; spritz with cooking spray. Cook until a thermometer reads at least 145°, 5-6 minutes, turning once.
NOTE In our testing, we find cook times vary dramatically among brands of air fryers. As a result, we give wider than normal ranges on suggested cook times. Begin checking at the first time listed and adjust as needed.
2 PORK CHOPS 297 cal., 9g fat (3g sat. fat), 101mg chol., 565mg sod., 22g carb. (1g sugars, 1g fiber), 27g pro. **DIABETIC EXCHANGES** 3 lean meat, 1½ starch, 1 fat.

SKILLET CASSOULET

This quick skillet version of a French classic is chock-full of flavor. Kielbasa, ham and cannellini beans make the stew a hearty meal-in-one dinner.
—*Barbara Brittain, Santee, CA*

TAKES: 30 min. • **MAKES:** 3 servings

- 2 tsp. canola oil
- ¼ lb. smoked turkey kielbasa, cut into ½-in. slices
- ¼ lb. fully cooked boneless ham, cubed
- 2 medium carrots, sliced
- 1 celery rib, sliced
- ½ medium red onion, sliced
- 2 garlic cloves, minced
- 1 can (15 oz.) cannellini beans, rinsed and drained
- 1 can (14½ oz.) no-salt-added diced tomatoes, undrained
- ¾ tsp. dried thyme
- ⅛ tsp. pepper

1. In a large skillet, heat oil over medium-high heat. Add kielbasa, ham, carrots, celery and onion; cook and stir until the sausage is browned and vegetables are tender. Add garlic; cook 1 minute longer.
2. Stir in remaining ingredients. Bring to a boil. Reduce heat; simmer, uncovered, 4-5 minutes or until heated through.
1⅓ CUPS 282 cal., 8g fat (1g sat. fat), 43mg chol., 901mg sod., 33g carb. (9g sugars, 10g fiber), 22g pro.

BRATWURST BURGERS WITH BRAISED ONIONS

BRATWURST BURGERS WITH BRAISED ONIONS

This is a fun mashup of a bratwurst with onion and peppers, chicken-fried steak and beef burger. The best of three dishes, bratwurst burgers are guaranteed to be family-pleasing.
—Priscilla Yee, Concord, CA

TAKES: 30 min. • **MAKES:** 4 servings

- 1 Tbsp. canola oil
- 1 large onion, sliced
- 1 medium sweet red pepper, sliced
- 1 medium sweet yellow pepper, sliced
- 1 cup dark beer or chicken broth

BURGERS
- ½ lb. ground beef
- ½ lb. uncooked bratwurst links, casings removed
- 1 large egg, lightly beaten
- 1 Tbsp. 2% milk
- ¾ cup seasoned bread crumbs
- 4 slices Muenster cheese
- 4 hamburger buns, split and toasted
- 8 tsp. spicy brown mustard

1. In a large skillet, heat oil over medium heat. Add onion and peppers; cook and stir 5 minutes. Stir in the beer. Bring to a boil. Reduce heat; simmer, uncovered, until vegetables are tender and liquid is almost evaporated, 15-20 minutes. Remove and keep warm.
2. In a small bowl, combine the beef and bratwurst, mixing lightly but thoroughly. Shape into four ¾-in.-thick patties.
3. In a shallow bowl, mix the egg and milk. Place bread crumbs in a separate shallow bowl. Dip patties into the egg mixture, then roll in the crumb mixture to coat.
4. In the same skillet over medium heat, cook the burgers until a thermometer reads 160° for medium doneness and juices run clear, 3-4 minutes on each side; top with cheese during the last 1-2 minutes of cooking. Serve burgers on buns with mustard and onion mixture.
1 BURGER 659 cal., 36g fat (13g sat. fat), 145mg chol., 1409mg sod., 41g carb. (10g sugars, 3g fiber), 32g pro.

BUCATINI WITH SAUSAGE & KALE Spinach

I was short on time but wanted to make an elegant dinner for my husband and me. That night, we ate this simple pasta starring spicy sausage and our homegrown kale.
—Angela Lemoine, Howell, NJ

TAKES: 30 min. • **MAKES:** 6 servings

- 1 pkg. (12 oz.) bucatini pasta or fettuccine
- 2 tsp. plus 3 Tbsp. olive oil, divided
- 1 lb. regular or spicy bulk Italian sausage
- 5 garlic cloves, thinly sliced
- 8 cups chopped fresh kale (about 5 oz.)
- ¾ tsp. salt
- ¼ tsp. pepper
  Shredded Romano cheese

1. Cook the pasta according to package directions, decreasing time by 3 minutes. Drain, reserving 2 cups pasta water. Toss pasta with 2 tsp. oil.
2. In a 6-qt. stockpot, cook the sausage over medium heat until no longer pink, 5-7 minutes, breaking sausage into large crumbles. Add garlic and remaining oil; cook and stir 2 minutes. Stir in the kale, S salt and pepper; cook, covered, over medium-low heat until kale is tender, about 10 minutes, stirring occasionally.
3. Add pasta and reserved pasta water; bring to a boil. Reduce heat; simmer, uncovered, until the pasta is al dente and liquid is absorbed, about 3 minutes, tossing to combine. Sprinkle with the shredded cheese.
1⅓ CUPS 512 cal., 30g fat (8g sat. fat), 51mg chol., 898mg sod., 43g carb. (2g sugars, 3g fiber), 19g pro.

BUCATINI WITH
SAUSAGE & KALE

SMOKED SAUSAGE & VEGGIE SHEET-PAN SUPPER

This recipe is tasty, quick and easily doubled for last-minute dinner guests. Cook it in the oven or on the grill, and add the veggies of your choice.
—Judy Batson, Tampa, FL

TAKES: 30 min. • **MAKES:** 4 servings

- 1 pkg. (13½ oz.) smoked sausage, cut into ½-in. slices
- 8 fresh Brussels sprouts, thinly sliced
- 1 large sweet onion, halved and sliced
- 1 medium yellow summer squash, halved and sliced
- 1 medium zucchini, halved and sliced
- 1 medium sweet yellow pepper, chopped
- 1 medium green pepper, chopped
- 1 medium tomato, chopped
- ¾ cup sliced fresh mushrooms
- ½ cup Greek vinaigrette

Preheat oven to 400°. Place the first 9 ingredients into a greased 15x10x1-in. baking pan. Drizzle with vinaigrette; toss to coat. Bake, uncovered, 15 minutes. Remove pan from oven; preheat broiler. Broil sausage mixture 3-4 in. from heat until vegetables are lightly browned, 3-4 minutes.

2 CUPS 491 cal., 37g fat (13g sat. fat), 64mg chol., 1430mg sod., 22g carb. (13g sugars, 5g fiber), 18g pro.

TEST KITCHEN TIP
Use smoked turkey sausage or fully-cooked chicken sausage for a lighter version.

SMOKED SAUSAGE & VEGGIE SHEET-PAN SUPPER

RIGATONI WITH SAUSAGE & PEAS

RIGATONI WITH SAUSAGE & PEAS

With a hearty tomato sauce and tangy goat cheese, this weeknight wonder is my version of comfort food. You'll want to have bowl after bowl.
—*Lizzie Munro, Brooklyn, NY*

TAKES: 30 min. • **MAKES:** 6 servings

- 12 oz. uncooked rigatoni or large tube pasta
- 1 lb. bulk Italian sausage
- 4 garlic cloves, minced
- ¼ cup tomato paste
- 1 can (28 oz.) crushed tomatoes
- ½ tsp. dried basil
- ¼ to ½ tsp. crushed red pepper flakes
- 1½ cups frozen peas *green beans*
- ½ cup heavy whipping cream
- ½ cup crumbled goat or feta cheese
  Thinly sliced fresh basil, optional

1. Cook rigatoni according to package directions.
2. Meanwhile, in a Dutch oven, cook sausage over medium heat 6-8 minutes or until no longer pink, breaking into crumbles. Add garlic; cook 1 minute longer. Drain. Add tomato paste; cook and stir 2-3 minutes or until meat is coated. Stir in tomatoes, dried basil and pepper flakes; bring to a boil. Reduce heat; simmer, uncovered, 10-15 minutes or until thickened, stirring occasionally.
3. Drain rigatoni; stir into sausage mixture. Add peas and cream; heat through. Top with cheese, and fresh basil if desired.

1⅔ CUPS 563 cal., 28g fat (12g sat. fat), 75mg chol., 802mg sod., 60g carb. (11g sugars, 7g fiber), 23g pro.

BEEFY CHILI DOGS ✓

For years people have told me I make the best chili dogs out there. It's timeless and family-friendly, and I usually carry the recipe with me because people ask for it.
—*Vicki Boyd, Mechanicsville, VA*

TAKES: 30 min.
MAKES: 8 servings (2 cups chili)

- 1 lb. ground beef
- 1 tsp. chili powder
- ½ tsp. garlic powder
- ½ tsp. paprika
- ¼ tsp. cayenne pepper
- 1 cup ketchup
- 8 hot dogs
- 8 hot dog buns, split
  Optional: Shredded cheddar cheese and chopped onion

1. For chili, in a large skillet, cook beef over medium heat 5-7 minutes or until no longer pink, breaking into crumbles; drain. Transfer beef to a food processor; pulse until finely chopped.
2. Return beef to skillet; stir in the seasonings and ketchup. Bring to a boil. Reduce heat; simmer, covered, 15-20 minutes to allow flavors to blend, stirring occasionally.
3. Meanwhile, cook hot dogs according to package directions. Serve in buns with the chili. If desired, top with the cheese and onion.

FREEZE OPTION Freeze cooled chili in a freezer container. To use, partially thaw in refrigerator overnight. Heat through in a saucepan, stirring occasionally; add water if necessary.

1 HOT DOG WITH ¼ CUP CHILI 400 cal., 22g fat (9g sat. fat), 60mg chol., 1092mg sod., 31g carb. (11g sugars, 1g fiber), 19g pro.

CHAPTER 8

FISH & SEAFOOD FAVORITES

P. 168

P. 166

P. 175

P. 170

MEDITERRANEAN SOLE ✓

Steaming in parchment is an easy and healthy way to cook fish and veggies. This simple recipe is really elegant and incredibly flavorful. Any white fish will work in place of the sole.
—*Andrea Potischman, Menlo Park, CA*

TAKES: 25 min. • **MAKES:** 4 servings

- 1 lb. sole fillets, cut into 4 portions
- ¼ tsp. pepper
- 1 medium lemon, sliced
- 2 Tbsp. dry white wine or chicken broth
- 2 Tbsp. olive oil, divided
- 2 cups cherry tomatoes, halved
- ½ cup Greek olives, halved
- 1 Tbsp. capers, drained
- 1 Tbsp. lemon juice
- 2 garlic cloves, minced
- 2 Tbsp. minced fresh parsley

1. Preheat oven to 400°. Place each fillet on a piece of heavy-duty foil or parchment (about 12 in. square). Sprinkle fillets with pepper; top with lemon slices. Drizzle with wine and 1 Tbsp. oil.
2. In a small bowl, combine tomatoes, olives, capers, lemon juice, garlic and remaining 1 Tbsp. oil; spoon over fillets. Fold foil or parchment around the fish, sealing tightly.
3. Place packets on a baking sheet. Bake until fish just begins to flake easily with a fork, 10-12 minutes. Open packets carefully to allow steam to escape. Sprinkle with parsley.
1 PACKET 211 cal., 14g fat (2g sat. fat), 51mg chol., 669mg sod., 7g carb. (2g sugars, 2g fiber), 15g pro. **DIABETIC EXCHANGES** 3 lean meat, 3 fat, 1 vegetable.

AIR-FRYER SCALLOPS

AIR-FRYER SCALLOPS ✓

I never liked seafood until my husband urged me to try scallops. Now, I love it! With crunchy breading, these air-fryer scallops are the best you'll ever have.
—*Martina Preston, Willow Grove, PA*

TAKES: 25 min. • **MAKES:** 2 servings

- 1 large egg
- ⅓ cup mashed potato flakes
- ⅓ cup seasoned bread crumbs
- ⅛ tsp. salt
- ⅛ tsp. pepper
- 6 sea scallops (about ¾ lb.), patted dry
- 2 Tbsp. all-purpose flour
  Butter-flavored cooking spray

1. Preheat air fryer to 400°. In a shallow bowl, lightly beat egg. In another bowl, toss together the potato flakes, bread crumbs, salt and pepper. In a third bowl, toss scallops with flour to coat lightly.

Dip into egg, then into potato mixture, patting to adhere.
2. Arrange scallops in a single layer on greased tray in air-fryer basket; spritz with cooking spray. Cook until golden brown, 3-4 minutes. Turn; spritz with cooking spray. Cook until the breading is golden brown and scallops are firm and opaque, 3-4 minutes longer.
3 SCALLOPS 298 cal., 5g fat (1g sat. fat), 134mg chol., 1138mg sod., 33g carb. (2g sugars, 2g fiber), 28g pro.

TEST KITCHEN TIP
Bring a little flair to the scallops by adding a dash of dried basil or oregano to the potato flakes-bread crumb mixture.

AIR-FRYER PRETZEL-CRUSTED CATFISH

I love the flavor of this air-fried catfish. I'm not a big fish lover, so any recipe that has me loving fish is a keeper in my book. It's wonderful served with a nice buttery, herbed rice pilaf and corn muffins with butter and honey!
—Kelly Williams, Forked River, NJ

PREP: 15 min. • **COOK:** 10 min./batch
MAKES: 4 servings

- 4   catfish fillets (6 oz. each)
- ½ tsp. salt
- ½ tsp. pepper
- 2   large eggs
- ⅓ cup Dijon mustard
- 2   Tbsp. 2% milk
- ½ cup all-purpose flour
- 4   cups honey mustard miniature pretzels, coarsely crushed
    Cooking spray
    Lemon slices, optional

1. Preheat air fryer to 325°. Sprinkle catfish with salt and pepper. Whisk eggs, mustard and milk in a shallow bowl. Place the flour and pretzels in separate shallow bowls. Coat fillets with flour, then dip into egg mixture and coat with crushed pretzels.
2. In batches, place the fillets in a single layer on greased tray in air-fryer basket; spritz with cooking spray. Cook until fish flakes easily with a fork, 10-12 minutes. If desired, serve with lemon slices.
1 FILLET 466 cal., 14g fat (3g sat. fat), 164mg chol., 1580mg sod., 45g carb. (2g sugars, 2g fiber), 33g pro.

TEST KITCHEN TIP

If you don't have an air fryer, you can make this recipe in a deep fryer, electric skillet or on the stovetop.

CRAB-TOPPED TOMATO SLICES

When camping, my wife and I top large beefsteak tomatoes with spicy chunks of crab. Then we warm this summer treat over the fire.
—Thomas Faglon, Somerset, NJ

TAKES: 30 min. • **MAKES:** 4 servings

- 1   carton (8 oz.) mascarpone cheese
- 2   Tbsp. finely chopped sweet red pepper
- 1½ tsp. grated lemon zest
- 2   Tbsp. lemon juice
- 1   tsp. seafood seasoning
- 1   tsp. hot pepper sauce
- ½ tsp. salt
- ¼ tsp. freshly ground pepper
- 2   cans (6 oz. each) lump crabmeat, drained
- 8   slices tomato (½ in. thick)
    Minced chives

1. Preheat oven to 375°. In a large bowl, combine the first 8 ingredients; gently stir in crab.
2. Place tomato slices on a foil-lined baking sheet; top with crab mixture. Bake until heated through, 12-15 minutes. Sprinkle with chives.
1 SERVING 325 cal., 27g fat (14g sat. fat), 153mg chol., 980mg sod., 3g carb. (1g sugars, 1g fiber), 20g pro.

AIR-FRYER PRETZEL-CRUSTED CATFISH

ONE-PAN SWEET CHILI SHRIMP & VEGGIES

This recipe has everything I'm looking for in a weeknight family dinner: A quick and nutritious meal that my kids will eat! My oldest son loves shrimp and I thought it could work really well as a complete sheet-pan supper.
—*Elisabeth Larsen, Pleasant Grove, UT*

TAKES: 30 min. • **MAKES:** 4 servings

1   lb. uncooked shrimp (16-20 per lb.), peeled and deveined
2   medium zucchini, halved and sliced
½   lb. sliced fresh mushrooms
1   medium sweet orange pepper, julienned
3   Tbsp. sweet chili sauce
1   Tbsp. canola oil
1   Tbsp. lime juice
1   Tbsp. reduced-sodium soy sauce
3   green onions, chopped
¼   cup minced fresh cilantro

1. Preheat oven to 400°. Place shrimp, zucchini, mushrooms and pepper in a greased 15x10x1-in. baking pan. Combine chili sauce, oil, lime juice and soy sauce. Pour over shrimp mixture and toss to coat.
2. Bake until the shrimp turn pink and vegetables are tender, 12-15 minutes. Sprinkle with green onions and cilantro.
1 SERVING 199 cal., 6g fat (1g sat. fat), 138mg chol., 483mg sod., 15g carb. (11g sugars, 3g fiber), 22g pro.

ONE-PAN SWEET CHILI SHRIMP & VEGGIES

PORTUGUESE SHRIMP ✓

I received this recipe nearly 40 years ago from a co-worker who was raised in Portugal. She made it for an office potluck luncheon and everyone wanted the recipe! It is easy to make, impressive to serve and delicious. The sauce is also good served on fish fillets.
—*Kristine Chayes, Smithtown, NY*

TAKES: 30 min. • **MAKES:** 6 servings

2 Tbsp. olive oil
1 medium onion, sliced
½ cup chopped green pepper
1 cup tomato sauce
½ cup orange juice
¼ cup diced pimientos, drained
½ tsp. grated orange zest
½ tsp. salt
¼ tsp. pepper
2 lbs. uncooked shrimp (16-20 per lb.), peeled and deveined
4 cups hot cooked rice
 Minced fresh parsley, optional

In a large skillet, heat oil over medium-high heat. Add onion and green pepper; cook until onion starts to turn brown, about 10 minutes. Stir in tomato sauce, orange juice, pimientos, zest, salt and pepper. Bring mixture to a boil, reduce heat and simmer 5 minutes. Add shrimp; simmer, covered, until shrimp turn pink, 4-5 minutes. Serve with rice. Sprinkle with parsley if desired.

1 SERVING 336 cal., 7g fat (1g sat. fat), 184mg chol., 566mg sod., 38g carb. (4g sugars, 2g fiber), 29g pro. **DIABETIC EXCHANGES** 4 lean meat, 2½ starch, 1 fat.

PORTUGUESE SHRIMP

PRESSURE-COOKER BUFFALO SHRIMP MAC & CHEESE

Rich, creamy and slightly spicy, this shrimp and pasta dish does it all. It's a nice new twist on popular Buffalo chicken dishes.
—*Robin Haas, Cranston, RI*

PREP: 15 min. • **COOK:** 10 min. + releasing
MAKES: 6 servings

- 2 cups 2% milk
- 1 cup half-and-half cream
- 1 Tbsp. unsalted butter
- 1 tsp. ground mustard
- ½ tsp. onion powder
- ¼ tsp. white pepper
- ¼ tsp. ground nutmeg
- 1½ cups uncooked elbow macaroni
- 2 cups shredded cheddar cheese
- 1 cup shredded Gouda or Swiss cheese
- ¾ lb. frozen cooked salad shrimp, thawed
- 1 cup crumbled blue cheese
- 2 Tbsp. Louisiana-style hot sauce
- 2 Tbsp. minced fresh chives
- 2 Tbsp. minced fresh parsley
   Additional Louisiana-style hot sauce, optional

1. In a 6-qt. electric pressure cooker, combine the first 7 ingredients; stir in macaroni. Lock lid; close pressure-release valve. Adjust to pressure-cook on high for 3 minutes. Allow pressure to naturally release for 4 minutes, then quick-release any remaining pressure.
2. Select saute setting and adjust for medium heat. Stir in shredded cheeses, shrimp, blue cheese and hot sauce. Cook until heated through, 5-6 minutes. Just before serving, stir in chives, parsley and, if desired, additional hot sauce.
1 SERVING 551 cal., 34g fat (20g sat. fat), 228mg chol., 1269mg sod., 22g carb. (7g sugars, 1g fiber), 38g pro.

AIR-FRYER COD ✓

This air-fryer cod recipe will tempt even the biggest fish skeptic. It's healthy and delicious—no breading needed!
—*Kim Russell, North Wales, PA*

TAKES: 30 min. • **MAKES:** 2 servings

- ¼ cup fat-free Italian salad dressing
- ½ tsp. sugar
- ⅛ tsp. salt
- ⅛ tsp. garlic powder
- ⅛ tsp. curry powder
- ⅛ tsp. paprika
- ⅛ tsp. pepper
- 2 cod fillets (6 oz. each)
- 2 tsp. butter

1. Preheat air fryer to 370°. In a shallow bowl, mix the first 7 ingredients; add cod, turning to coat. Let stand 10-15 minutes.
2. Place the fillets in a single layer on a greased tray in air-fryer basket; discard remaining marinade. Cook until the fish just begins to flake easily with a fork, 8-10 minutes. Top with butter.
1 FILLET 168 cal., 5g fat (3g sat. fat), 75mg chol., 366mg sod., 2g carb. (2g sugars, 0 fiber), 27g pro. **DIABETIC EXCHANGES** 4 lean meat, 1 fat.

TEST KITCHEN TIP

Go ahead and experiment with the seasonings for this dish. Try cumin, coriander, five-spice powder or red pepper flakes.

SPAGHETTI CARBONARA

ROSEMARY SALMON & VEGGIES

My husband and I eat a lot of salmon. One night, I created this meal in a rush to get dinner on the table. It's a keeper! You can use zucchini, small cauliflower florets or even fresh green beans.
—Elizabeth Bramkamp, Gig Harbor, WA

TAKES: 30 min. • **MAKES:** 4 servings

- 1½ lbs. salmon fillets, cut into 4 portions
- 2 Tbsp. melted coconut oil or olive oil
- 2 Tbsp. balsamic vinegar
- 2 tsp. minced fresh rosemary or ¾ tsp. dried rosemary, crushed
- 1 garlic clove, minced
- ½ tsp. salt
- 1 lb. fresh asparagus, trimmed
- 1 medium sweet red pepper, cut into 1-in. pieces
- ¼ tsp. pepper
   Lemon wedges

1. Preheat oven to 400°. Place salmon in a greased 15x10x1-in. baking pan. Combine oil, vinegar, rosemary, garlic and salt. Pour half over salmon. Place asparagus and red pepper in a large bowl; drizzle with remaining oil mixture and toss to coat. Arrange around salmon in pan; sprinkle with pepper.
2. Bake until salmon flakes easily with a fork and vegetables are tender, 12-15 minutes. Serve with lemon wedges.
1 SERVING 357 cal., 23g fat (9g sat. fat), 85mg chol., 388mg sod., 7g carb. (4g sugars, 2g fiber), 31g pro. **DIABETIC EXCHANGES** 4 lean meat, 1½ fat, 1 vegetable.

SPAGHETTI CARBONARA

This is a classic Italian recipe. The key is to use the hot pasta water to make the dish creamy. If made properly, there is no need to add cream or milk. The dish is luxurious, satisfying, comforting and easy to make. You can also add peas after you have cooked the pancetta and garlic. Additionally, you can use any pasta you like. But the consistency is usually best with a thicker spaghetti.
—Luisa Webb, Fort Collins, CO

TAKES: 30 min. • **MAKES:** 8 servings

- 1 pkg. (16 oz.) spaghetti
- 2 large eggs
- 1 cup grated Parmesan cheese
- 1 Tbsp. olive oil
- 4 oz. chopped pancetta
- 2 garlic cloves, minced
- ¼ tsp. salt
- ¼ tsp. freshly ground pepper
   Chopped fresh parsley

1. Cook spaghetti according to package directions for al dente. Meanwhile, in a large bowl, whisk eggs and Parmesan; set aside.
2. In a large skillet, heat oil over medium heat. Add pancetta; cook and stir until crispy, 5-6 minutes. Add garlic; cook 1 minute longer.
3. Drain spaghetti, reserving ¾ cup pasta water. Add spaghetti to skillet; toss to coat. Slowly add egg mixture, stirring constantly. Add salt, pepper and enough pasta water for sauce to reach desired consistency. Sprinkle with parsley, and additional Parmesan if desired.
1 CUP 337 cal., 11g fat (4g sat. fat), 66mg chol., 539mg sod., 44g carb. (2g sugars, 2g fiber), 14g pro.

ROSEMARY
SALMON & VEGGIES

AIR-FRYER CRUMB-TOPPED SOLE

Looking for a low-carb supper you can make in a flash? These buttery sole fillets are covered with a rich sauce and topped with toasty bread crumbs. They're super speedy thanks to your air fryer.
—Taste of Home *Test Kitchen*

PREP: 10 min. • **COOK:** 10 min./batch
MAKES: 4 servings

- 3 Tbsp. reduced-fat mayonnaise
- 3 Tbsp. grated Parmesan cheese, divided
- 2 tsp. mustard seed
- ¼ tsp. pepper
- 4 sole fillets (6 oz. each)
- 1 cup soft bread crumbs
- 1 green onion, finely chopped
- ½ tsp. ground mustard
- 2 tsp. butter, melted
  Cooking spray

1. Preheat air fryer to 375°. Combine mayonnaise, 2 Tbsp. cheese, mustard seed and pepper; spread over tops of the fillets.
2. In batches, place fish in a single layer on a greased tray in air-fryer basket. Cook until the fish flakes easily with a fork, 3-5 minutes.
3. Meanwhile, in a small bowl, combine the bread crumbs, onion, ground mustard and remaining 1 Tbsp. cheese; stir in butter. Spoon over fillets, patting gently to adhere; spritz topping with cooking spray. Cook until golden brown, 2-3 minutes longer. If desired, sprinkle with additional green onion.

1 FILLET 233 cal., 11g fat (3g sat. fat), 89mg chol., 714mg sod., 8g carb. (1g sugars, 1g fiber), 24g pro.

TEST KITCHEN TIP
If you don't have an air fryer, you can bake these crumb-topped fillets in an oven.

AIR-FRYER CRUMB-TOPPED SOLE

**SHRIMP SPAGHETTI
WITH CHERRY TOMATOES**

THAI SCALLOP SAUTE

Just open a bottle of Thai peanut sauce to give this seafood stir-fry some serious authenticity.
—Taste of Home *Test Kitchen*

PREP: 15 min. • **COOK:** 20 min.
MAKES: 4 servings

- 3 tsp. olive oil, divided
- 1½ lbs. sea scallops
- 2 cups fresh broccoli florets
- 2 medium onions, halved and sliced
- 1 medium zucchini, sliced
- 4 small carrots, sliced
- ¼ cup Thai peanut sauce
- ¼ tsp. salt
   Hot cooked rice
   Lime wedges, optional

1. In a large skillet, heat 1 tsp. oil over medium-high heat. Add half the scallops; stir-fry until firm and opaque. Remove from pan. Repeat with an additional 1 tsp. oil and remaining scallops.
2. In same skillet, heat the remaining oil over medium-high heat. Add vegetables; stir-fry until crisp-tender, 7-9 minutes. Stir in peanut sauce and salt. Return scallops to pan; heat through. Serve with rice, and lime wedges if desired.

1½ CUPS 268 cal., 8g fat (1g sat. fat), 41mg chol., 1000mg sod., 24g carb. (10g sugars, 4g fiber), 25g pro.

SHRIMP SPAGHETTI WITH CHERRY TOMATOES

This is a very tasty pasta dish, full of umami flavors and, if done properly, an insanely silky sauce. Shut your eyes and you will swear you're in Sicily.
—Hassan Nurullah, Hapeville, GA

PREP: 15 min. • **COOK:** 25 min.
MAKES: 6 servings

- 1 lb. uncooked spaghetti
- 3 Tbsp. olive oil
- 2 garlic cloves, smashed
- 1 tsp. crushed red pepper flakes
- 4 cups heirloom cherry tomatoes
- 2 shallots, thinly sliced
- 1 can anchovy fillets (2 oz.)
- ¾ cup muffuletta mix or olive bruschetta topping
- 4 Tbsp. unsalted butter
- 1 lb. uncooked shrimp (26-30 per lb.), peeled and deveined
- 1½ cups grated Romano cheese
- 2 Tbsp. minced fresh parsley

1. In a Dutch oven, cook pasta according to package directions; drain, reserving 1 cup cooking liquid. Set aside.
2. In same Dutch oven, heat oil over medium-high heat. Add garlic and red pepper flakes until fragrant. Discard garlic cloves; add tomatoes, shallots, anchovy fillets, muffuletta mix and butter. Cook until tomatoes begin to burst, 4-5 minutes. Add shrimp; cook until shrimp turn pink, 4-5 minutes. Add the pasta, reserved pasta water and Romano cheese to pan; stir until creamy. Garnish with parsley and additional Romano.

1¾ CUPS 726 cal., 35g fat (13g sat. fat), 150mg chol., 1163mg sod., 66g carb. (5g sugars, 4g fiber), 38g pro.

COPYCAT CHEESECAKE FACTORY SHRIMP SCAMPI

Make this simply elegant recipe with a dry white wine, or chicken broth and lemon juice if you don't want to open a new bottle. Plate it as they do at the restaurant by arranging the shrimp around a mound of angel hair pasta.
—Taste of Home *Test Kitchen*

TAKES: 30 min. • **MAKES:** 4 servings

- 12 oz. uncooked angel hair pasta
- ½ cup all-purpose flour
- 2 Tbsp. grated Parmesan cheese
- ½ tsp. salt
- ¼ tsp. pepper
- 1½ lbs. uncooked shrimp (26-30 per lb.), peeled and deveined
- 3 Tbsp. butter

SAUCE

- 2 Tbsp. olive oil
- 1 small shallot, chopped
- 5 garlic cloves
- 1 cup dry white wine
- 2 cups heavy whipping cream
- 2 plum tomatoes, diced
- 6 fresh basil leaves, thinly sliced
- ½ tsp. salt
- ¼ tsp. pepper
- 2 Tbsp. grated Parmesan cheese

1. Cook the pasta according to package directions. Meanwhile, in a shallow dish, combine flour, Parmesan cheese, salt and pepper. Add shrimp; turn to coat, shaking off excess flour mixture. In a large skillet, melt butter over medium heat; add shrimp. Cook and stir until the shrimp turn pink, 3-5 minutes. Remove and keep warm.

2. In the same skillet, heat the oil over medium heat; add shallot. Cook and stir until tender, 2-3 minutes. Add the garlic, cook 1 minute longer. Stir in the wine. Bring to a boil. Reduce heat; simmer, uncovered, until reduced by about half, 3-4 minutes. Stir in cream; simmer, uncovered, until slightly thickened, about 5 minutes. Remove and discard garlic cloves. Stir in tomatoes, basil, salt, pepper and Parmesan cheese.

3. Drain pasta. To serve, spoon sauce into shallow dishes. Top with pasta and shrimp and, if desired, additional basil.
2½ CUPS 1121 cal., 64g fat (36g sat. fat), 370mg chol., 993mg sod., 86g carb. (7g sugars, 4g fiber), 46g pro.

TEST KITCHEN TIP

We recommend a dry, crisp white wine, such as sauvignon blanc, pinot grigio, unoaked chardonnay or another high-quality white wine. Select one with a moderate acidity, so it doesn't overwhelm the dish.

SWISS & CRAB SUPPER PIE

SWISS & CRAB SUPPER PIE

Though some parts of Alaska are suitable for farming, we're on the Gulf, where commercial fishing is the main industry. Crab is plentiful here, and so is salmon, halibut, shrimp and sea herring. You don't need fresh crab for this tasty, easy-to-make supper pie. With canned crabmeat, it becomes a terrific off-the-shelf meal. Hope your family enjoys it as much as mine does!
—*Kathy Crow, Cordova, AK*

PREP: 15 min. • **BAKE:** 45 min. + standing
MAKES: 8 servings

- 1   sheet refrigerated pie crust
- 1   can (6 oz.) lump crabmeat, drained
- 1   cup shredded Swiss cheese
- 2   green onions, thinly sliced
- 3   large eggs, beaten
- 1   cup half-and-half cream
- ½   tsp. salt
- ½   tsp. grated lemon zest
- ¼   tsp. ground mustard
-     Dash mace
- ¼   cup sliced almonds

1. Preheat oven to 450°. Line a 9-in. tart pan with unpricked crust; line with heavy-duty foil. Bake 5 minutes. Remove foil; reduce oven temperature to 325°.
2. Arrange crab evenly in baked crust; top with the cheese and green onion. Combine remaining ingredients except almonds; pour into tart shell. Sprinkle top with almonds.
3. Bake until set, 45 minutes. Let stand for 10 minutes before serving.

1 PIECE 276 cal., 18g fat (8g sat. fat), 123mg chol., 435mg sod., 15g carb. (2g sugars, 0 fiber), 13g pro.

GOES GREAT WITH ...
Dill & Chive Peas (p. 298) make colorful complements to this entree, and they only take 10 minutes.

**SPINACH & SHRIMP
FRA DIAVOLO**

**GOES GREAT
WITH ...**
Hot buttered
pasta is a fast,
no-fuss side
you can easily
prepare on the
stovetop while
this dish is
simmering.

SPINACH & SHRIMP FRA DIAVOLO

This quick dish is spicy, garlicky, saucy and loaded with delicious shrimp. Plus, with the addition of spinach, you're also getting a serving of veggies. When you need a perfect low-fat weeknight meal that is easy to pull together, this is it. You can substitute arugula or kale for the spinach if you like.
—*Julie Peterson, Crofton, MD*

TAKES: 30 min. • **MAKES:** 4 servings

- 2 Tbsp. olive oil
- 1 medium onion, chopped
- 5 garlic cloves, minced
- ½ to 1 tsp. crushed red pepper flakes
- 1 cup dry white wine
- 1 can (14½ oz.) diced tomatoes, undrained
- 1 can (8 oz.) tomato sauce
- 3 Tbsp. minced fresh basil or 1 Tbsp. dried basil
- 1 tsp. dried oregano
- ¼ tsp. salt
- ¼ tsp. pepper
- 1 lb. uncooked shrimp (26-30 per lb.), peeled and deveined
- 3 cups finely chopped fresh spinach
   Grated Parmesan cheese, optional

1. In a large skillet, heat oil over medium-high heat. Add the onion; cook and stir until tender, 5-7 minutes. Add garlic and pepper flakes; cook 1 minute longer. Stir in wine. Bring to a boil; cook until liquid is reduced by half. Stir in the tomatoes, tomato sauce, basil, oregano, salt and pepper. Cook and stir until sauce is slightly thickened, about 10 minutes.
2. Add the shrimp and spinach; cook and stir until shrimp turn pink and spinach is wilted, 3-5 minutes. Sprinkle with cheese if desired.

1½ CUPS 235 cal., 9g fat (1g sat. fat), 138mg chol., 727mg sod., 14g carb. (6g sugars, 4g fiber), 22g pro. **DIABETIC EXCHANGES** 3 lean meat, 2 vegetable, 1½ fat.

AIR-FRYER SALMON

AIR-FRYER SALMON

Preparing salmon in the air fryer is, hands down, one of the easiest ways to cook it. The salmon stays succulent, but still gets lightly browned on the outside. Use this simple recipe as a starting point for different flavors and styles. The possibilities are endless!
—Taste of Home *Test Kitchen*

PREP: 10 min. • **COOK:** 15 min.
MAKES: 4 servings

- 1 Tbsp. olive oil
- 4 salmon fillets (6 oz. each)
- ½ tsp. salt
- ¼ tsp. garlic powder
- ¼ tsp. pepper
- ⅛ tsp. paprika

Preheat air fryer to 400°. Drizzle oil over salmon. Combine salt, garlic powder, pepper and paprika; sprinkle over fish.

Place salmon in a single layer in air-fryer basket. Cook until fish is lightly browned and just beginning to flake easily with a fork, 7-9 minutes.

1 FILLET 296 cal., 19g fat (4g sat. fat), 85mg chol., 381mg sod., 0 carb. (0 sugars, 0 fiber), 29g pro. **DIABETIC EXCHANGES** 4 lean meat, 1 fat.

TEST KITCHEN TIP

You can cook frozen salmon in the air fryer without thawing it. Frozen salmon takes longer to cook, though, so the timing depends on the size of the fish fillets and your air fryer. Check the salmon at the high end of the suggested cooking time, and consider adding a few minutes on top of that.

PRESSURE-COOKER RED CLAM SAUCE

This recipe tastes as if you've been working on it all day. What a classy way to jazz up pasta sauce!
—*JoAnn Brown, Latrobe, PA*

PREP: 20 min. • **COOK:** 5 min.
MAKES: 4 servings

- 1 Tbsp. canola oil
- 1 medium onion, chopped
- 2 garlic cloves, minced
- 2 cans (6½ oz. each) chopped clams, undrained
- 1 can (14½ oz.) diced tomatoes, undrained
- 1 can (6 oz.) tomato paste
- ¼ cup minced fresh parsley
- 1 bay leaf
- 1 tsp. sugar
- 1 tsp. dried basil
- ½ tsp. dried thyme
- 6 oz. linguine, cooked and drained

1. Select saute setting on a 6-qt. electric pressure cooker and adjust for medium heat. Add oil. When oil is hot, add onion; saute until tender. Add the garlic; cook 1 minute longer. Press cancel.
2. Stir in the next 8 ingredients. Lock lid; close pressure-release vale. Adjust to pressure-cook on high for 3 minutes. Allow the pressure to naturally release for 5 minutes, then quick-release any remaining pressure. Discard bay leaf. Serve with linguine.
1 SERVING 302 cal., 5g fat (0 sat. fat), 33mg chol., 667mg sod., 50g carb. (11g sugars, 5g fiber), 17g pro.

AIR-FRYER TUNA BURGERS

My family was hesitant to try these, but any skepticism disappeared after a bite.
—*Kim Stoller, Smithville, OH*

TAKES: 30 min. • **MAKES:** 4 servings

- 1 large egg, lightly beaten
- ½ cup dry bread crumbs
- ½ cup finely chopped celery
- ⅓ cup mayonnaise
- ¼ cup finely chopped onion
- 2 Tbsp. chili sauce
- 1 pouch (6.4 oz.) light tuna in water
- 4 hamburger buns, split and toasted
  Optional: Lettuce leaves and sliced tomato

1. Preheat air fryer to 350°. In a small bowl, combine first 6 ingredients; fold in tuna. Shape into 4 patties.
2. In batches, place patties in a single layer on greased tray in air-fryer basket. Cook until lightly browned, 5-6 minutes per side. Serve on buns. If desired, top with lettuce and tomato.
1 BURGER 366 cal., 17g fat (3g sat. fat), 64mg chol., 665mg sod., 35g carb. (6g sugars, 2g fiber), 17g pro.

TEST KITCHEN TIP
Chili sauce is the secret to these patties, but you can replace it with mustard, relish or even additional mayonnaise.

PRESSURE-COOKER RED CLAM SAUCE

COCONUT CITRUS SAUCED COD

I love to make this fusion meal on weeknights when I'm short on time but want something big in flavor.
—*Roxanne Chan, Albany, CA*

TAKES: 30 min. • **MAKES:** 4 servings

- 4 cod fillets (6 oz. each)
- 1 Tbsp. cornstarch
- 1 cup canned coconut milk
- ½ cup orange juice
- 2 Tbsp. sweet chili sauce
- 1 tsp. minced fresh gingerroot
- 1 tsp. soy sauce
- 1 can (11 oz.) mandarin oranges, drained
- 1 green onion, chopped
- 2 Tbsp. sliced almonds
- 1 Tbsp. sesame oil
  Minced fresh cilantro

In a large saucepan, place a steamer basket over 1 in. water. Place cod in basket. Bring water to a boil. Reduce heat to maintain a low boil; steam, covered, until the fish just begins to flake easily with a fork, 8-10 minutes. Meanwhile, in a small saucepan, whisk cornstarch, coconut milk and orange juice until smooth. Add chili sauce, ginger and soy sauce. Cook and stir over medium heat until thickened, 1-2 minutes. Stir in oranges, green onion, almonds and sesame oil; heat through. Serve with cod; sprinkle with cilantro.

1 SERVING 330 cal., 15g fat (10g sat. fat), 65mg chol., 316mg sod., 19g carb. (15g sugars, 1g fiber), 29g pro.

COCONUT CITRUS SAUCED COD

SHEET-PAN SHRIMP FAJITAS ✓

I love easy, weeknight dinners like this. This one comes together so quickly and is customizable with your favorite toppings.
—Carla Hubl, Hastings, NE

PREP: 30 min. • **COOK:** 20 min.
MAKES: 6 servings

- 1½ lbs. uncooked shrimp (31-40 per lb.), peeled and deveined
- 1 each medium green, sweet red and yellow peppers, cut into ½-in. strips
- 1 sweet onion, cut into ½-in. strips
- 2 garlic cloves, minced
- 2 Tbsp. olive oil
- 2 tsp. chili powder
- 1 tsp. ground cumin
- ¾ tsp. salt
- 12 corn tortillas (6 in.), warmed
  Optional: Lime wedges, crema, fresh cilantro and sliced avocado

1. Preheat oven to 425°. In a large bowl, combine shrimp, peppers, onion and garlic. Drizzle with oil; sprinkle with chili powder, cumin and salt. Toss to coat. Spread evenly between 2 greased 15x10x1-in. baking pans.
2. Roast 10 minutes, rotating pans halfway through cooking. Remove pans from oven; preheat broiler.
3. Broil shrimp mixture, 1 pan at a time, 3-4 in. from heat until vegetables are lightly browned and shrimp turn pink, 4-5 minutes. Serve in tortillas with toppings as desired.

2 FAJITAS 280 cal., 8g fat (1g sat. fat), 138mg chol., 484mg sod., 31g carb. (5g sugars, 5g fiber), 22g pro. **DIABETIC EXCHANGES** 3 lean meat, 1½ starch, 1 vegetable, 1 fat.

TEST KITCHEN TIP
You don't have to remove the shrimp tails for this sheet-pan dinner. Just make sure they're peeled and deveined before cooking.

SHEET-PAN SHRIMP FAJITAS

🕐 5️⃣
SCALLOPS WITH WILTED SPINACH

Two of my favorite foods are bacon and seafood. In this dish, I get them together with white wine, shallots and some baby spinach. Serve with bread to soak up the tasty broth.
—*Deborah Williams, Peoria, AZ*

TAKES: 25 min. • **MAKES:** 4 servings

- 4   bacon strips, chopped
- 12   sea scallops (about 1½ lbs.), side muscles removed
- 2   shallots, finely chopped
- ½   cup white wine or chicken broth
- 8   cups fresh baby spinach (about 8 oz.)

1. In a large nonstick skillet, cook the bacon over medium heat until crisp, stirring occasionally. Remove with a slotted spoon; drain on paper towels. Discard drippings, reserving 2 Tbsp. Wipe skillet clean if necessary.
2. Pat scallops dry with paper towels. In same skillet, heat 1 Tbsp. drippings over medium-high heat. Add scallops; cook until golden brown and firm, 2-3 minutes on each side. Remove from the pan; keep warm.
3. Heat remaining drippings in same pan over medium-high heat. Add the shallots; cook and stir until tender, 2-3 minutes. Add wine; bring to a boil, stirring to loosen browned bits from pan. Add spinach; cook and stir until wilted, 1-2 minutes. Stir in the bacon. Serve with scallops.

3 SCALLOPS WITH ½ CUP SPINACH MIXTURE 247 cal., 11g fat (4g sat. fat), 56mg chol., 964mg sod., 12g carb. (1g sugars, 1g fiber), 26g pro.

🕐
BASIL-LEMON CRAB LINGUINE

I love using fresh herbs to punch up pasta dishes. This linguine looks and tastes like a meal from a five-star restaurant.
—*Tonya Burkhard, Palm Coast, FL*

TAKES: 25 min. • **MAKES:** 4 servings

- 1   pkg. (9 oz.) refrigerated linguine
- ⅓   cup butter, cubed
- 1   jalapeno pepper, seeded and finely chopped
- 1   garlic clove, minced
- 1   tsp. grated lemon zest
- 3   Tbsp. lemon juice
- 2   cans (6 oz. each) lump crabmeat, drained
- ¼   cup loosely packed basil leaves, thinly sliced
- ½   tsp. sea salt
- ¼   tsp. freshly ground pepper

1. Cook linguine according to package directions. Meanwhile, in a large skillet, heat butter over medium heat. Add jalapeno and garlic; cook and stir 1-2 minutes or until tender. Stir in lemon zest and juice. Add the crab; heat through, stirring gently.
2. Drain the linguine; add to skillet. Sprinkle with basil, salt and pepper; toss to combine.

NOTE Wear disposable gloves when cutting hot peppers; the oils can burn skin. Avoid touching your face.

1¼ CUPS 392 cal., 18g fat (11g sat. fat), 161mg chol., 856mg sod., 35g carb. (1g sugars, 2g fiber), 23g pro.

BLEND OF THE BAYOU

BLEND OF THE BAYOU ✓

My sister-in-law shared this easy recipe with me. It has been handed down in my husband's family for generations. It's quick to prepare, nutritious and flavorful. I have now passed it on to my children too.
—*Ruby Williams, Bogalusa, LA*

PREP: 20 min. • **BAKE:** 25 min.
MAKES: 8 servings

1 pkg. (8 oz.) cream cheese, cubed
4 Tbsp. butter, divided
1 large onion, chopped
2 celery ribs, chopped
1 large green pepper, chopped
1 lb. cooked shrimp (31-40 per lb.), peeled and deveined
2 cans (6 oz. each) crabmeat, drained, flaked and cartilage removed
1 can (10¾ oz.) condensed cream of mushroom soup, undiluted
¾ cup cooked rice
1 jar (4½ oz.) sliced mushrooms, drained
1 tsp. garlic salt
¾ tsp. hot pepper sauce
½ tsp. cayenne pepper
¾ cup shredded cheddar cheese
½ cup crushed butter-flavored crackers (about 12 crackers)

1. Preheat oven to 350°. In a saucepan, cook and stir cream cheese and 2 Tbsp. butter over low heat until melted and smooth.
2. In a large cast-iron or other ovenproof skillet, saute the onion, celery and green pepper in the remaining butter until tender. Stir in the shrimp, crab, soup, rice, mushrooms, garlic salt, pepper sauce, cayenne and cream cheese mixture.
3. Combine the cheddar cheese and cracker crumbs; sprinkle over top. Bake, uncovered, for 25-30 minutes or until bubbly.
1 CUP 366 cal., 23g fat (13g sat. fat), 164mg chol., 981mg sod., 17g carb. (3g sugars, 2g fiber), 23g pro.

SICILIAN PIZZA (SFINCIONE) ✓

My favorite pizza from childhood is still my favorite today. The crunchy breadcrumb topping sets it apart from its American counterpart. I like to top this pie with fresh basil.
—*Susan Falk, Sterling Heights, MI*

PREP: 20 min. • **BAKE:** 20 min.
MAKES: 12 servings

2 loaves (1 lb. each) fresh or frozen pizza dough, thawed
3 Tbsp. olive oil, divided
1 can (28 oz.) whole tomatoes, drained and crushed
1 medium onion, finely chopped
1 can (2 oz.) anchovy fillets, drained and broken into ¼-in. pieces
1 cup shredded mozzarella cheese
½ cup soft bread crumbs
   Fresh torn basil leaves

1. Preheat the oven to 425°. Grease a 15x10x1-in. baking pan. Press dough to fit bottom and ½ in. up sides of pan. Brush with 2 Tbsp. oil; top with tomatoes, onion and anchovies. Sprinkle with mozzarella. Combine bread crumbs and remaining 1 Tbsp. oil; sprinkle over pizza.
2. Bake on a lower oven rack until edges are golden brown and cheese is melted, 20-25 minutes. Sprinkle with the basil before serving.
1 PIECE 277 cal., 9g fat (2g sat. fat), 11mg chol., 527mg sod., 38g carb. (4g sugars, 3g fiber), 11g pro.

GOES GREAT WITH ...
Pick up a Caesar salad kit at the grocery store to round out this yummy pizza.

SICILIAN PIZZA (SFINCIONE)

BLOCK ISLAND LITTLENECKS WITH CHORIZO

Every summer my family digs clams on the shores of Block Island, Rhode Island. This dish highlights fresh clam's sweet and salty flavor, and chorizo adds a little kick. The Swiss chard greens from our garden, corn and cannellini beans round out the flavor profile. The best part is dipping crusty bread into the delicious broth! Quick and easy to put together, it's the perfect dinner on a summer night!
—*Pamela Gelsomini, Wrentham, MA*

PREP: 20 min. • **COOK:** 20 min.
MAKES: 8 servings (4 qt.)

- 3   lbs. fresh littleneck clams
- 1   bunch Swiss chard, stems removed and chopped (about 4 cups)
- ½   lb. fully cooked Spanish chorizo links, chopped
- 1   can (15 oz.) cannellini beans, rinsed and drained
- 1   medium onion, chopped
- 1   cup fresh or frozen corn
- 4   garlic cloves, minced
- 1   tsp. salt
- 1   tsp. pepper
- 1   bottle (12 oz.) beer
- ⅓   cup olive oil
     Grilled French bread baguette slices

1. Place the clams in a stockpot; top with the next 8 ingredients. Add beer and oil; bring to a boil. Reduce the heat; simmer, covered, for 10 minutes.
2. Stir; cook, covered, until the clams open, 5-7 minutes longer. Discard any unopened clams. Ladle into bowls; serve with grilled bread.

2 CUPS 265 cal., 17g fat (4g sat. fat), 28mg chol., 729mg sod., 16g carb. (3g sugars, 4g fiber), 12g pro.

BLOCK ISLAND LITTLENECKS WITH CHORIZO

SHEET-PAN SOY-GINGER SALMON WITH VEGGIES

This salmon and veggie sheet-pan dinner is packed with Asian flavors, and is so easy to make. It's high in protein, omega-3 fatty acids, fiber and so many other nutrients, and it's delicious! We like to serve it over brown rice or quinoa.
—*Pamela Gelsomini, Wrentham, MA*

PREP: 20 min+ marinating
BAKE: 20 min. • **MAKES:** 6 servings

½ cup thinly sliced green onions, divided
⅓ cup reduced-sodium soy sauce
¼ cup packed brown sugar
¼ cup honey
2 Tbsp. sesame seeds, divided
2 Tbsp. rice vinegar
3 garlic cloves, chopped
1 Tbsp. sesame oil
1 tsp. crushed red pepper flakes
1 tsp. minced fresh gingerroot
1 salmon fillet (2 lbs.)

4 cups fresh broccoli florets
3 medium zucchini, halved lengthwise and cut into ½-in. slices (about 4 cups)
¼ cup olive oil
½ tsp. salt
½ tsp. pepper
   Hot cooked rice, optional

1. In a large bowl, whisk ¼ cup green onion, soy sauce, brown sugar, honey, 1 Tbsp. sesame seeds, vinegar, garlic, sesame oil, pepper flakes and ginger until blended. Pour ½ cup marinade into a shallow dish. Add salmon; turn to coat. Refrigerate, covered, 2-3 hours. Cover and refrigerate remaining marinade.
2. Preheat oven to 400°. Drain salmon, discarding marinade in dish. Place salmon on a greased rimmed baking sheet. Toss broccoli and zucchini with oil, salt and pepper; arrange in a single layer around salmon. Bake until salmon just begins to flake easily with a fork and vegetables are crisp-tender, 20-25 minutes.
3. Meanwhile, transfer the reserved marinade to a small saucepan. Bring to a boil; cook until liquid is reduced by half, 10-12 minutes. Serve salmon and vegetables with sauce and, if desired, rice. Top with remaining ¼ cup green onions and 1 Tbsp. sesame seeds.

4 OZ. COOKED SALMON WITH 1 CUP VEGETABLES 426 cal., 26g fat (5g sat. fat), 76mg chol., 627mg sod., 20g carb. (15g sugars, 3g fiber), 29g pro. **DIABETIC EXCHANGES** 4 lean meat, 2 fat, 1 vegetable, ½ starch.

SHEET-PAN SOY-GINGER SALMON WITH VEGGIES

CHAPTER 9

MEATLESS MAINSTAYS

P. 194

P. 190

P. 185

P. 190

GOES GREAT WITH ...
Store-bought cornbread muffins are perfect with this main course.

CHILES RELLENOS SOUFFLE

CHILES RELLENOS SOUFFLE

After we spent the night at our friends' house in Arizona, we awoke to the tantalizing aroma of an egg souffle. This lovely Southwest-inspired dish brings back wonderful memories.
—*Pat Coyne, Las Vegas, NV*

G-N

PREP: 15 min. • **BAKE:** 45 min.
MAKES: 8 servings

- 2 cans (4 oz. each) chopped green chiles
- ¼ cup sliced ripe olives
- ¼ cup finely chopped onion
- 2 cups sharp shredded cheddar cheese
- 4 large eggs
- 1½ cups biscuit/baking mix
- 2 cups 2% milk
- ¼ tsp. pepper
- 1 cup 4% small-curd cottage cheese
  Optional: Salsa and sour cream

1. Preheat oven to 350°. Spread green chiles in a greased 11x7-in. baking dish; sprinkle with olives, onion and cheese. In a large bowl, whisk eggs, biscuit mix, milk and pepper until blended. Stir in cottage cheese; pour over top.
2. Bake, uncovered, until golden brown, puffed and a knife inserted in the center comes out clean, 45-50 minutes. Let stand 5-10 minutes before serving. If desired, serve with the salsa and sour cream.

TO MAKE AHEAD Refrigerate unbaked souffle, covered, several hours or overnight. To use, preheat oven to 350°. Remove souffle from refrigerator while oven heats. Bake, as directed, increasing time as necessary until golden and puffed, and a knife inserted in center comes out clean. Let stand for 5-10 minutes before serving.
1 PIECE 305 cal., 17g fat (8g sat. fat), 128mg chol., 708mg sod., 23g carb. (5g sugars, 1g fiber), 16g pro.

ROASTED PUMPKIN LASAGNA

ROASTED PUMPKIN LASAGNA

This is a hearty meatless meal my family enjoys. If you prefer butternut squash, it can be used instead of pumpkin.
—*Wendy Masters, East Garafraxa, ON*

PREP: 1 hour • **BAKE:** 1 hour + standing
MAKES: 12 servings

- 1 medium pie pumpkin (about 3 lbs.)
- 2 Tbsp. olive oil
- 1 tsp. salt, divided
- ¼ tsp. ground nutmeg
- 12 uncooked lasagna noodles
- ½ cup butter, cubed
- 1 cup chopped onion
- 3 garlic cloves, minced
- ½ cup all-purpose flour
- 4½ cups 2% milk
- ¼ cup chopped fresh sage
- ½ cup grated Parmesan cheese
- 2 cups shredded mozzarella cheese
  Crushed red pepper flakes, optional

1. Preheat oven to 400°. Peel pumpkin; cut in half lengthwise. (Discard seeds or save for toasting.) Cut into ¼-in.-thick slices. Place in a single layer on 2 greased 15x10x1-in. baking pans. Drizzle with oil; sprinkle with ¼ tsp. salt and nutmeg. Roast until tender, 30-35 minutes. Reduce the oven temperature to 350°.
2. Meanwhile, cook lasagna noodles according to package directions for al dente. In a large saucepan, melt butter over medium heat. Add onion; cook and stir until tender, 6-7 minutes. Add garlic; cook 1 minute longer. Stir in flour and remaining ¾ tsp. salt until smooth; gradually whisk in milk and sage. Bring to a boil, stirring constantly; cook and stir until thickened, 8-10 minutes. Remove from heat; stir in Parmesan cheese. Drain noodles.
3. Place 3 noodles in a greased 13x9-in. baking dish. Layer with one-third of pumpkin, 1⅓ cups sauce and ½ cup mozzarella cheese. Repeat layers twice. Top with remaining noodles, sauce and mozzarella cheese.
4. Bake, covered, 30 minutes. Uncover and bake until golden brown and bubbly, 30-35 minutes longer. Let stand 10-15 minutes before serving. If desired, sprinkle with red pepper flakes.
1 PIECE 350 cal., 17g fat (9g sat. fat), 45mg chol., 481mg sod., 37g carb. (8g sugars, 2g fiber), 13g pro.

MUSHROOM & SWEET POTATO POTPIE

The last time I was in the U.S., I had a mushroom and beer potpie at a small brewpub. It was rich and comforting. I tried numerous versions when I got home and I think I've come pretty close!
—Iben Ravn, Copenhagen, Denmark

PREP: 45 min. • **BAKE:** 30 min.
MAKES: 8 servings

⅓ cup olive oil, divided
1 lb. sliced fresh shiitake mushrooms
1 lb. sliced baby portobello mushrooms
2 large onions, chopped
2 garlic cloves, minced
1 tsp. minced fresh rosemary, plus more for topping
1 bottle (12 oz.) porter or stout beer
1½ cups mushroom broth or vegetable broth, divided
2 bay leaves
1 Tbsp. balsamic vinegar
2 Tbsp. reduced-sodium soy sauce
¼ cup cornstarch
3 to 4 small sweet potatoes, peeled and thinly sliced
¾ tsp. coarsely ground pepper
½ tsp. salt

1. Preheat oven to 400°. In a Dutch oven, heat 1 Tbsp. oil over medium heat. Add shiitake mushrooms and cook in batches until dark golden brown, 8-10 minutes; remove with a slotted spoon. Repeat with 1 Tbsp. oil and the portobello mushrooms.

2. In the same pan, heat 1 Tbsp. oil over medium heat. Add onions; cook and stir 8-10 minutes or until tender. Add garlic and 1 tsp. rosemary; cook 30 seconds longer. Stir in the beer, 1 cup broth, bay leaves, vinegar, soy sauce and sauteed mushrooms.

3. Bring to a boil. Reduce heat; simmer, uncovered, 10 minutes. In a small bowl, mix cornstarch and remaining broth until smooth; stir into mushroom mixture. Return to a boil, stirring constantly; cook and stir until thickened, 1-2 minutes. Remove and discard the bay leaves; transfer the mushroom mixture to 8 greased 8-oz. ramekins. Place on a rimmed baking sheet.

4. Layer sweet potatoes in a circular pattern on top of each ramekin; brush with remaining oil and sprinkle with pepper, salt and additional rosemary. Bake, covered, until potatoes are tender, 20-25 minutes. Remove cover and bake until the potatoes are lightly browned, 8-10 minutes. Let stand for 5 minutes before serving.

1 SERVING 211 cal., 10g fat (1g sat. fat), 0 chol., 407mg sod., 26g carb. (10g sugars, 4g fiber), 5g pro.

MUSHROOM & SWEET POTATO POTPIE

TEST KITCHEN TIP

We're not sticklers for specific types of mushrooms. Go ahead and experiment with whatever mushrooms you have; just be sure to saute them until they turn a rich golden brown. This really adds a lot of flavor.

PINTO BEAN ZUCCHINI BOATS

PINTO BEAN ZUCCHINI BOATS

Zucchini shells take center stage when filled with vegetables, beans and sauce.
—Taste of Home *Test Kitchen*

TAKES: 30 min. • **MAKES:** 4 servings

4	large zucchini
8	cups water
1	tsp. salt
½	cup chopped red onion
1	Tbsp. olive oil
1	can (15 oz.) pinto beans, rinsed and drained
1	can (11 oz.) Mexicorn, drained
1	can (8 oz.) tomato sauce
½	cup chili sauce
1	tsp. dried cilantro flakes
½	tsp. ground cumin
3	oz. Gouda cheese, shredded
½	cup chopped tomato

1. Cut zucchini in half lengthwise. Scoop out flesh, leaving a ⅜-in. shell. Chop flesh and set aside. In a Dutch oven, bring water and salt to a boil. Add zucchini shells; cook until crisp-tender, 5-8 minutes. Drain and set aside.
2. In a large skillet, saute the onion and zucchini flesh in oil until crisp-tender. Stir in the beans, corn, tomato sauce, chili sauce, cilantro and cumin. Cook over medium heat until heated through, about 5 minutes. Sprinkle with cheese; cover and cook until cheese is melted, about 1 minute. Spoon into zucchini shells; sprinkle with tomato.

2 ZUCCHINI HALVES 377 cal., 11g fat (4g sat. fat), 24mg chol., 1310mg sod., 55g carb. (22g sugars, 9g fiber), 17g pro.

FARMERS MARKET STREET TACOS

No matter what I bring home from the local farmers market, I always end up stuffing it into a taco for a fresh veggie-filled treat. You really can't go wrong.
—*Ralph Jones, San Diego, CA*

TAKES: 30 min. • **MAKES:** 4 servings

- 2 bunches bok choy, halved
- 1 medium zucchini, cut into 3-in. sticks
- ½ lb. fresh asparagus spears
- 2 medium ripe avocados, peeled and quartered
- 1 bunch green onions
- 2 jalapeno peppers, halved and seeded
- 2 Tbsp. olive oil
- ½ tsp. kosher salt
- ½ tsp. pepper
- 8 mini corn tortillas
    Fresh cilantro leaves
    Optional: Pickled red onions, lime wedges, sliced radishes and salsa verde

1. Prepare grill for medium-high heat. Brush bok choy, zucchini, asparagus, avocados, green onions and jalapenos with the olive oil; sprinkle with salt and pepper. Transfer to a greased grill rack.
2. Grill, covered, or broil 4 in. from heat until vegetables are crisp-tender and slightly charred, 4-5 minutes, turning occasionally. Grill tortillas until warmed and slightly charred, 30-45 seconds per side. Cut vegetables to desired sizes; serve in tortillas with cilantro and toppings of your choice.
NOTE Wear disposable gloves when cutting hot peppers; the oils can burn skin. Avoid touching your face.
2 TACOS 319 cal., 19g fat (3g sat. fat), 0 chol., 536mg sod., 33g carb. (9g sugars, 13g fiber), 11g pro.

GOES GREAT WITH ...
Pop open a can of refried beans to serve with these tasty tacos.

FARMERS MARKET STREET TACOS

SWEET POTATO CHILI BAKE

I am vegetarian and wanted to develop some dishes that are a little heartier than traditional vegetarian fare. Here's one that I think is delicious!
—Jillian Tournoux, Massillon, OH

PREP: 30 min. • **BAKE:** 20 min.
MAKES: 7 servings

- 2 cups cubed peeled sweet potato
- 1 medium sweet red pepper, chopped
- 1 Tbsp. olive oil
- 1 garlic clove, minced
- 1 can (28 oz.) diced tomatoes, undrained
- 2 cups vegetable broth
- 1 can (15 oz.) black beans, rinsed and drained
- 4½ tsp. brown sugar
- 3 tsp. chili powder
- 1 tsp. salt
- ½ tsp. pepper
- 1 pkg. (6½ oz.) cornbread/muffin mix
- ½ cup shredded cheddar cheese
  Optional toppings: Sour cream, shredded cheddar cheese and chopped seeded jalapeno pepper

1. In a Dutch oven, saute sweet potato and red pepper in oil until pepper is crisp-tender. Add garlic; cook 1 minute longer. Add tomatoes, broth, beans, brown sugar, chili powder, salt and pepper. Bring to a boil. Reduce heat; simmer, uncovered, 15-20 minutes or until potatoes are tender.
2. Meanwhile, preheat the oven to 400°. Prepare cornbread batter according to package directions; stir in cheese. Drop by tablespoonfuls over chili.
3. Cover and bake 18-20 minutes or until a toothpick inserted in the center comes out clean. Serve with toppings of your choice.
NOTE Wear disposable gloves when cutting hot peppers; the oils can burn skin. Avoid touching your face.
1 CUP 324 cal., 11g fat (5g sat. fat), 54mg chol., 1204mg sod., 47g carb. (16g sugars, 6g fiber), 10g pro.

MUFFIN-TIN LASAGNAS

This is a super fun way to serve lasagna and a nice way to surprise everyone at the table. Easy and quick, these cups can be made with whatever ingredients your family likes best.
—Sally Kilkenny, Granger, IA

TAKES: 30 min. • **MAKES:** 1 dozen

- 1 large egg, lightly beaten
- 1 carton (15 oz.) part-skim ricotta cheese
- 2 cups shredded Italian cheese blend, divided
- 1 Tbsp. olive oil
- 24 wonton wrappers
- 1 jar (24 oz.) garden-style pasta sauce
  Minced fresh parsley, optional

1. Preheat oven to 375°. In a bowl, mix egg, ricotta cheese and 1¼ cups Italian cheese blend.
2. Generously grease 12 muffin cups with oil; line each with a wonton wrapper. Fill each with 1 Tbsp. ricotta mixture and 1½ Tbsp. pasta sauce. Top each with a second wrapper, rotating corners and pressing down centers. Repeat ricotta and sauce layers. Sprinkle with the remaining cheese blend.
3. Bake until cheese is melted, 20-25 minutes. If desired, sprinkle with parsley.
2 MINI LASAGNAS 414 cal., 19g fat (9g sat. fat), 83mg chol., 970mg sod., 36g carb. (8g sugars, 2g fiber), 22g pro.

VEGETARIAN
SKILLET
ENCHILADAS

PORTOBELLO & CHICKPEA SHEET-PAN SUPPER

This is a fantastic meatless dinner or an amazing side dish. It works well with a variety of sheet-pan-roasted veggies. We enjoy using zucchini or summer squash, and you can also change up the herbs in the dressing.
—*Elisabeth Larsen, Pleasant Grove, UT*

PREP: 15 min. • **BAKE:** 35 min.
MAKES: 4 servings

- ¼ cup olive oil
- 2 Tbsp. balsamic vinegar
- 1 Tbsp. minced fresh oregano
- ¾ tsp. garlic powder
- ½ tsp. salt
- ¼ tsp. pepper
- 1 can (15 oz.) chickpeas or garbanzo beans, rinsed and drained
- 4 large portobello mushrooms (4 to 4½ in.), stems removed
- 1 lb. fresh asparagus, trimmed and cut into 2-in. pieces
- 8 oz. cherry tomatoes

1. Preheat oven to 400°. In a small bowl, combine the first 6 ingredients. Toss chickpeas with 2 Tbsp. oil mixture. Transfer to a 15x10x1-in. baking pan. Bake 20 minutes.
2. Brush the mushrooms with 1 Tbsp. oil mixture; add to pan. Toss the asparagus and tomatoes with remaining oil mixture; arrange around mushrooms. Bake until the vegetables are tender, 15-20 minutes longer.
1 MUSHROOM WITH 1 CUP VEGETABLES
279 cal., 16g fat (2g sat. fat), 0 chol., 448mg sod., 28g carb. (8g sugars, 7g fiber), 8g pro. **DIABETIC EXCHANGES** 3 fat, 2 starch.

VEGETARIAN SKILLET ENCHILADAS

Whether served for meatless Monday or your family's everyday vegetarian meal, these unconventional enchiladas will leave everyone asking for more.
—*Susan Court, Pewaukee, WI*

TAKES: 25 min. • **MAKES:** 4 servings

- 1 Tbsp. canola oil
- 1 medium onion, chopped
- 1 medium sweet red pepper, chopped
- 2 garlic cloves, minced
- 1 can (15 oz.) black beans, rinsed and drained
- 1 can (10 oz.) enchilada sauce
- 1 cup frozen corn
- 2 tsp. chili powder
- ½ tsp. ground cumin
- ⅛ tsp. pepper
- 8 corn tortillas (6 in.), cut into ½-in. strips

- 1 cup shredded Mexican cheese blend Optional: Chopped fresh cilantro, sliced avocado, sliced radishes, sour cream and lime wedges

1. Preheat the oven to 400°. Heat oil in a 10-in. cast-iron or other ovenproof skillet over medium-high heat. Add the onion and pepper; cook and stir until tender, 2-3 minutes. Add garlic; cook 1 minute longer. Stir in beans, enchilada sauce, corn, chili powder, cumin and pepper. Stir in tortilla strips.
2. Bring to a boil. Reduce heat; simmer, uncovered, until the tortilla strips are softened, 3-5 minutes. Sprinkle with cheese. Bake, uncovered, until sauce is bubbly and the cheese is melted, 3-5 minutes. Garnish with optional ingredients as desired.
1½ CUPS 307 cal., 14g fat (5g sat. fat), 25mg chol., 839mg sod., 33g carb. (5g sugars, 7g fiber), 14g pro.

GOES GREAT WITH ... Grilled Naan (p. 297) is a quick and easy addition to this sheet-pan main course.

Taste of Home

PORTOBELLO & CHICKPEA SHEET-PAN SUPPER

KIMCHI FRIED RICE

Forget ordinary fried rice! Kimchi fried rice is just as easy, but it packs a flavorful punch. It is a fantastic use for leftovers, and you can also freeze it for up to three months. When cooking your defrosted rice, add a little extra soy sauce so it doesn't dry out.
—Taste of Home *Test Kitchen*

TAKES: 20 min. • **MAKES:** 4 servings

- 2 Tbsp. canola oil, divided
- 1 small onion, chopped
- 1 cup kimchi, coarsely chopped
- ½ cup matchstick carrots
- ¼ cup kimchi juice
- 1 garlic cloves, minced
- 1 tsp. minced fresh gingerroot
- 3 cups leftover short grain rice
- 2 green onions, thinly sliced
- 3 tsp. soy sauce
- 1 tsp. sesame oil
- 4 large eggs
   Optional toppings: Sliced nori, black sesame seeds and green onions

1. In large skillet, heat 1 Tbsp. oil over medium-high heat. Add onion; cook and stir until tender, 2-4 minutes. Add kimchi, carrots, kimchi juice, garlic and ginger; cook 2 minutes longer. Add rice, green onion, soy sauce and sesame oil; heat through, stirring frequently.
2. In another large skillet, heat the remaining 1 Tbsp. oil over medium-high heat. Break eggs, 1 at a time, into pan; reduce heat to low. Cook to desired doneness, turning after whites are set if desired. Serve over rice. If desired, sprinkle with nori, sesame seeds and additional green onion.

1 CUP FRIED RICE WITH 1 EGG 331 cal., 14g fat (2g sat. fat), 186mg chol., 546mg sod., 41g carb. (4g sugars, 2g fiber), 11g pro.

GOES GREAT WITH ...
Bake up some frozen spring rolls or egg rolls to enjoy with this Kimchi Fried Rice.

KIMCHI FRIED RICE

FRIED
LASAGNA

2. In an electric skillet or deep fryer, heat oil to 375°. In a shallow bowl, mix bread crumbs, ⅔ cup Italian cheese blend and remaining 1 tsp. Italian seasoning. Place remaining 4 eggs in a separate shallow bowl. Dip lasagna bundles into the eggs, then into crumb mixture, patting to help coating adhere.

3. Fry the bundles in batches until golden brown, 8-10 minutes, turning once. Drain on paper towels. Serve with marinara, Alfredo, the remaining Italian cheese blend and, if desired, additional Italian seasoning.

2 LASAGNA ROLLS 876 cal., 54g fat (19g sat. fat), 195mg chol., 1011mg sod., 61g carb. (11g sugars, 4g fiber), 37g pro.

SPINACH-TOPPED PITAS

Customizable pitas are a terrific way to please the whole family for dinner. Try using different vegetables and cheese blends to change things up. You can also use sliced zucchini instead of tomato.
—*Doris Allers, Portage, MI*

TAKES: 30 min. • **MAKES:** 4 servings

- 4 pita breads (6 in.)
- 1 cup reduced-fat ricotta cheese
- ½ tsp. garlic powder
- 1 pkg. (10 oz.) frozen chopped spinach, thawed and squeezed dry
- 3 medium tomatoes, sliced
- ¾ cup crumbled feta cheese
- ¾ tsp. dried basil

1. Place pita breads on a baking sheet. Combine the ricotta cheese and garlic powder; spread over pitas. Top with the spinach, tomatoes, feta cheese and basil.
2. Bake at 400° for 12-15 minutes or until bread is lightly browned.

1 PIZZA 320 cal., 7g fat (4g sat. fat), 26mg chol., 642mg sod., 46g carb. (7g sugars, 6g fiber), 17g pro. **DIABETIC EXCHANGES** 2 starch, 2 vegetable, 1 lean meat, 1 fat.

FRIED LASAGNA

One of my favorite dishes at Olive Garden is their fried lasagna. On a whim, I tried to re-create it at home. After a few tries, I think I got it pretty close to the original.
—*Jolene Martinelli, Fremont, NH*

PREP: 45 min. + freezing
COOK: 10 min./batch
MAKES: 10 servings

- 20 uncooked lasagna noodles
- 1 carton (32 oz.) whole-milk ricotta cheese
- 2½ cups shredded Italian cheese blend, divided
- 2 cups shredded part-skim mozzarella cheese
- 6 large eggs, beaten, divided use
- 4 tsp. Italian seasoning, divided
  Oil for deep-fat frying
- 2½ cups panko bread crumbs
- 1 jar (24 oz.) marinara sauce, warmed
- 1 jar (15 oz.) Alfredo sauce, warmed

1. Cook lasagna noodles according to package directions for al dente. In a large bowl, combine ricotta, 1¼ cups Italian cheese blend, mozzarella, 2 eggs and 3 tsp. Italian seasoning. Drain noodles. If desired, cut off the ribboned edges (discard or save for another use). Spread about ¼ cup filling on each noodle. Starting with a short side, fold each in thirds. Place all on a parchment-lined baking sheet, seam side down. Freeze just until firm, about 1 hour.

VEGAN BECHAMEL SAUCE

As one of the original mother sauces, bechamel is a vital part of a wide variety of recipes, including casseroles, white lasagnas and mac and cheese.
—Taste of Home *Test Kitchen*

TAKES: 20 min.
MAKES: 4 servings (2 cups)

- 3 Tbsp. vegan butter-style sticks
- 2 Tbsp. all-purpose flour
- 1½ cups unsweetened refrigerated soy milk
- 2 Tbsp. nutritional yeast
- ½ tsp. salt
- ¼ tsp. pepper
  Dash ground nutmeg
  Hot cooked pasta

In a small saucepan, melt vegan butter over medium heat. Stir in flour until smooth; gradually whisk in soy milk. Bring to a boil, stirring constantly. Remove from heat; stir in nutritional yeast, salt, pepper and nutmeg until smooth. Let rest 3 minutes or until thickened. Serve with pasta.

½ CUP 135 cal., 10g fat (4g sat. fat), 0 chol., 433mg sod., 7g carb. (2g sugars, 1g fiber), 4g pro.

PRESSURE-COOKER STUFFED PEPPERS

Here's a good-for-you dinner that's also a meal-in-one classic.
—Michelle Gurnsey, Lincoln, NE

PREP: 15 min. • **COOK:** 5 min. + releasing
MAKES: 4 servings

- 4 medium sweet red peppers
- 1 can (15 oz.) black beans, rinsed and drained
- 1 cup shredded pepper jack cheese
- ¾ cup salsa
- 1 small onion, chopped
- ½ cup frozen corn
- ⅓ cup uncooked converted long grain rice
- 1¼ tsp. chili powder
- ½ tsp. ground cumin
  Reduced-fat sour cream, optional

1. Place trivet insert and 1 cup water in a 6-qt. electric pressure cooker.
2. Cut and discard tops from peppers; remove seeds. In a large bowl, mix the beans, cheese, salsa, onion, corn, rice, chili powder and cumin; spoon into peppers. Set peppers on trivet.
3. Lock the lid; close pressure-release valve. Adjust to pressure-cook on high for 5 minutes. Let pressure release naturally. Serve with sour cream if desired.

1 STUFFED PEPPER 333 cal., 10g fat (5g sat. fat), 30mg chol., 582mg sod., 45g carb. (8g sugars, 8g fiber), 15g pro.
DIABETIC EXCHANGES 2 starch, 2 vegetable, 2 lean meat, 1 fat.

TEST KITCHEN TIP

Use yellow and green peppers in addition to the red to amp up the presentation of this delightful main course.

EGGPLANT
FLATBREADS

🕐 EGGPLANT FLATBREADS

I loved to make these back in the day.
Now I'm a chef and still enjoy them.
—*Christine Wendland, Browns Mills, NJ*

TAKES: 30 min. • **MAKES:** 4 servings

- 3 Tbsp. olive oil, divided
- 2½ cups cubed eggplant (½ in.)
- 1 small onion, halved and thinly sliced
- ½ tsp. salt
- ⅛ tsp. pepper
- 1 garlic clove, minced
- 2 naan flatbreads
- ½ cup part-skim ricotta cheese
- 1 tsp. dried oregano
- ½ cup roasted garlic tomato sauce
- ½ cup loosely packed basil leaves
- 1 cup shredded part-skim mozzarella cheese
- 2 Tbsp. grated Parmesan cheese
  Sliced fresh basil, optional

1. Preheat oven to 400°. In a large skillet, heat 1 Tbsp. oil over medium-high heat; saute eggplant and onion with salt and pepper until eggplant begins to soften, 4-5 minutes. Stir in garlic; remove from the heat.
2. Place the naans on a baking sheet. Spread with ricotta cheese; sprinkle with oregano. Spread with the tomato sauce. Top with eggplant mixture and whole basil leaves. Sprinkle with the mozzarella cheese and Parmesan cheese; drizzle with remaining oil.
3. Bake until the crust is golden brown and the cheese is melted, 12-15 minutes. Top with sliced basil if desired. Cut each naan in half.
½ PIZZA 340 cal., 21g fat (7g sat. fat), 32mg chol., 996mg sod., 25g carb. (5g sugars, 3g fiber), 14g pro.
NOTE A meatless pasta sauce or any flavored tomato sauce may be substituted for the roasted garlic tomato sauce.

SLOW-COOKER
BAKED ZITI

**GOES GREAT
WITH ...**
Keep a loaf of
frozen garlic
bread on hand
to serve with
entrees such
as this one.

SLOW-COOKER BAKED ZITI

I don't know one family that doesn't have some crazy, hectic evening. This recipe is an easy fix for a busy weeknight dinner.
—Christy Addison, Clarksville, OH

PREP: 10 min. • **COOK:** 2 hours
MAKES: 6 servings

- 1 container (15 oz.) whole-milk ricotta cheese
- 1 large egg, beaten
- 1 tsp. dried basil
- ½ tsp. crushed red pepper flakes, optional
- 1 jar (24 oz.) meatless pasta sauce
- 2 cups uncooked ziti
- ¼ cup water
- 2 cups shredded mozzarella cheese
- ¼ cup minced fresh basil
  Grated Parmesan cheese, optional

1. In a small bowl, stir together ricotta cheese, egg, basil and, if desired, red pepper flakes. Pour pasta sauce into a 5-qt. slow cooker. Evenly top sauce with pasta; pour water over top. Drop heaping tablespoonfuls of ricotta cheese mixture over pasta. Sprinkle with mozzarella cheese.
2. Cook, covered, on high until heated through and pasta is tender, 2-2½ hours. Top with fresh basil and, if desired, Parmesan cheese and additional red pepper flakes. Serve immediately.
1½ CUPS 379 cal., 17g fat (10g sat. fat), 89mg chol., 886mg sod., 36g carb. (13g sugars, 3g fiber), 23g pro.

TEST KITCHEN TIP
This slow-cooked recipe was developed with enough liquid to rehydrate the dry, uncooked pasta during the 2½ hours it spends in the slow cooker. This way, no prep is necessary.

RAMEN VEGGIE STIR-FRY

RAMEN VEGGIE STIR-FRY

This ramen stir-fry is perfect for using up veggies that you have in your refrigerator. The total amount should be about 4 cups of vegetables that you can mix and match each time you make the recipe. For a heartier dish, add leftover chicken, pork or beef.
—Taste of Home *Test Kitchen*

PREP: 20 min. • **COOK:** 15 min.
MAKES: 4 servings

- 2 pkg. (3 oz. each) ramen noodles
- 2 tsp. cornstarch
- 3 Tbsp. soy sauce
- 2 Tbsp. rice vinegar
- 2 Tbsp. hoisin sauce
- 1 tsp. minced gingerroot
- 1 tsp. minced garlic
- ¼ tsp. salt
- ¼ tsp. pepper
- 2 Tbsp. sesame oil
- 1 cup fresh broccoli florets
- 1 cup fresh sugar snap peas
- 1 medium carrot, cut into matchsticks
- 1 medium sweet red pepper, julienned
  Optional: Sesame seeds and green onions

1. Discard ramen noodle seasoning packets or save for another use. Cook noodles according to package directions.
2. Meanwhile, in a small bowl, combine cornstarch, soy sauce, vinegar, hoisin sauce, ginger, garlic, salt and pepper until blended; set aside.
3. In a large skillet, heat oil over medium-high heat. Add the vegetables; cook and stir until crisp-tender, 5-7 minutes.
4. Stir the soy sauce mixture and add to pan. Bring to a boil; cook and stir until thickened, 1-2 minutes. Drain noodles; stir into vegetable mixture. If desired, garnish with the sesame seeds and green onions.
1¼ CUPS 332 cal., 14g fat (5g sat. fat), 0 chol., 1257mg sod., 41g carb. (8g sugars, 3g fiber), 8g pro.

SAMOSA POTPIE

The go-to appetizer at any Indian restaurant, samosas are reimagined as this delicious main-dish potpie. The heavily spiced potato and pea filling is surrounded by a flaky homemade crust. Serve with green or tamarind chutney.
—*Shri Repp, Seattle, WA*

PREP: 40 min. + chilling
BAKE: 40 min. + cooling
MAKES: 8 servings

- 2½ cups all-purpose flour
- 1 tsp. salt
- 1 tsp. dried ajwain seeds or dried thyme
- 1 cup cold unsalted butter
- 6 to 8 Tbsp. ice water

FILLING

- 4 cups cubed peeled potatoes
- ½ cup frozen peas, thawed
- 1 Tbsp. lemon juice
- 1 Tbsp. chat masala seasoning
- 1 tsp. ground cumin
- 1 tsp. ground coriander
- ½ tsp. chili powder
- ¼ tsp. ground turmeric
- ½ tsp. salt
- 1 to 2 red chili peppers, minced, optional
  Green or tamarind chutney, optional

1. In a large bowl, mix flour, salt and ajwain seeds; cut in butter until crumbly. Gradually add the ice water, tossing with a fork until dough holds together when pressed. Divide dough in half. Shape each into a disk; refrigerate, covered, 1 hour or overnight.

2. Preheat oven to 375°. For filling, place potatoes in a large saucepan; add water to cover. Bring to a boil. Reduce heat; cook, uncovered, until tender, 15-20 minutes. Drain; return to pan. Mash potatoes gently, leaving some chunks. Stir in peas, lemon juice, seasonings and, if desired, chili peppers.

3. On a lightly floured surface, roll half of dough to a ⅛-in.-thick circle; transfer to a 9-in. pie plate greased well with butter. Trim even with rim. Add filling. Roll remaining dough to a ⅛-in.-thick circle. Place over filling. Trim, seal and flute edge. Cut slits in top.

4. Bake until crust is golden brown, 40-45 minutes. Cool for 10 minutes before cutting. If desired, serve with chutney.

1 PIECE 430 cal., 24g fat (14g sat. fat), 61mg chol., 715mg sod., 48g carb. (1g sugars, 3g fiber), 6g pro.

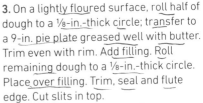

SAUCY VEGETABLE TOFU

This is my daughter Tonya's favorite dish. Sometimes we make it with rigatoni and call it "Riga-Tonya." Either way, it's a quick and wonderful way to prepare your kids some yummy vegetables.
—*Sandra Eckert, Pottstown, PA*

TAKES: 20 min. • **MAKES:** 6 servings

- 8 oz. uncooked whole wheat spiral pasta
- 1 large onion, coarsely chopped
- 1 large green or sweet red pepper, coarsely chopped
- 1 medium zucchini, halved lengthwise and sliced
- 1 Tbsp. olive oil
- 1 pkg. (16 oz.) firm tofu, drained and cut into ½-in. cubes
- 2 cups meatless spaghetti sauce

1. Cook pasta according to package directions. Meanwhile, in a large skillet, saute the onion, pepper and zucchini in oil until crisp-tender.

2. Stir in tofu and spaghetti sauce; heat through. Drain pasta; serve with tofu mixture.

1¼ CUPS TOFU MIXTURE WITH ⅔ CUP PASTA 274 cal., 7g fat (1g sat. fat), 0 chol., 380mg sod., 41g carb. (9g sugars, 7g fiber), 14g pro. **DIABETIC EXCHANGES** 2 starch, 2 lean meat, 1 vegetable, ½ fat.

SAMOSA POTPIE

BAKED FETA PASTA

BAKED FETA PASTA

There's a reason this recipe went viral on TikTok! It's simple to throw together and incredibly creamy and delicious.
—*Sarah Tramonte, Milwaukee, WI*

PREP: 15 min. • **BAKE:** 30 min.
MAKES: 8 servings

- 2 pints cherry tomatoes
- 3 garlic cloves, halved
- ½ cup olive oil
- 1 pkg. (8 oz.) block feta cheese
- 1 tsp. sea salt
- ¼ tsp. coarsely ground pepper
- 1 pkg. (16 oz.) rigatoni or other short pasta
  Fresh basil leaves, coarsely chopped

1. Preheat oven to 400°. In a 13x9-in. baking dish, combine tomatoes, garlic and ¼ cup olive oil. Place the block of feta in center, moving tomatoes so the cheese is sitting on the bottom of dish. Drizzle the feta with remaining oil and sprinkle with salt and pepper. Bake until tomato skins start to split and the garlic has softened, 30-40 minutes.
2. Meanwhile, cook pasta according to package directions for al dente. Drain, reserving 1 cup pasta water.
3. Stir the feta mixture, lightly pressing tomatoes, until combined. Add pasta and toss to combine. Stir in enough reserved pasta water to reach desired consistency. Sprinkle with basil.
1 SERVING 373 cal., 16g fat (6g sat. fat), 25mg chol., 507mg sod., 46g carb. (5g sugars, 3g fiber), 12g pro.

TEST KITCHEN TIP

Just like other cheeses, feta melts better if you start with a block first, instead of buying already crumbled cheese at the store. Crumbled feta may also burn and stick to the bottom of the baking dish.

MAYAN POTATO QUESADILLAS

I make potato-filled rolled tacos all the time, but I wanted to switch it up and made quesadillas out of my original recipe. I serve the crispy quesadillas with salsa and sour cream. For an extra surprise serve homemade guacamole.
—*Marina Castle Kelley, Canyon Country, CA*

PREP: 20 min. • **COOK:** 15 min.
MAKES: 4 servings

- 1 cup mashed potatoes (without added milk and butter)
- 1 cup tomatillo salsa, divided
- ¼ cup thinly sliced green onions
- 2 flour tortillas (10 in.)
- 1 cup shredded cheddar cheese
- 2 Tbsp. butter, softened
- ½ cup sour cream

1. In a large bowl, combine mashed potatoes, ½ cup tomatillo salsa and green onion. Top half of each tortilla with half the potato mixture; sprinkle each with ½ cup cheese. Fold tortilla to close. Lightly butter top and bottom of quesadillas.

2. In a large cast-iron skillet or griddle, in batches, cook the quesadillas over medium heat until golden brown and heated through, 2-3 minutes on each side. Cut each into 4 wedges. Serve with sour cream and remaining ½ cup tomatillo salsa. If desired, sprinkle with additional green onion.

2 WEDGES 394 cal., 24g fat (14g sat. fat), 64mg chol., 877mg sod., 32g carb. (5g sugars, 5g fiber), 11g pro.

TEST KITCHEN TIP

While these quesadillas already have lots of flavor, you can experiment with adding bacon bits, chopped pickled jalapenos or some garlic powder—or all of the above!

MAYAN POTATO QUESADILLAS

MEDITERRANEAN CHICKPEAS

Add this to your meatless Monday lineup. It's fantastic with feta cheese on top.
—*Elaine Ober, Brookline, MA*

TAKES: 25 min. • **MAKES:** 4 servings

- 1 cup water
- ¾ cup uncooked whole wheat couscous
- 1 Tbsp. olive oil
- 1 medium onion, chopped
- 2 garlic cloves, minced
- 1 can (15 oz.) chickpeas or garbanzo beans, rinsed and drained
- 1 can (14½ oz.) no-salt-added stewed tomatoes, cut up
- 1 can (14 oz.) water-packed artichoke hearts, rinsed, drained and chopped
- ½ cup pitted Greek olives, coarsely chopped
- 1 Tbsp. lemon juice
- ½ tsp. dried oregano
  Dash pepper
  Dash cayenne pepper

1. In a small saucepan, bring water to a boil. Stir in couscous. Remove from heat; let stand, covered, 5-10 minutes or until water is absorbed. Fluff with a fork.
2. Meanwhile, in a large nonstick skillet, heat oil over medium-high heat. Add onion; cook and stir until tender. Add garlic; cook 1 minute longer. Sir in the remaining ingredients; heat through, stirring occasionally. Serve with the couscous.

1 CUP CHICKPEA MIXTURE WITH ⅔ CUP COUSCOUS 340 cal., 10g fat (1g sat. fat), 0 chol., 677mg sod., 51g carb. (9g sugars, 9g fiber), 11g pro.

COPYCAT MAC & CHEESE

My kids and I love mac and cheese. We always get it in the bread bowls when we're at Panera, but with three cheeses, these white cheddar shells are filling on their own.
—*Steven Schend, Grand Rapids, MI*

TAKES: 25 min. • **MAKES:** 6 servings

- 3½ cups uncooked pipetti pasta or medium pasta shells
- ¼ cup butter, cubed
- ¼ cup all-purpose flour
- 2½ cups 2% milk
- ¼ tsp. pepper
- 2 cups shredded white cheddar cheese
- 4 slices white American cheese, chopped
- ¼ cup grated Parmesan cheese
  Bread bowls, optional

Cook the pasta according to package directions; drain and set aside. In a large saucepan, melt the butter over low heat; whisk in flour until smooth. Whisk in the milk and pepper. Bring to a boil; cook and stir for 2 minutes or until thickened. Stir in the cheeses until melted; stir in pasta. Serve in bread bowls if desired.

1 CUP 538 cal., 27g fat (16g sat. fat), 79mg chol., 565mg sod., 50g carb. (7g sugars, 2g fiber), 23g pro.

AIR-FRYER CHICKPEA
& RED ONION BURGERS

VEGETARIAN PAD THAI

Here's my version of pad thai loaded with crisp, colorful veggies and zesty flavor. Give fresh and simple a twirl.
—*Colleen Doucette, Truro, NS*

TAKES: 30 min. • **MAKES:** 4 servings

- 6   oz. uncooked thick rice noodles
- 2   Tbsp. brown sugar
- 3   Tbsp. reduced-sodium soy sauce
- 4   tsp. rice vinegar
- 2   tsp. lime juice
- 2   tsp. olive oil
- 3   medium carrots, shredded
- 1   medium sweet red pepper, cut into thin strips
- 4   green onions, chopped
- 3   garlic cloves, minced
- 4   large eggs, lightly beaten
- 2   cups bean sprouts
- ⅓   cup chopped fresh cilantro
     Chopped peanuts, optional
     Lime wedges

1. Prepare the noodles according to package directions. Drain; rinse well and drain again. In a small bowl, mix together the brown sugar, soy sauce, vinegar and lime juice.
2. In a large nonstick skillet, heat oil over medium-high heat; stir-fry carrots and pepper until crisp-tender, 3-4 minutes. Add green onion and garlic; cook and stir 2 minutes. Remove from pan.
3. Reduce heat to medium. Pour eggs into same pan; cook and stir until no liquid egg remains. Stir in carrot mixture, noodles and sauce mixture; heat through. Add bean sprouts; toss to combine. Top with cilantro, and peanuts if desired. Serve with lime wedges.
1¼ CUPS 339 cal., 8g fat (2g sat. fat), 186mg chol., 701mg sod., 55g carb. (15g sugars, 4g fiber), 12g pro.

AIR-FRYER CHICKPEA & RED ONION BURGERS

When chilly days arrive and we retire the grill to the garage, I make a batch of air-fryer chickpea burgers that even die-hard meat eaters can't resist.
—*Lily Julow, Lawrenceville, GA*

TAKES: 30 min. • **MAKES:** 6 servings

- 1   large red onion, thinly sliced
- ¼   cup fat-free red wine vinaigrette
- 2   cans (15 oz. each) chickpeas or garbanzo beans, rinsed and drained
- ⅓   cup chopped walnuts
- ¼   cup toasted wheat germ or dry bread crumbs
- ¼   cup packed fresh parsley sprigs
- 2   large eggs
- 1   tsp. curry powder
- ½   tsp. pepper
     Cooking spray
- ⅓   cup fat-free mayonnaise
- 2   tsp. Dijon mustard

- 6   sesame seed hamburger buns, split and toasted
- 6   lettuce leaves
- 3   Tbsp. thinly sliced fresh basil leaves

1. Preheat air fryer to 375°. In a small bowl, mix onion and vinaigrette; set aside. Place chickpeas, walnuts, wheat germ and parsley in a food processor; pulse until blended. Add the eggs, curry powder and pepper; process until smooth.
2. Shape into 6 patties. In batches, place patties in a single layer on a greased tray in air-fryer basket, spray with cooking spray. Cook until a thermometer reads 160°, 8-10 minutes, flipping halfway through.
3. In a small bowl, mix mayonnaise and mustard; spread over cut sides of buns. Serve patties on buns with lettuce, basil and onion mixture.
1 BURGER 381 cal., 13g fat (2g sat. fat), 62mg chol., 697mg sod., 54g carb. (10g sugars, 9g fiber), 16g pro.

VEGETARIAN
PAD THAI

**GOES GREAT
WITH ...**
Glazed Pear
Shortcakes
(p. 312) cap
off this meal
wonderfully.

CHAPTER 10

CASSEROLES & HOT BAKES

P. 216

P. 219

P. 212

P. 222

GOES GREAT WITH ...
Simple Waldorf Salad (p. 302) is a 10-minute fix that works well with this casserole.

BISCUIT NUGGET CHICKEN BAKE

BISCUIT NUGGET CHICKEN BAKE

Topped with seasoned biscuits, this yummy casserole is an easy way to please the family.
—Kayla Dempsey, O'Fallon, IL

TAKES: 30 min. • **MAKES:** 6 servings

- 3 cups cubed cooked chicken
- 1 can (10¾ oz.) condensed cream of chicken soup, undiluted
- 1 cup 2% milk
- 1 jar (4½ oz.) sliced mushrooms, drained
- ½ tsp. dill weed
- ½ tsp. paprika

TOPPING

- ¼ cup grated Parmesan cheese
- 1 Tbsp. dried minced onion
- 1 tsp. dried parsley flakes
- ½ tsp. paprika
- 2 tubes (6 oz. each) refrigerated buttermilk biscuits

1. In a large saucepan, combine the first 6 ingredients. Cook and stir over medium heat until heated through, 5-7 minutes; keep warm.
2. In a large bowl, combine Parmesan cheese, onion, parsley and paprika. Separate biscuits and cut into quarters; add to bowl and toss to coat. Place on an ungreased baking sheet. Bake at 400° for 5 minutes.
3. Transfer the chicken mixture to a greased 8-in. square baking dish; top with biscuits. Bake, uncovered, 10-13 minutes or until bubbly and biscuits are golden brown.

1 CUP 570 cal., 25g fat (12g sat. fat), 75mg chol., 3144mg sod., 57g carb. (6g sugars, 2g fiber), 30g pro.

REUBEN BREAD PUDDING

REUBEN BREAD PUDDING

Aunt Renee always brought this tasty casserole to family picnics in Chicago. It became so popular that she started bringing two or three. I have also made it using dark rye bread or marbled rye, and ham instead of corned beef—all the variations are delicious!
—Johnna Johnson, Scottsdale, AZ

PREP: 20 min. • **BAKE:** 35 min.
MAKES: 6 servings

- 4 cups cubed rye bread (about 6 slices)
- 2 Tbsp. butter, melted
- 2 cups cubed or shredded cooked corned beef (about ½ lb.)
- 1 can (14 oz.) sauerkraut, rinsed and well drained
- 1 cup shredded Swiss cheese, divided
- 3 large eggs
- 1 cup 2% milk
- ⅓ cup prepared Thousand Island salad dressing
- 1½ tsp. prepared mustard
- ¼ tsp. pepper

1. Preheat oven to 350°. In a large bowl, toss bread cubes with butter. Stir in corned beef, sauerkraut and ½ cup cheese; transfer to a greased 11x7-in. baking dish.
2. In same bowl, whisk eggs, milk, salad dressing, mustard and pepper; pour over the top. Bake, uncovered, 30 minutes. Sprinkle with the remaining cheese. Bake until the top is golden and a knife inserted in the center comes out clean, 5-7 minutes longer.

1 PIECE 390 cal., 25g fat (10g sat. fat), 165mg chol., 1295mg sod., 21g carb. (7g sugars, 3g fiber), 19g pro.

PUFF PASTRY CHICKEN POTPIE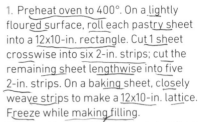

When my wife is craving comfort food, I whip up my chicken potpie. It is easy to make, sticks to your ribs and delivers soul-satisfying flavor.
—*Nick Iverson, Denver, CO*

PREP: 45 min. • **BAKE:** 45 min. + standing
MAKES: 8 servings

- 1 pkg. (17.3 oz.) frozen puff pastry, thawed
- 2 lbs. boneless skinless chicken breasts, cut into 1-in. pieces
- 1 tsp. salt, divided
- 1 tsp. pepper, divided
- 4 Tbsp. butter, divided
- 1 large onion, chopped
- 2 garlic cloves, minced
- 1 tsp. minced fresh thyme or ¼ tsp. dried thyme
- 1 tsp. minced fresh sage or ¼ tsp. rubbed sage
- ½ cup all-purpose flour
- 1½ cups chicken broth
- 1 cup plus 1 Tbsp. half-and-half cream, divided
- 2 cups frozen mixed vegetables (about 10 oz.)
- 1 Tbsp. lemon juice
- 1 large egg yolk

1. Preheat oven to 400°. On a lightly floured surface, roll each pastry sheet into a 12x10-in. rectangle. Cut 1 sheet crosswise into six 2-in. strips; cut the remaining sheet lengthwise into five 2-in. strips. On a baking sheet, closely weave strips to make a 12x10-in. lattice. Freeze while making filling.
2. Toss chicken with ½ tsp. each salt and pepper. In a large skillet, heat 1 Tbsp. butter over medium-high heat; saute chicken until browned, 5-7 minutes. Remove from pan.
3. In same skillet, heat remaining butter over medium-high heat; saute onion until tender, 5-7 minutes. Stir in garlic and herbs; cook 1 minute. Stir in flour until blended; cook and stir 1 minute. Gradually stir in broth and 1 cup cream. Bring to a boil, stirring constantly; cook and stir until thickened, about 2 minutes.
4. Stir in vegetables, lemon juice, chicken and the remaining salt and pepper; return to a boil. Transfer to a greased 2½-qt. oblong baking dish. Top with lattice, trimming to fit.
5. Whisk together the egg yolk and remaining cream; brush over pastry. Bake, uncovered, until filling is bubbly and pastry is golden brown, 45-55 minutes. Cover loosely with foil if the pastry starts getting too dark. Let stand 15 minutes before serving.

1 SERVING 523 cal., 25g fat (10g sat. fat), 118mg chol., 768mg sod., 42g carb. (4g sugars, 6g fiber), 30g pro.

PUFF PASTRY CHICKEN POTPIE

TEST KITCHEN TIP

Instead of raw chicken, use prepared rotisserie chicken and shred it. It's a quick and flavorful alternative to cooking the chicken yourself. Simply skip step 2 in this chicken potpie recipe if you choose to use rotisserie chicken.

**CHEESY FIESTA
BEEF CASSEROLE**

CHEESY FIESTA BEEF CASSEROLE

Over the years I've tweaked this recipe to end up with a delicious, quick weeknight meal. Spice it up with jalapenos if you prefer a little heat.
—*Joan Hallford, Fort Worth, TX*

PREP: 25 min. • **COOK:** 15 min.
MAKES: 8 servings

- 1 lb. ground beef
- 1 medium onion, chopped
- 1 can (15 oz.) black beans, rinsed and drained
- 1 cup picante sauce
- ½ tsp. chili powder
- 1 can (10½ oz.) reduced-fat reduced-sodium condensed cream of chicken soup, undiluted
- 1 can (10 oz.) diced tomatoes and green chiles, undrained
- 1 can (4 oz.) chopped green chiles
- 1 pkg. (9¾ oz.) nacho-flavored tortilla chips or plain tortilla chips, crushed
- 1 cup shredded sharp cheddar cheese
- 1 cup shredded Monterey Jack cheese
  Optional: Cubed avocado and sour cream

1. In a large skillet, cook beef and onion over medium heat until beef is no longer pink, 6-8 minutes, breaking up beef into crumbles; drain. Stir in beans, picante sauce and chili powder.
2. In a bowl, combine soup and tomatoes. In a lightly greased 2½-qt. baking dish, layer half the chips, beef mixture, soup mixture and cheeses. Repeat layers.
3. Microwave on medium high, uncovered, until heated through and cheese is melted, about 12 minutes. If desired, top with cubed avocado and sour cream.

1¼ CUPS 477 cal., 26g fat (9g sat. fat), 63mg chol., 1119mg sod., 37g carb. (4g sugars, 5g fiber), 23g pro.

EASY GROUND BEEF STROGANOFF

This ground beef Stroganoff is one of the dishes my family requests most often whenever I ask what they would like for dinner. It takes only minutes and tastes terrific, so I always honor their request.
—Julie Curfman, Chehalis, WA

TAKES: 25 min. • **MAKES:** 3 servings

- ½ lb. ground beef
- 1 cup sliced fresh mushrooms
- 1 medium onion, chopped
- 1 garlic clove, minced
- 1 can (10¾ oz.) condensed cream of mushroom or cream of chicken soup, undiluted
- ¼ tsp. pepper
- 1 cup sour cream
- 3 cups cooked egg noodles
  Chopped fresh parsley, optional

In a large skillet, cook beef, mushrooms, onion and garlic over medium heat until meat is crumbly and no longer pink; drain. Stir in soup and pepper. Cook until heated through, 2-3 minutes. Reduce heat. Stir in the sour cream; cook until heated through. Serve with noodles. If desired, top with chopped fresh parsley.

1 SERVING 554 cal., 28g fat (14g sat. fat), 141mg chol., 797mg sod., 44g carb. (7g sugars, 3g fiber), 26g pro.

TEST KITCHEN TIP
To make the ground beef stroganoff dairy free, mix in coconut milk or unsweetened almond milk, plus lemon juice and mustard to taste.

EASY GROUND BEEF STROGANOFF

MOUSSAKA

Moussaka is traditionally made with lamb, but I often use ground beef instead. The recipe looks a bit daunting, but if you prepare one step while working on another, it will save time.
—Kim Powell, Knoxville, TN

PREP: 45 min. • **BAKE:** 30 min. + standing
MAKES: 8 servings

- 3 medium potatoes, peeled and cut into ¼-in. slices
- 1 medium eggplant, cut into ½-in. slices
- 1½ lbs. ground lamb or ground beef
- 1 small onion, chopped
- 2 garlic cloves, minced
- 2 plum tomatoes, chopped
- 1¼ cups hot water
- 1 can (6 oz.) tomato paste
- 1¼ tsp. salt, divided
- ½ tsp. dried oregano
- ½ tsp. paprika
- ½ tsp. ground cinnamon
- ½ tsp. ground nutmeg, divided
- 3 Tbsp. butter
- ¼ cup all-purpose flour
- 4 cups 2% milk
- 2 cups shredded mozzarella cheese

1. Preheat the oven to 450°. Arrange the potato and eggplant in 2 greased 15x10x1-in. baking pans, overlapping as needed. Bake 20 minutes or until cooked through. Set aside; reduce oven setting to 400°.
2. In a large skillet, cook the lamb, onion and garlic over medium heat until meat is no longer pink, 7-9 minutes, breaking into crumbles; drain. Stir in the tomatoes, water, tomato paste, ¼ tsp. salt, oregano, paprika, cinnamon and ¼ tsp. nutmeg. Bring to a boil. Reduce heat; simmer, uncovered, 5 minutes.
3. In a large saucepan, melt butter over medium heat. Stir in flour until smooth; gradually whisk in milk. Bring to a boil, stirring constantly; cook and stir until thickened, 2-3 minutes. Stir in remaining 1 tsp. salt and ¼ tsp. nutmeg.

4. Arrange the parcooked potatoes in a greased 13x9-in. baking dish, overlapping as needed. Top with the lamb mixture. Arrange eggplant over top, overlapping as needed.
5. Top with bechamel sauce. Sprinkle with the mozzarella cheese. Bake, uncovered, until bubbly and golden brown, about 30 minutes. Let stand 20 minutes before serving.
1 SERVING 453 cal., 25g fat (13g sat. fat), 99mg chol., 700mg sod., 30g carb. (12g sugars, 4g fiber), 28g pro.

BAKED ORANGE ROUGHY & RICE

You have to love a delectable fish dinner with veggies and rice that only uses one dish. Your family will be lining up to dig in!
—Taste of Home *Test Kitchen*

PREP: 10 min. • **BAKE:** 30 min.
MAKES: 4 servings   375°

- 2 cups uncooked instant rice
- 1 pkg. (16 oz.) frozen broccoli-cauliflower blend, thawed
- 4 orange roughy fillets (6 oz. each)
- 1 can (14½ oz.) chicken broth
- 1 can (14½ oz.) fire-roasted diced tomatoes, undrained
- 1 tsp. garlic powder
- 1 tsp. lemon-pepper seasoning
- ¼ to ½ tsp. cayenne pepper
- ½ cup shredded cheddar cheese

1. Place rice in a greased 13x9-in. baking dish. Layer with the vegetables and fish. Pour the broth and tomatoes over the top; sprinkle with seasonings.
2. Cover and bake at 375° until fish flakes easily with a fork and rice is tender, 25-30 minutes. Sprinkle with the cheese; bake until cheese is melted, 5 minutes longer.
1 SERVING 442 cal., 7g fat (3g sat. fat), 119mg chol., 1047mg sod., 51g carb. (3g sugars, 3g fiber), 38g pro.

**CREAMY NOODLE
CASSEROLE**

CREAMY NOODLE CASSEROLE

My husband, Ronald, works long hours and frequently doesn't arrive home until past 7 p.m. This stovetop casserole is a smart choice for those late nights—it's just as tasty after it's been warmed in the microwave.
—*Barb Marshall, Pickerington, OH*

TAKES: 25 min. • **MAKES:** 8 servings

- 1 pkg. (12 oz.) egg noodles
- 1 pkg. (16 oz.) frozen broccoli cuts
- 3 cups cubed fully cooked ham
- 1 cup shredded part-skim mozzarella cheese
- 1 cup shredded Parmesan cheese
- ⅓ cup butter, cubed
- ½ cup half-and-half cream
- ¼ tsp. each garlic powder, salt and pepper

1. In a Dutch oven, cook the noodles in boiling water for 5 minutes. Add broccoli and ham; cook until noodles are tender, 5-10 minutes longer.
2. Drain; return to pan. Stir in the remaining ingredients. Cook and stir over low heat until butter is melted and mixture is heated through.
FREEZE OPTION Freeze cooled noodle mixture in freezer containers. To use, partially thaw in refrigerator overnight. Microwave, covered, on high in a microwave-safe dish until heated through, gently stirring; add broth or milk if necessary.
1 SERVING 428 cal., 20g fat (11g sat. fat), 112mg chol., 1087mg sod., 35g carb. (3g sugars, 3g fiber), 25g pro.

THAI PEANUT CHICKEN CASSEROLE

I used traditional pizza sauce and toppings in this recipe for years. After becoming a fan of Thai peanut chicken pizza, I decided to use those flavors instead. Serve with some stir-fried vegetables or a salad with sesame dressing for an easy yet tasty meal.
—*Katherine Wollgast, Troy, MO*

PREP: 30 min. • **BAKE:** 40 min.
MAKES: 10 servings

- 2 tubes (12 oz. each) refrigerated buttermilk biscuits
- 3 cups shredded cooked chicken
- 1 cup sliced fresh mushrooms
- 1 bottle (11½ oz.) Thai peanut sauce, divided
- 2 cups shredded mozzarella cheese, divided
- ½ cup chopped sweet red pepper
- ½ cup shredded carrot
- 4 green onions, sliced
- ¼ cup honey-roasted peanuts, coarsely chopped

1. Preheat the oven to 350°. Cut each biscuit into 4 pieces. Place in a greased 13x9-in. baking pan.
2. In a large bowl, combine chicken, mushrooms and 1 cup peanut sauce; spread over biscuits. Top with 1 cup cheese, red pepper, carrot and green onion. Sprinkle with the remaining 1 cup cheese.
3. Bake until topping is set, cheese is melted and biscuits have cooked all the way through, about 40 minutes. Sprinkle with peanuts and serve with remaining peanut sauce.
1 SERVING 490 cal., 25g fat (8g sat. fat), 55mg chol., 1013mg sod., 43g carb. (13g sugars, 1g fiber), 26g pro.

**GOES GREAT
WITH ...**
Serve Orange
& Olives Salad
(p. 303) with this
main dish.

CRESCENT BEEF CASSEROLE ✓

This flavorful meal-in-one dish is all you need to serve a satisfying and quick weeknight dinner. It's on the table in just 30 minutes.
—Taste of Home *Test Kitchen*

TAKES: 30 min. • **MAKES:** 6 servings

- 1 lb. lean ground beef (90% lean)
- 2 tsp. olive oil
- 1 cup diced zucchini
- ¼ cup chopped onion
- ¼ cup chopped green pepper
- 1 cup tomato puree
- 1 tsp. dried oregano
- ¼ tsp. salt
- ⅛ tsp. pepper
- 1½ cups mashed potatoes
- 1 cup (4 oz.) crumbled feta cheese
- 1 tube (8 oz.) refrigerated crescent rolls
- 1 large egg, beaten, optional

1. Preheat oven to 375°. In a large skillet, cook the beef over medium heat until no longer pink, crumble beef; drain and set aside. In the same skillet, heat oil over medium-high heat. Add zucchini, onion and green pepper; cook and stir until crisp-tender, 4-5 minutes. Stir in the beef, tomato puree, oregano, salt and pepper; heat through.
2. Spread mashed potatoes in an 11x7-in. baking dish coated with cooking spray. Top with beef mixture; sprinkle with feta cheese.
3. Unroll crescent dough. Separate into 4 rectangles; arrange 3 rectangles over the casserole. If desired, brush with egg wash. Bake until top is browned, 12-15 minutes. Roll the remaining dough into 2 crescent rolls; bake for another use.

1 SERVING 443 cal., 22g fat (7g sat. fat), 67mg chol., 981mg sod., 31g carb. (6g sugars, 3g fiber), 26g pro.

CRESCENT
BEEF CASSEROLE

CHICKEN PARMESAN STUFFED SHELLS

CHICKEN PARMESAN STUFFED SHELLS

When chicken Parmesan meets stuffed shells, it is love at first bite. The texture of the chicken holds up in the deliciously creamy cheese mixture.
—Cyndy Gerken, Naples, FL

PREP: 45 min. • **BAKE:** 40 min.
MAKES: 12 servings

- 1 pkg. (12 oz.) uncooked jumbo pasta shells
- 2 Tbsp. olive oil

FILLING

- 1 lb. boneless skinless chicken breasts, cut into ½-in. cubes
- 1½ tsp. Italian seasoning
- 1 tsp. salt, divided
- ½ tsp. pepper, divided
- 1 Tbsp. olive oil
- 2 Tbsp. butter
- ⅓ cup seasoned bread crumbs
- 3 cups part-skim ricotta cheese
- 1 cup shredded part-skim mozzarella cheese

- ½ cup grated Parmesan cheese
- ½ cup 2% milk
- ¼ cup chopped fresh Italian parsley

ASSEMBLY

- 4 cups meatless pasta sauce
- ¼ cup grated Parmesan cheese
- 8 oz. fresh mozzarella cheese, thinly sliced and halved

1. Preheat oven to 375°. Cook shells according to package directions for al dente; drain. Toss with oil; spread in an even layer on a baking sheet.

2. For filling, toss chicken with Italian seasoning, ½ tsp. salt and ¼ tsp. pepper. In a large skillet, heat oil over medium-high heat; saute chicken just until lightly browned, about 2 minutes. Reduce heat to medium; stir in butter until melted. Stir in bread crumbs; cook until crumbs are slightly toasted, 2-3 minutes, stirring occasionally. Cool slightly.

3. In a large bowl, mix cheeses, milk, parsley and the remaining salt and pepper. Fold in chicken.

4. Spread 2 cups pasta sauce into a greased 13x9-in. baking dish. Fill each shell with 2½ Tbsp. cheese mixture; place over sauce. Top with remaining sauce and cheeses (dish will be full).

5. Cover with greased foil; bake 30 minutes. Uncover; bake until heated through, 10-15 minutes.

1 SERVING 431 cal., 19g fat (10g sat. fat), 71mg chol., 752mg sod., 36g carb. (8g sugars, 2g fiber), 28g pro.

CATCH-OF-THE-DAY CASSEROLE

This super salmon recipe comes from my dear mother-in-law. She's one of the best cooks I know and one of the best mothers—a real gem.
—Cathy Clugston, Cloverdale, IN

PREP: 15 min. • **BAKE:** 30 min.
MAKES: 4 servings

- 4 oz. uncooked small shell pasta
- 1 can (10¾ oz.) condensed cream of celery soup, undiluted
- ½ cup mayonnaise
- ¼ cup milk
- ¼ cup shredded cheddar cheese
- 1 pkg. (10 oz.) frozen peas, thawed
- 1 can (7½ oz.) salmon, drained, bones and skin removed
- 1 Tbsp. finely chopped onion

1. Cook the pasta according to package directions. Meanwhile, in a large bowl, combine the soup, mayonnaise, milk and cheese until blended. Stir in peas, salmon and onion.

2. Drain pasta; add to salmon mixture. Transfer to a greased 2-qt. baking dish. Bake, uncovered, at 350° for 30-35 minutes or until bubbly.

1 CUP 532 cal., 32g fat (7g sat. fat), 46mg chol., 1120mg sod., 38g carb. (6g sugars, 5g fiber), 21g pro.

BEEFY FRENCH ONION POTPIE ✓

I came up with this dish knowing my husband loves French onion soup. It makes a perfect base for the hearty, beefy potpie.
—Sara Hutchens, Du Quoin, IL

TAKES: 30 min. • **MAKES:** 4 servings

- 1 lb. ground beef
- 1 small onion, chopped
- 1 can (10½ oz.) condensed French onion soup, undiluted
- 1½ cups shredded part-skim mozzarella cheese
- 1 tube (12 oz.) refrigerated buttermilk biscuits

1. Preheat oven to 350°. In a large skillet, cook the beef and onion over medium heat 6-8 minutes or until beef is no longer pink, breaking the meat into crumbles; drain. Stir in soup; bring to a boil.
2. Transfer mixture to an ungreased 9-in. deep-dish pie plate; sprinkle with mozarella cheese. Bake 5 minutes or until cheese is melted. Top with biscuits. Bake 15-20 minutes longer or until the biscuits are golden brown.
1 SERVING 553 cal., 23g fat (10g sat. fat), 98mg chol., 1550mg sod., 47g carb. (4g sugars, 1g fiber), 38g pro.

FRITO PIE ✓

Frito pie is legendary in the Southwest for being spicy, savory and cheesy fabulous. Here is my easy take on this crunchy classic.
—Jan Moon, Alamogordo, NM

TAKES: 30 min. • **MAKES:** 6 servings

- 1 lb. ground beef
- 1 medium onion, chopped
- 2 cans (15 oz. each) Ranch Style beans (pinto beans in seasoned tomato sauce)
- 1 pkg. (9¼ oz.) Frito corn chips
- 2 cans (10 oz. each) enchilada sauce
- 2 cups shredded cheddar cheese
  Thinly sliced green onions, optional

1. Preheat oven to 350°. In a large skillet, cook beef and onion over medium heat 6-8 minutes or until beef is no longer pink and onion is tender, crumbling meat; drain. Stir in beans; heat through.
2. Reserve 1 cup corn chips for topping. Place remaining corn chips in a greased 13x9-in. baking dish. Layer with meat mixture, enchilada sauce and cheese; top with reserved chips.
3. Bake, uncovered, 15-20 minutes or until cheese is melted. If desired, sprinkle with green onion.
1 SERVING 731 cal., 41g fat (14g sat. fat), 84mg chol., 1733mg sod., 54g carb. (6g sugars, 8g fiber), 34g pro.

TEST KITCHEN TIP

Frito pie is a flexible casserole that you can customize with stir-ins such as minced green chiles, sliced black olives, diced tomatoes, chopped onion and frozen corn kernels. You can't go wrong with delicious toppings such as guacamole and roasted tomato salsa.

SAUSAGE & APPLE QUINOA CASSEROLE

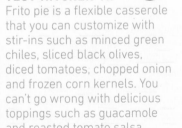

SAUSAGE & APPLE QUINOA CASSEROLE

My family loves the variety this casserole offers. It's unlike anything else I've made.
—*Brenna Norby, Grand Forks, ND*

PREP: 20 min. • **COOK:** 10 min.
MAKES: 6 servings

- 1   Tbsp. olive oil
- 1   pkg. (14 oz.) smoked kielbasa or Polish sausage, cut into ½-in. slices
- 1   small onion, chopped
- 1   cup chicken broth
- 1   cup apple cider or juice
- ¼   tsp. salt
- 1   pkg. (16 oz.) frozen cut kale or frozen chopped spinach
- 1   cup quinoa, rinsed
- 1   medium apple, chopped
- ¼   cup chopped pecans
- ¼   cup dried cranberries
- 1   tsp. dried sage leaves

1. Select saute setting on a 6-qt. electric pressure cooker. Adjust for medium heat; add oil. When the oil is hot, cook and stir sausage, adding the onion after 5 minutes, until sausage is browned and onion is crisp-tender, about 10 minutes total. Remove and keep warm. Add broth, cider and salt to the pressure cooker. Cook for 1 minute, stirring to loosen browned bits from pan. Press cancel.
2. Stir in kale, quinoa and the sausage mixture. Lock lid; close pressure-release valve. Adjust to pressure-cook on high for 7 minutes. Quick-release pressure. Stir in the remaining ingredients; cover and let stand 5 minutes.

1¼ CUPS 443 cal., 29g fat (7g sat. fat), 44mg chol., 701mg sod., 40g carb. (15g sugars, 5g fiber), 15g pro.

GOES GREAT WITH ...

Pop open a tube of biscuits or crescent rolls to enjoy alongside this hearty dish.

SLOPPY JOE TATER TOT CASSEROLE

SLOPPY JOE TATER TOT CASSEROLE

This simple casserole is an easy dinner for both you and the kids. Serve with carrot and celery sticks for a fuss-free feast. You can also stir in some spicy brown mustard if the adults want a bit more zing.
—Laura Wilhelm, West Hollywood, CA

PREP: 20 min. • **COOK:** 4 hours + standing
MAKES: 10 servings

1 bag (32 oz.) frozen Tater Tots, divided
2 lbs. ground beef or turkey
1 can (15 oz.) tomato sauce
1 bottle (8 oz.) sweet chili sauce
2 Tbsp. packed brown sugar
1 Tbsp. Worcestershire sauce
1 Tbsp. dried minced garlic
1 Tbsp. dried minced onion
½ tsp. salt
½ tsp. pepper
1¼ cups shredded Colby-Monterey Jack cheese
¼ tsp. paprika

1. Place half the Tater Tots in bottom of a 5-qt. slow cooker.
2. In a large skillet, cook the beef over medium-high heat until no longer pink, 5-6 minutes, breaking into crumbles; drain. Stir in the next 8 ingredients; reduce heat and simmer 2-3 minutes. Place beef mixture in the slow cooker; top with the remaining Tater Tots. Cook, covered, on low 4 hours.
3. Top with the cheese. Sprinkle with the paprika. Let stand, uncovered, 15 minutes before serving.
1 CUP 466 cal., 24g fat (9g sat. fat), 69mg chol., 1332mg sod., 41g carb. (18g sugars, 4g fiber), 22g pro.

TACO CORNBREAD CASSEROLE

TACO CORNBREAD CASSEROLE

A whole can of chiles adds fire to this casserole. For less heat, you can use just enough of the can for your taste.
—Lisa A. Paul, Terre Haute, IN

PREP: 25 min. • **BAKE:** 1 hour
MAKES: 8 servings

2 lbs. ground beef
2 envelopes taco seasoning
2 cans (14½ oz. each) diced tomatoes, drained
1 cup water
1 cup cooked rice
1 can (4 oz.) chopped green chiles
2 pkg. (8½ oz. each) cornbread/muffin mix
1 can (8¾ oz.) whole kernel corn, drained
1 cup sour cream
2 cups corn chips
2 cups shredded Mexican cheese blend or cheddar cheese, divided
1 can (2¼ oz.) sliced ripe olives, drained
Optional: Shredded lettuce, chopped tomatoes and chopped red onion

1. Preheat oven to 400°. In a Dutch oven, cook the beef over medium heat until no longer pink, 8-10 minutes, breaking it into crumbles; drain. Stir in taco seasoning. Add tomatoes, water, rice and green chiles; heat through, stirring occasionally.
2. Meanwhile, prepare cornbread mix according to package directions; stir in corn. Pour half the batter into a greased 13x9-in. baking dish. Layer with half the meat mixture, all the sour cream, half the corn chips and 1 cup cheese. Top with the remaining batter and meat mixture, and the olives.
3. Bake, uncovered, until cornbread is cooked through, 55-60 minutes. Sprinkle with remaining 1 cup corn chips and 1 cup cheese; bake until cheese is melted, 3-5 minutes longer. If desired, serve with lettuce, tomatoes and red onion.
1½ CUPS 817 cal., 40g fat (17g sat. fat), 183mg chol., 1982mg sod., 74g carb. (20g sugars, 4g fiber), 36g pro.

BEEF STEW SKILLET PIE

Puff pastry makes a pretty topping for this homey skillet potpie.
—*Josh Rink, Milwaukee, WI*

PREP: 1½ hours
BAKE: 30 min. + standing
MAKES: 6 servings

- 6 Tbsp. all-purpose flour, divided
- 1½ tsp. salt
- ½ tsp. pepper
- 1 lb. boneless beef round steak, cut into 1-in. pieces
- 2 Tbsp. canola oil
- 1 large onion, chopped
- 2 garlic cloves, minced
- ¼ cup dry red wine
- 2 cups beef broth, divided
- 1 Tbsp. tomato paste
- ½ tsp. Italian seasoning
- ½ tsp. dried basil
- 1 bay leaf
- 2 medium potatoes, cubed
- 3 large carrots, peeled and sliced
- 1 sheet frozen puff pastry, thawed
- ½ cup frozen peas *green beans*
- 2 Tbsp. minced fresh parsley
- 1 large egg, beaten

1. In a large resealable container, combine 3 Tbsp. flour, salt and pepper. Add beef in batches; shake to coat. Invert a 10-in. cast-iron or other ovenproof skillet onto parchment; trace circle around pan ¼ in. larger than rim. Cut out circle and set aside. In same skillet, saute the beef in oil until browned. Add onion and garlic; cook and stir until the onion is tender. Add the wine, stirring to loosen browned bits.
2. Combine 1½ cups broth, tomato paste, Italian seasoning and basil; stir into skillet. Add bay leaf. Bring to a boil. Reduce heat; cover and simmer until meat is tender, about 45 minutes. Add the potatoes and carrots; cook until the vegetables are tender, 20-25 minutes longer.
3. Meanwhile, roll out puff pastry to fit skillet, using parchment circle as a guide; cut venting slits in pastry. Keep chilled until ready to use.
4. Combine the remaining flour and broth until smooth; gradually stir into skillet. Bring to a boil; cook and stir until thickened and bubbly, about 2 minutes. Discard bay leaf. Stir in peas and parsley.
5. Brush beaten egg around edge of the skillet to help pastry adhere; carefully place pastry over filling. Using a fork, press pastry firmly onto rim of pan; brush with egg. Bake pie at 425° until pastry is dark golden brown, 30-35 minutes. Let stand for 10 minutes before serving.

1 SERVING 473 cal., 19g fat (4g sat. fat), 73mg chol., 1088mg sod., 49g carb. (4g sugars, 6g fiber), 25g pro.

BEEF STEW SKILLET PIE

CHICKEN BACON RANCH CASSEROLE

CHICKEN BACON RANCH CASSEROLE

This casserole is a dinner that both of my wonderful (but picky!) children will eat. I can easily make it ahead and then bake it right before serving. Sometimes I add cooked veggies, such as peas or chopped broccoli, for a complete meal.
—*Rebekah Schultz, Mantua, NJ*

PREP: 30 min. • **COOK:** 15 min.
MAKES: 10 cups

- 1 pkg. (16 oz.) uncooked spiral pasta
- 1½ cups 2% milk
- ½ cup ranch salad dressing
- 1 envelope ranch salad dressing mix
- 1 pkg. (8 oz.) cream cheese, cubed
- 2 cups cubed cooked chicken
- 8 bacon strips, cooked and crumbled
- 2 cups shredded Colby cheese, divided
  Sliced green onions, optional

1. Preheat oven to 400°. Cook pasta according to the package directions. Drain and transfer to a large bowl.
2. In the same pan, combine milk, ranch salad dressing and salad dressing mix until smooth. Stir in cream cheese. Cook and stir over medium heat until cream cheese is melted; pour over pasta. Stir in chicken, bacon and 1 cup Colby cheese. Transfer to a greased 13x9-in. baking dish. Top with remaining 1 cup Colby cheese. Bake, uncovered, until heated through and cheese is melted, 15-20 minutes. If desired, sprinkle with green onion.
1 CUP 495 cal., 26g fat (12g sat. fat), 80mg chol., 710mg sod., 40g carb. (4g sugars, 1g fiber), 24g pro.

TEST KITCHEN TIP
Add more flavor by sprinkling parsley or minced garlic into your casserole.

SALSA VERDE CHICKEN CASSEROLE

This is a rich, surprisingly tasty rendition of a number of Tex-Mex dishes melded into a single packed, beautiful casserole. Best of all, it's ready in hardly any time!
—*Janet McCormick, Proctorville, OH*

400°

TAKES: 30 min. • **MAKES:** 6 servings

- 2 cups shredded rotisserie chicken
- 1 cup sour cream
- 1½ cups salsa verde, divided
- 8 corn tortillas (6 in.)
- 2 cups chopped tomatoes
- ¼ cup minced fresh cilantro
- 2 cups shredded Monterey Jack cheese
  Optional toppings: Additional salsa verde, avocado slices, thinly sliced green onions and fresh cilantro leaves

1. In a small bowl, combine chicken, sour cream and ¾ cup salsa. Spread ¼ cup salsa on the bottom of a greased 8-in. square baking dish.
2. Layer with half the tortillas and chicken mixture; sprinkle with half the tomatoes, all the minced cilantro and half the cheese. Repeat layers with the remaining tortillas, chicken mixture, tomatoes and cheese.
3. Bake, uncovered, at 400° until bubbly, 20-25 minutes. Serve with remaining salsa and toppings of your choice.

1 SERVING 400 cal., 23g fat (13g sat. fat), 102mg chol., 637mg sod., 22g carb. (5g sugars, 3g fiber), 26g pro.

TEST KITCHEN TIP

If substituting canned tomatoes for the fresh, drain them well first so you don't end up with a soupy dish.

SALSA VERDE
CHICKEN
CASSEROLE

MEATBALL SUBMARINE CASSEROLE

We were hosting a bunch of friends, and after a comedy of errors, I had to come up with a plan B for dinner. Much-loved meatball subs are even better as a hearty casserole—so delicious!
—*Rick Friedman, Palm Springs, CA*

TAKES: 30 min. • **MAKES:** 4 servings

- 1 pkg. (12 oz.) frozen fully cooked Italian meatballs
- 4 slices sourdough bread
- 1½ tsp. olive oil
- 1 garlic clove, halved
- 1½ cups pasta sauce with mushrooms
- ½ cup shredded part-skim mozzarella cheese, divided
- ½ cup grated Parmesan cheese, divided

1. Preheat broiler. Microwave meatballs, covered, on high until heated through, 4-6 minutes. Meanwhile, place bread on an ungreased baking sheet; brush 1 side of bread with oil. Broil 4-6 in. from heat until golden brown, 1-2 minutes. Rub the bread with cut surface of garlic; discard garlic. Tear bread into bite-sized pieces; transfer to a greased 11x7-in. baking dish. Reduce oven setting to 350°.
2. Add pasta sauce, ¼ cup mozzarella cheese and ¼ cup Parmesan cheese to meatballs; toss to combine. Pour the mixture over bread pieces; sprinkle with remaining cheeses. Bake, uncovered, until cheeses are melted, 15-18 minutes.
1 SERVING 417 cal., 28g fat (13g sat. fat), 59mg chol., 1243mg sod., 22g carb. (8g sugars, 3g fiber), 23g pro.

MILLION-DOLLAR CHICKEN CASSEROLE

Everyone at the table will love this family-friendly dish. This chicken casserole is so easy to mix together and quickly serve on the dinner table on busy weeknights. Stir in some shredded cheddar, mozzarella or Monterey Jack cheese for extra flavor.
—*Taste of Home Test Kitchen*

PREP: 30 min. • **BAKE:** 25 min.
MAKES: 8 servings

- 4 oz. cream cheese, softened
- ½ cup sour cream
- 1 can (10½ oz.) condensed cream of chicken soup, undiluted
- ½ tsp. onion powder
- ½ tsp. garlic powder
- 4 cups shredded cooked chicken
- 1 cup 2% cottage cheese
- 25 Ritz crackers, crushed
- 3 Tbsp. butter, melted
- 2 green onions, chopped

1. Preheat oven to 350°. In a large bowl, beat cream cheese and sour cream until smooth. Beat in soup, onion powder and garlic powder. Stir in chicken and cottage cheese. Transfer to a greased 9-in. square baking dish. Combine crackers and butter; sprinkle over casserole.
2. Bake, uncovered, until heated through, 25-30 minutes. Sprinkle with green onion.
1¼ CUPS 363 cal., 24g fat (11g sat. fat), 105mg chol., 593mg sod., 12g carb. (3g sugars, 1g fiber), 26g pro.

CHAPTER 11

SLOW-COOKED, AIR-FRIED & INSTANT POT® ENTREES

P. 245

P. 244

P. 234

P. 249

PRESSURE-COOKER
CHICKPEA & POTATO CURRY

PRESSURE-COOKER CHICKPEA & POTATO CURRY

Here's a classic Indian dish.
—Anjana Devasahayam, San Antonio, TX

PREP: 25 min. • **COOK:** 5 min. + releasing
MAKES: 6 servings

- 1 Tbsp. canola oil
- 1 medium onion, chopped
- 2 garlic cloves, minced
- 2 tsp. minced fresh gingerroot
- 2 tsp. ground coriander
- 1 tsp. garam masala
- 1 tsp. chili powder
- ½ tsp. salt
- ½ tsp. ground cumin
- ¼ tsp. ground turmeric
- 2½ cups vegetable stock
- 2 cans (15 oz. each) chickpeas or garbanzo beans, rinsed and drained
- 1 can (15 oz.) crushed tomatoes
- 1 large baking potato, peeled and cut into ¾-in. cubes
- 1 Tbsp. lime juice
  Chopped fresh cilantro
  Hot cooked rice
  Optional: Sliced red onion and lime wedges

1. Select saute setting on a 6-qt. electric pressure cooker. Adjust for medium heat; add oil. When oil is hot, cook and stir onion until crisp-tender, 2-4 minutes. Add garlic, ginger and dry seasonings; cook and stir 1 minute. Add stock to the pressure cooker. Cook for 30 seconds, stirring to loosen browned bits from pan. Press cancel. Add the next 3 ingredients. Lock lid; close pressure-release valve
2. Adjust to pressure-cook on high for 3 minutes. Let the pressure release naturally for 10 minutes; quick-release any remaining pressure.
3. Stir in lime juice; sprinkle with cilantro. Serve with rice and, if desired, red onion and lime wedges.
1¼ CUPS 240 cal., 6g fat (0 sat. fat), 0 chol., 767mg sod., 42g carb. (8g sugars, 9g fiber), 8g pro.

AIR-FRYER PORK SCHNITZEL

AIR-FRYER PORK SCHNITZEL

This pork recipe is one of my husband's favorites because it reminds him of his German roots. Cooking pork schnitzel in an air fryer is genius because we can eat in a jiffy.
—Joyce Folker, Paraowan, UT

PREP: 20 min. • **COOK:** 10 min.
MAKES: 4 servings

- ¼ cup all-purpose flour
- 1 tsp. seasoned salt
- ¼ tsp. pepper
- 1 large egg
- 2 Tbsp. 2% milk
- ¾ cup dry bread crumbs
- 1 tsp. paprika
- 4 pork sirloin cutlets (4 oz. each)
  Cooking spray

DILL SAUCE
- 1 Tbsp. all-purpose flour
- ¾ cup chicken broth
- ½ cup sour cream
- ¼ tsp. dill weed

1. Preheat air fryer to 375°. In a shallow bowl, mix flour, seasoned salt and pepper. In a second shallow bowl, whisk egg and milk until blended. In a third bowl, mix bread crumbs and paprika.
2. Pound pork cutlets with a meat mallet to ¼-in. thickness. Dip cutlets into flour mixture to coat both sides; shake off excess. Dip into the egg mixture, then into the crumb mixture, patting to help the coating adhere.
3. Place the pork in a single layer on a greased tray in air-fryer basket; spritz with cooking spray. Cook until golden brown, 4-5 minutes. Turn; spritz with cooking spray. Cook until golden brown, 4-5 minutes longer. Remove to a serving plate; keep warm.
4. Meanwhile, in a small saucepan, whisk the flour and broth until smooth. Bring to a boil, stirring constantly; cook and stir 2 minutes or until thickened. Reduce heat to low. Stir in sour cream and dill; heat through (do not boil). Serve with pork.
1 SERVING 309 cal., 13g fat (5g sat. fat), 91mg chol., 572mg sod., 17g carb. (2g sugars, 1g fiber), 30g pro.

SLOW-COOKER AL PASTOR BOWLS

You'll love this really simple version of a traditional Mexican favorite. It is easy to serve as bowls over rice or in tortillas with your favorite toppings.
—Taste of Home *Test Kitchen*

PREP: 10 min. • **COOK:** 6 hours
MAKES: 8 cups

    2   cans (7 oz. each) whole green chiles
    1   can (20 oz.) pineapple chunks, drained
    1   medium onion, chopped
    ½   cup orange juice
    ¼   cup white vinegar
    3   garlic cloves, peeled
    2   Tbsp. chili powder
    2   tsp. salt
  1½   tsp. smoked paprika
    1   tsp. dried oregano
    1   tsp. ground cumin
    ½   tsp. ground coriander
    4   lbs. boneless pork loin roast
        Hot cooked rice
        Optional toppings: Black beans, chopped avocado, corn, sliced radishes, lime and Mexican crema

1. In a blender, puree first 12 ingredients. In a 5- or 6-qt. slow cooker, combine the pork and pineapple mixture. Cook, covered, on low until the pork is very tender, 6-8 hours. Stir to break up pork.
2. Serve the pork in bowls over rice. Add optional toppings as desired.
⅔ CUP 232 cal., 7g fat (3g sat. fat), 75mg chol., 512mg sod., 11g carb. (8g sugars, 1g fiber), 30g pro. **DIABETIC EXCHANGES** 4 lean meat, ½ starch.

**SLOW-COOKER
AL PASTOR BOWLS**

AIR-FRYER
QUICK TATER TOTS BAKE

I like to prepare this easy dish when I'm short on time. You can also make the bake a little fancier by assembling it in a few individual ramekins instead of one 2-quart baking dish.
—*Jean Ferguson, Elverta, CA*

PREP: 15 min. • **COOK:** 30 min.
MAKES: 4 servings

- ¾ to 1 lb. ground beef or turkey
- 1 small onion, chopped
   Salt and pepper to taste
- 1 pkg. (16 oz.) frozen Tater Tots
- 1 can (10¾ oz.) condensed cream of mushroom soup, undiluted
- ⅔ cup 2% milk or water
- 1 cup shredded cheddar cheese

1. Preheat air fryer to 350°. In a large skillet, cook the beef and onion over medium heat until meat is no longer pink; crumble beef; drain. Season with salt and pepper.
2. Transfer to a greased 2-qt. baking dish that will fit in the air-fryer basket. Top with Tater Tots. Combine the soup and milk; pour over potatoes. Sprinkle with cheese.
3. Fold an 18x12-in. piece of foil lengthwise into thirds, making a sling. Use sling to lower dish into air fryer. Cook, uncovered, until heated through, 30-40 minutes.
1½ CUPS 570 cal., 35g fat (12g sat. fat), 87mg chol., 1357mg sod., 37g carb. (5g sugars, 4g fiber), 26g pro.

> ## TEST KITCHEN TIP
> Spice things up a bit by stirring ground cumin, curry powder, hot pepper sauce, red pepper flakes or even taco seasoning into the ground beef mixture.

PRESSURE-COOKER
SWISS STEAK

Swiss steak has a been a standby for family cooks for decades, and this no-fuss way to cook it promises to keep the entree popular for years to come. Best of all, it's low in calories and fat.
—*Sarah Burks, Wathena, KS*

PREP: 10 min. • **COOK:** 20 min. + releasing
MAKES: 6 servings

- 1½ lbs. beef round steak, cut into 6 pieces
- ½ tsp. salt
- ¼ tsp. pepper
- 1 medium onion, cut into ¼-in. slices
- 1 celery rib, cut into ½-in. slices
- 2 cans (8 oz. each) tomato sauce

Sprinkle the steak with salt and pepper. Place onion in a 6-qt. electric pressure cooker. Top with celery, tomato sauce and steak. Lock lid; close the pressure-release valve. Adjust to pressure-cook on high 20 minutes. Let pressure release naturally 5 minutes; quick-release any remaining pressure. A thermometer inserted into the steak should read at least 145°.
1 SERVING 167 cal., 4g fat (1g sat. fat), 63mg chol., 581mg sod., 6g carb. (2g sugars, 2g fiber), 27g pro. **DIABETIC EXCHANGES** 3 lean meat, 1 vegetable.

SLOW-COOKER THAI PEANUT CHICKEN WITH NOODLES

I serve this Thai favorite with noodles mixed into the sauce, but it is also wonderful served over rice. Garnish with green onion or cilantro for a pop of color and fresh flavor.
—Catherine Cebula, Littleton, MA

PREP: 35 min. • **COOK:** 2½ hours
MAKES: 6 servings

- 1½ lbs. boneless skinless chicken breasts, cut into ¾ in. cubes
- 1 medium onion, chopped
- ¾ cup salsa
- ¼ cup creamy peanut butter
- 2 Tbsp. black bean sauce
- 1 Tbsp. reduced-sodium soy sauce
- 8 oz. uncooked linguine
- 1 Tbsp. canola oil
- ½ lb. sliced baby portobello mushrooms
- Thinly sliced green onions, optional

1. Place the chicken and onion in a 4-qt. slow cooker. Combine the salsa, peanut butter, black bean sauce and soy sauce; add to slow cooker. Cook, covered, on low 2½-3½ hours or until chicken is tender.
2. Meanwhile, prepare pasta according to package directions; drain. In a large skillet, heat oil over medium-high heat. Add mushrooms; cook and stir until tender, 6-8 minutes; set aside. During the last 10 minutes of cooking, stir the cooked pasta and mushrooms into slow cooker. If desired, sprinkle with green onion.

1⅓ CUPS 378 cal., 11g fat (2g sat. fat), 63mg chol., 436mg sod., 37g carb. (5g sugars, 2g fiber), 32g pro. **DIABETIC EXCHANGES** 4 lean meat, 2 starch, 2 fat, 1 vegetable.

AIR-FRYER ROASTED SALMON WITH SAUTEED BALSAMIC SPINACH

This is my favorite way to eat salmon. The dish is healthy, affordable, fast and delicious.
—Susan Hall, Sparks, MD

TAKES: 30 min. • **MAKES:** 4 servings

- 3 tsp. olive oil, divided
- 4 salmon fillets (6 oz. each)
- 1½ tsp. reduced-sodium seafood seasoning
- ¼ tsp. pepper
- 1 garlic clove, sliced
- Dash crushed red pepper flakes
- 10 cups fresh baby spinach (about 10 oz.)
- 6 small tomatoes, seeded and cut into ½-in. pieces
- ½ cup balsamic vinegar

1. Preheat air fryer to 450°. Rub 1 tsp. oil over both sides of the salmon; sprinkle with the seafood seasoning and pepper. In batches if necessary, place salmon on a greased tray in air-fryer basket. Cook until the fish just begins to flake easily with a fork, 10-12 minutes.
2. Meanwhile, place garlic, pepper flakes and the remaining oil in a 6-qt. stockpot; heat over medium-low heat until garlic is softened, 3-4 minutes. Increase heat to medium-high. Add spinach; cook and stir until wilted, 3-4 minutes. Stir in the tomatoes; heat through. Divide among 4 serving dishes.
3. In a small saucepan, bring vinegar to a boil. Cook until vinegar is reduced by half, 2-3 minutes. Immediately remove from heat.
4. To serve, place salmon over spinach mixture. Drizzle with balsamic glaze.

1 SERVING 348 cal., 19g fat (4g sat. fat), 85mg chol., 286mg sod., 12g carb. (9g sugars, 2g fiber), 31g pro.

SLOW-COOKER THAI PEANUT CHICKEN WITH NOODLES

AIR-FRYER GARLIC-BUTTER STEAK

This quick and easy entree is definitely restaurant quality and sure to become a staple at your house!
—*Lily Julow, Lawrenceville, GA*

TAKES: 20 min. • **MAKES:** 2 servings

- 1 beef flat iron steak or boneless top sirloin steak (¾ lb.)
- ⅛ tsp. salt
- ⅛ tsp. pepper
- 1 Tbsp. butter, softened
- 1 tsp. minced fresh parsley
- ½ tsp. minced garlic
- ¼ tsp. reduced-sodium soy sauce

1. Preheat the air fryer to 400°. Sprinkle steak with salt and pepper. Place steak on a tray in air-fryer basket. Cook until meat reaches desired doneness (for medium-rare, a thermometer should read 135°; medium, 140°; medium-well, 145°), 8-10 minutes, turning halfway through cooking.
2. Meanwhile, combine butter, parsley, garlic and soy sauce. Serve with steak.
4 OZ. COOKED BEEF WITH 2 TSP. GARLIC BUTTER 353 cal., 24g fat (11g sat. fat), 125mg chol., 322mg sod., 0 carb. (0 sugars, 0 fiber), 33g pro.

READER RAVES
"Very tasty! I cut the steak into strips so it cooked quicker."

—JENNIFER084, TASTEOFHOME.COM

AIR-FRYER GARLIC-BUTTER STEAK

AIR-FRYER COCONUT-CRUSTED TURKEY STRIPS

PRESSURE-COOKER TEX-MEX RISOTTO

I absolutely love food with lots of flavor and a Mexican twist, but I'm too lazy to stand over a pot of risotto. My pressure cooker gave me the opportunity to marry my love of Mexican foods and creamy risotto with no fuss.
—*Sharon Marx, Grand Blanc, MI*

PREP: 20 min. • **COOK:** 10 min.
MAKES: 6 servings

- 1   Tbsp. olive oil
- ½   large sweet orange pepper, chopped
- 1   jalapeno pepper, seeded and minced, optional
- 1½ cups uncooked arborio rice
- 2½ cups reduced-sodium chicken broth
- ½   lb. boneless skinless chicken breasts, cut into 1½-in. cubes
- 1   can (10 oz.) diced tomatoes and green chiles, undrained
- 1   can (15 oz.) black beans, rinsed and drained
- 1½ cups shredded Manchego cheese
- 1   cup frozen corn, thawed
- ½   cup chopped fresh cilantro

1. Select saute setting on a 6-qt. electric pressure cooker. Adjust for medium heat; add oil. When oil is hot, add orange pepper and, if desired, jalapeno; cook and stir until crisp-tender, 2-3 minutes. Add rice, cook and stir 1 minute longer. Press cancel. Add the broth, chicken and tomatoes.
2. Lock lid; close the pressure-release valve. Adjust to pressure-cook on high for 6 minutes. Allow pressure to release naturally for 5 minutes; quick-release any remaining pressure. Stir in beans, Manchego cheese, corn and cilantro; heat through. Garnish with additional cilantro if desired.

1⅓ CUPS 446 cal., 13g fat (7g sat. fat), 49mg chol., 742mg sod., 57g carb. (2g sugars, 5g fiber), 23g pro.

AIR-FRYER COCONUT-CRUSTED TURKEY STRIPS

My granddaughter shared these tasty change-of-pace turkey strips with me. With a plum dipping sauce, they're just the thing for a light supper.
—*Agnes Ward, Stratford, ON*

PREP: 20 min. • **COOK:** 10 min./batch
MAKES: 6 servings

- 2   large egg whites
- 2   tsp. sesame oil
- ½   cup sweetened shredded coconut, lightly toasted
- ½   cup dry bread crumbs
- 2   Tbsp. sesame seeds, toasted
- ½   tsp. salt
- 1½ lbs. turkey breast tenderloins, cut into ½-in. strips
     Cooking spray

DIPPING SAUCE
- ½   cup plum sauce
- ⅓   cup unsweetened pineapple juice
- 1½ tsp. prepared mustard
- 1   tsp. cornstarch

Optional: Grated lime zest and lime wedges

1. Preheat air fryer to 400°. In a shallow bowl, whisk the egg whites and oil. In another shallow bowl, mix the coconut, bread crumbs, sesame seeds and salt. Dip the turkey into the egg mixture, then into the coconut mixture, patting to help coating adhere.
2. Working in batches, place turkey in a single layer on a greased tray in air-fryer basket; spritz with cooking spray. Cook until golden brown, 3-4 minutes. Turn; spritz with cooking spray. Cook until golden brown and turkey is no longer pink, 3-4 minutes longer.
3. Meanwhile, in a small saucepan, mix sauce ingredients. Bring to a boil; cook and stir until thickened, 1-2 minutes. Serve turkey with sauce. If desired, top the turkey strips with grated lime zest and serve with lime wedges.
3 OZ. COOKED TURKEY WITH 2 TBSP. SAUCE 292 cal., 9g fat (3g sat. fat), 45mg chol., 517mg sod., 24g carb. (5g sugars, 1g fiber), 31g pro.

GOES GREAT WITH ... Prepare a can of chicken tortilla soup or corn chowder to enjoy with this risotto.

PRESSURE-COOKER TEX-MEX RISOTTO

SLOW-COOKER MILK-CAN SUPPER ✓

Here's a hearty slow-cooked version of a campfire classic. Cowboys and ranchers would cook this meal over a milk can on an open fire, letting the flavors and textures blend together.
—*Nick Iverson, Denver, CO*

PREP: 20 min. • **COOK:** 6 hours
MAKES: 8 servings

- 1 Tbsp. canola oil
- 8 uncooked bratwurst links
- 2 lbs. small Yukon Gold potatoes, quartered
- 1 small head cabbage, coarsely chopped
- 2 medium onions, quartered
- 3 medium carrots, peeled and cut into 2-in. lengths
- 3 medium parsnips, peeled and cut into 2-in. lengths
- 6 fresh thyme sprigs
- 2 garlic cloves, crushed
- 2 bay leaves
- ½ tsp. salt
- ½ tsp. pepper
- 1 cup light beer
- 1 cup reduced-sodium chicken broth

1. Heat the oil in a large skillet over medium heat; add sausages and cook until browned, 3-4 minutes. Remove from heat; set aside.
2. Place potatoes in a single layer on the bottom of a 6-qt. slow cooker. Top with cabbage, onions, carrots and parsnips. Add thyme, garlic, bay leaves, salt and pepper. Add sausages; pour beer and chicken broth over top. Cook, covered, *on low* 6-8 hours or until vegetables are tender. Remove bay leaves before serving.
1 SERVING 457 cal., 27g fat (9g sat. fat), 63mg chol., 967mg sod., 37g carb. (6g sugars, 4g fiber), 15g pro.

SLOW-COOKER MILK-CAN SUPPER

PRESSURE-COOKER COQ AU VIN

Don't be daunted by the elegant name. This classic French dish is now made easier in one appliance! This recipe has all the classic flavors of a rich red wine-mushroom sauce but is so simple to make. My family loves it with whole grain country bread.
—*Julie Peterson, Crofton, MD*

PREP: 25 min. • **COOK:** 15 min.
MAKES: 6 servings

- 3 thick-sliced bacon strips, chopped
- 1½ lbs. boneless skinless chicken thighs
- 1 medium onion, chopped
- 2 Tbsp. tomato paste
- 5 garlic cloves, minced
- 1½ cups dry red wine or reduced-sodium chicken broth
- 4 medium carrots, chopped
- 2 cups sliced baby portobello mushrooms
- 1 cup reduced-sodium chicken broth
- 4 fresh thyme sprigs
- 2 bay leaves
- ½ tsp. kosher salt
- ¼ tsp. pepper

PRESSURE-COOKER COQ AU VIN

1. Select saute setting on a 6-qt. electric pressure cooker. Adjust for medium heat; add bacon. Cook and stir until crisp. Remove with a slotted spoon; drain on paper towels. Discard drippings, reserving 1 Tbsp. in the pressure cooker. Brown chicken on both sides in reserved drippings; remove and set aside.
2. Add onion, tomato paste and garlic to pressure cooker; cook and stir for 5 minutes. Add wine; cook 2 minutes. Press cancel.
3. Add chicken, carrots, mushrooms, broth, thyme, bay leaves, kosher salt and pepper to pressure cooker. Lock lid; close the pressure-release valve. Adjust to pressure-cook on high for 5 minutes. Quick-release pressure. A thermometer inserted into the chicken should read at least 170°.

4. Remove chicken and vegetables to a serving platter; keep warm. Discard thyme and bay leaves. Select the saute setting and adjust for low heat. Simmer the cooking juices, stirring constantly, until reduced by half, 10-15 minutes. Stir in bacon. Serve with the chicken and vegetables.

1 SERVING 244 cal., 11g fat (3g sat. fat), 78mg chol., 356mg sod., 9g carb. (4g sugars, 2g fiber), 23g pro. **DIABETIC EXCHANGES** 3 lean meat, 1 vegetable, ½ fat.

SLOW-COOKER OPTION In a large skillet, cook bacon over medium heat until crisp, stirring occasionally. Remove with a slotted spoon; drain on paper towels. Discard drippings, reserving 1 Tbsp. in pan. Brown chicken on both sides in reserved drippings; remove and set aside. Add onion, tomato paste and garlic to skillet; cook and stir over medium-high heat 5 minutes. Add wine; cook 2 minutes. Transfer to a 4- or 5-qt. slow cooker.

Add chicken, carrots, mushrooms, broth, thyme, bay leaves, salt and pepper. Cook, covered, on low 6-7 hours or until chicken is tender.

Remove chicken and vegetables to a serving platter; keep warm. Discard thyme and bay leaves. Transfer cooking juices to a large saucepan. Bring to a boil; cook until the liquid is reduced by half, 10-15 minutes. Stir in bacon. Serve with chicken and vegetables.

AIR-FRYER
MEAT LOAF

AIR-FRYER MEAT LOAF

If you're looking for a meal for two, then look no further. This entree cooks quickly in the air fryer. Plus, it's easy to double.
—*Michelle Beran, Claflin, KS*

PREP: 15 min. • **BAKE:** 30 min.
MAKES: 2 mini meat loaves

1   large egg
¼   cup 2% milk
⅓   cup crushed saltines
3   Tbsp. chopped onion
¼   tsp. salt
⅛   tsp. rubbed sage
      Dash pepper
½   lb. lean ground beef (90% lean)
¼   cup ketchup
2   Tbsp. brown sugar
¼   tsp. Worcestershire sauce

1. In a large bowl, beat egg. Add the milk, cracker crumbs, onion, salt, sage and pepper. Crumble beef over mixture and mix well. Preheat air fryer to 325°. Shape into 2 loaves; place on a greased tray in air-fryer basket. Cook 20 minutes.
2. Meanwhile, combine the ketchup, brown sugar and Worcestershire sauce; spoon over the meat loaves. Cook until a thermometer reads 160°, 10-15 minutes longer.
1 MEAT LOAF 352 cal., 13g fat (5g sat. fat), 164mg chol., 891mg sod., 32g carb. (22g sugars, 1g fiber), 26g pro.

TEST KITCHEN TIP

The easiest way to keep your air-fryer meat loaf juicy is to avoid slicing it right away. Let it rest for 10 minutes before digging in.

SLOW-COOKER CHICKEN TORTILLA SOUP

SLOW-COOKER CHICKEN TORTILLA SOUP

Don't be shy about loading up the spices and shredded chicken into your slow cooker. Chicken tortilla soup tastes amazing as leftovers the next day. Your family will thank you for this!
—*Karen Kelly, Germantown, MD*

PREP: 10 min. • **COOK:** 4 hours
MAKES: 8 servings (2 qt.)

1   lb. boneless skinless chicken breasts
1   Tbsp. canola oil
1   medium onion, chopped
3   garlic cloves, minced
1   carton (32 oz.) reduced-sodium chicken broth
1   can (15 oz.) black beans, rinsed and drained
1   can (14 oz.) fire-roasted diced tomatoes
1½   cups frozen corn
1   Tbsp. chili powder
1   Tbsp. ground cumin
1   tsp. paprika
½   tsp. salt
¼   tsp. pepper
¼   cup minced fresh cilantro
        Crushed tortilla chips
        Optional toppings: Chopped avocado, jalapeno peppers and lime wedges

1. In a large skillet over medium heat, brown chicken in oil. Remove chicken to 3-qt. slow cooker. Add onion to skillet; cook and stir until tender, 6-8 minutes. Add garlic; cook 1 minute longer. Transfer to slow cooker. Stir in next 9 ingredients. Cover and cook on low until the chicken is tender, 4-5 hours.
2. Remove the chicken and shred with 2 forks; return to the slow cooker. Stir in cilantro. Sprinkle with tortilla chips. Serve with toppings as desired.
1 CUP 176 cal., 4g fat (1g sat. fat), 31mg chol., 725mg sod., 19g carb. (3g sugars, 4g fiber), 17g pro. **DIABETIC EXCHANGES** 2 lean meat, 1 starch, ½ fat.

GREEK-STYLE STUFFED PEPPERS

Bountiful peppers found at the local farmers market in early fall, combined with some standard Greek ingredients, create a dish that bursts with color and fresh flavor.
—Renee Murby, Johnston, RI

PREP: 30 min. • **COOK:** 4½ hours
MAKES: 8 servings

- 2 Tbsp. olive oil
- 1 small fennel bulb, chopped
- 1 small red onion, chopped
- 1 pkg. (10 oz.) frozen chopped spinach, thawed and squeezed dry
- 3 garlic cloves, minced
- 2 each medium sweet yellow, orange, red and green peppers
- 1 can (28 oz.) crushed tomatoes, divided
- 1 lb. ground lamb
- 1 cup cooked barley
- 1 cup crumbled feta cheese, plus more for serving
- ½ cup Greek olives, chopped
- 1½ tsp. dried oregano
- ½ tsp. salt
- ½ tsp. crushed red pepper flakes
- ½ tsp. pepper
  Chopped fresh parsley, optional

1. In a large skillet, heat oil over medium-high heat. Add fennel and onion; cook and stir until tender, 6-8 minutes. Add spinach and garlic; cook 1 minute longer. Cool slightly.
2. Cut and reserve tops from peppers; remove and discard seeds. Pour 1 cup crushed tomatoes into the bottom of a 6- or 7-qt. slow cooker. In a large bowl, combine the lamb, barley, 1 cup cheese, olives and seasonings; add the fennel mixture. Spoon mixture into peppers; place in slow cooker. Pour remaining crushed tomatoes over peppers; replace the pepper tops. Cook, covered, on low 4½-5½ hours, until peppers are tender. Serve with additional feta, and chopped parsley if desired.

1 STUFFED PEPPER 313 cal., 16g fat (6g sat. fat), 45mg chol., 684mg sod., 26g carb. (11g sugars, 8g fiber), 17g pro. **DIABETIC EXCHANGES** 2 starch, 2 medium-fat meat, 1 fat.

GREEK-STYLE STUFFED PEPPERS

AIR-FRYER JAMAICAN JERK PORK CHOPS

These sweet, spicy chops can be thrown together in minutes, but they definitely don't taste that way. Served with a side of jasmine rice, every bite is like a trip to a tropical location.
—Allison Ulrich, Frisco, TX

TAKES: 25 min. • **MAKES:** 4 servings

- 1 Tbsp. butter, softened
- ¼ cup peach preserves
- 4 boneless thin-cut pork loin chops (2 to 3 oz. each)
- 3 tsp. Caribbean jerk seasoning
- ½ tsp. salt
- ¼ tsp. pepper
- ½ medium sweet orange pepper
- ½ medium sweet yellow pepper
- ½ medium sweet red pepper
  Hot cooked rice, optional

1. Preheat air fryer to 350°. In a small bowl, mix butter and peach preserves until combined.
2. Sprinkle the chops with seasonings. Place on a greased tray in air-fryer basket. Cook until no longer pink, 2-3 minutes on each side. Remove and keep warm.
3. Cut peppers into thin strips. Place on a greased tray in air-fryer basket. Cook until crisp-tender and lightly browned, 5-6 minutes, stirring occasionally. Return chops to air fryer with peppers; top with butter mixture. Cook until butter is melted, 1-2 minutes. If desired, serve with rice.

1 SERVING 368 cal., 14g fat (7g sat. fat), 84mg chol., 1099mg sod., 32g carb. (28g sugars, 2g fiber), 28g pro.

PRESSURE-COOKER GARDEN
CHICKEN CACCIATORE

PRESSURE-COOKER GARDEN CHICKEN CACCIATORE

Treat company to this perfect Italian meal. I get time to spend with my guests while it cooks in the pressure cooker, and it often earns me rave reviews. I like to serve it with couscous, green beans and a dry red wine—mangia!
—*Martha Schirmacher, Sterling Heights, MI*

PREP: 15 min. • **COOK:** 10 min.
MAKES: 12 servings

- 12 boneless skinless chicken thighs (about 3 lbs.)
- 2 medium green peppers, chopped
- 1 can (14½ oz.) diced tomatoes with basil, oregano and garlic, undrained
- 1 can (6 oz.) tomato paste
- 1 medium onion, chopped
- ½ cup reduced-sodium chicken broth
- ¼ cup dry red wine or additional reduced-sodium chicken broth
- 3 garlic cloves, minced
- ¾ tsp. salt
- ⅛ tsp. pepper
- 2 Tbsp. cornstarch
- 2 Tbsp. cold water
  Minced fresh parsley, optional

1. Place chicken in a 6- or 8-qt. electric pressure cooker. Combine the green peppers, tomatoes, tomato paste, onion, broth, wine, garlic, salt and pepper; pour over chicken. Lock lid; close pressure-release valve. Adjust to pressure-cook on high for 10 minutes. Quick-release pressure. A thermometer inserted into the chicken should read at least 170°. Remove chicken to a serving patter; keep warm.
2. In a small bowl, mix the cornstarch and water until smooth; stir into broth mixture. Select saute setting and adjust for low heat. Simmer, stirring constantly, until thickened, 1-2 minutes.
3 OZ. COOKED CHICKEN WITH ABOUT
½ CUP SAUCE 206 cal., 8g fat (2g sat. fat), 76mg chol., 353mg sod., 8g carb. (3g sugars, 2g fiber), 23g pro.

AIR-FRYER TILAPIA FILLETS

Cooking tilapia fillets in the air fryer means dinner will be on the table in less than half an hour. It's quick and easy, and it doesn't dry out the delicate fillets.
—*Dana Alexander, Lebanon, MO*

TAKES: 20 min. • **MAKES:** 2 servings

- 2 tilapia fillets (6 oz. each)
- 1 Tbsp. butter, melted
- 1 tsp. Montreal steak seasoning
- ½ tsp. dried parsley flakes
- ¼ tsp. paprika
- ¼ tsp. dried thyme
- ⅛ tsp. onion powder
- ⅛ tsp. salt
- ⅛ tsp. pepper
- Dash garlic powder

1. Preheat air fryer to 400°. Brush the fillets with butter. In a small bowl, mix remaining ingredients; sprinkle over the fillets.

2. Place fillets in a single layer on a greased tray in air-fryer basket. Cook until fish just begins to flake easily with a fork, 6-8 minutes.

NOTE In our testing, we find cook times vary dramatically among brands of air fryers. As a result, we give wider than normal ranges on the suggested cook times. Begin checking at the first time listed and adjust as needed.

1 FILLET 193 cal., 7g fat (4g sat. fat), 98mg chol., 594mg sod., 0 carb. (0 sugars, 0 fiber), 32g pro. **DIABETIC EXCHANGES** 5 lean meat, 1½ fat.

TEST KITCHEN TIP

Tilapia goes from the freezer to the air fryer easier than a fattier fish would. Just make sure that frozen fillets reach an internal temperature of 145°, no matter if you air-fry frozen or thawed fillets.

AIR-FRYER TILAPIA FILLETS

⏱ 🗑
PRESSURE-COOKER PORK TACOS WITH MANGO SALSA ✓

I've made quite a few tacos in my day, but you can't beat the tender filling made in a pressure cooker. These are by far the best pork tacos we've had—and we've tried plenty. Make the mango salsa from scratch if you have time!
—*Amber Massey, Argyle, TX*

PREP: 25 min. • **COOK:** 5 min.
MAKES: 12 servings

- 2 Tbsp. white vinegar
- 2 Tbsp. lime juice
- 3 cups cubed fresh pineapple
- 1 small red onion, coarsely chopped
- 3 Tbsp. chili powder
- 2 chipotle peppers in adobo sauce
- 2 tsp. ground cumin
- 1½ tsp. salt
- ½ tsp. pepper
- 1 bottle (12 oz.) dark Mexican beer
- 3 lbs. pork tenderloin, cut into 1-in. cubes
- ¼ cup chopped fresh cilantro
- 1 jar (16 oz.) mango salsa
- 24 corn tortillas (6 in.), warmed
  Optional toppings: Cubed fresh pineapple, cubed avocado and queso fresco

1. Puree the first 9 ingredients in a blender; stir in beer. In a 6-qt. electric pressure cooker, combine pork and pineapple mixture. Lock lid; close pressure-release valve. Adjust to pressure-cook on high for 3 minutes. Quick-release pressure. A thermometer inserted into pork should read at least 145°. Stir to break up pork.
2. Stir the cilantro into salsa. Using a slotted spoon, place the pork mixture in tortillas. Serve with salsa and your choice of optional toppings.
2 TACOS 284 cal., 6g fat (2g sat. fat), 64mg chol., 678mg sod., 30g carb. (5g sugars, 5g fiber), 26g pro. **DIABETIC EXCHANGES** 3 lean meat, 2 starch.

🍲
SLOW-COOKER ASIAN SHORT RIBS ✓

My slow cooker is my best friend, and I use it at least three times a week. This versatile recipe is one of my favorites. The sauce can be used for other cuts of meat too.
—*Carole Resnick, Cleveland, OH*

PREP: 15 min. • **COOK:** 6 hours
MAKES: 6 servings

- ¾ cup sugar
- ¾ cup ketchup
- ¾ cup reduced-sodium soy sauce
- ⅓ cup honey
- ¼ cup lemon juice
- 3 Tbsp. hoisin sauce
- 1 Tbsp. ground ginger
- 2 garlic cloves, minced
- 4 lbs. bone-in beef short ribs
  Optional: Hot cooked ramen noodles, sesame seeds, julienned green onions and carrots, and sliced cucumber, radishes, mushrooms and red chili peppers

In a greased 4- or 5-qt. slow cooker, whisk together the first 8 ingredients. Add short ribs and turn to coat; cook, covered, on low 6-7 hours or until meat is tender. If desired, serve with ramen noodles and optional toppings.
1 SERVING 460 cal., 15g fat (6g sat. fat), 73mg chol., 1706mg sod., 56g carb. (51g sugars, 0 fiber), 27g pro.

**PRESSURE-COOKER
BEEF & FARRO STEW**

APPLE BUTTER
PORK WITH WHITE BEANS

This enticing dish is an entire dinner with meat, vegetables and beans, wonderful to come home to after I've run the kids around to activities all afternoon. The apple butter with the pork is yummy and perfect for fall!
—*Elisabeth Larsen, Pleasant Grove, UT*

PREP: 20 min. • **COOK:** 4 hours
MAKES: 10 servings

12	oz. fresh baby carrots, coarsely chopped
1	small onion, chopped
1	boneless pork loin roast (3 lbs.)
1½	tsp. salt, divided
½	tsp. pepper, divided
1	Tbsp. olive oil
1	cup apple butter
2	Tbsp. apple cider vinegar
1	Tbsp. Dijon mustard
3	garlic cloves, minced
2	cans (15 oz. each) great northern beans, rinsed and drained

1. Place carrots and onion in a 6-qt. slow cooker. Sprinkle roast with 1 tsp. salt and ¼ tsp. pepper. In a large skillet, heat oil over medium-high heat; brown roast on all sides. Transfer to slow cooker.
2. In a small bowl, combine apple butter, vinegar, mustard, garlic, remaining salt and pepper; pour over the pork and vegetables. Cook, covered, on low until the vegetables are tender and a thermometer inserted into pork reads 145°, 3½-4½ hours.
3. Remove roast from slow cooker; tent with foil. Add beans to slow cooker; cook, covered, on high until heated through, about 30 minutes. Serve sliced pork with bean mixture.
4 OZ. COOKED PORK WITH ½ CUP BEAN MIXTURE 314 cal., 8g fat (3g sat. fat), 68mg chol., 579mg sod., 28g carb. (12g sugars, 5g fiber), 31g pro..

PRESSURE-COOKER
BEEF & FARRO STEW

This pressure-cooked stew is loaded with tender beef and lots of veggies. It's comforting and filling.
—*Kaylen Friederich, Reno, NV*

PREP: 40 min. • **COOK:** 30 min. + releasing
MAKES: 12 servings (4 qt.)

1	boneless beef chuck roast (about 2 lbs.), cut into 1-in. pieces
1½	tsp. salt
½	tsp. pepper
2	Tbsp. olive oil, divided
6	large carrots, cut into ½-in. pieces
3	celery ribs, chopped
1	large onion, chopped
6	garlic cloves, minced
¼	cup tomato paste
1	cup dry red wine
6	cups beef stock
4	large Yukon Gold potatoes, peeled and cut into 1-in. pieces
½	lb. fresh mushrooms, sliced
¾	cup farro, rinsed
3	bay leaves
1	tsp. garlic powder
1	tsp. dried thyme

1. Sprinkle beef with salt and pepper. Select saute or browning setting on a 6-qt. electric pressure cooker. Adjust for medium heat; add 1 Tbsp. oil. When oil is hot, brown beef in batches. Set aside.
2. Add remaining 1 Tbsp. oil and the carrots, celery and onion to pressure cooker; cook and stir until vegetables are crisp-tender, 5-7 minutes.
3. Add garlic; cook 1 minute longer. Add tomato paste; cook and stir until fragrant, about 1 minute. Add wine, stirring to loosen browned bits.
4. Return the beef to pressure cooker. Stir in stock, potatoes, mushrooms, farro, bay leaves, garlic powder and thyme. Press cancel.
5. Lock lid; close the pressure-release valve. Adjust to pressure-cook on high for 30 minutes. Let pressure release naturally for 15 minutes; quick-release any remaining pressure. If desired, skim fat from stew. Discard bay leaves.
1⅓ CUPS 360 cal., 10g fat (3g sat. fat), 49mg chol., 619mg sod., 43g carb. (6g sugars, 5g fiber), 22g pro. **DIABETIC EXCHANGES** 3 starch, 3 lean meat, ½ fat

APPLE BUTTER PORK WITH WHITE BEANS

AIR-FRYER BEEF TURNOVERS

My mom's recipe for these flavorful pockets called for dough made from scratch, but I streamlined it by using refrigerated crescent rolls and an air fryer. My children love the turnovers plain or dipped in ketchup, and they are also terrific with mustard.
—Claudia Bodeker, Ash Flat, AR

TAKES: 30 min. • **MAKES:** 1 dozen

- 1 lb. ground beef
- 1 medium onion, chopped
- 1 jar (16 oz.) sauerkraut, rinsed, drained and chopped
- 1 cup shredded Swiss cheese
- 3 tubes (8 oz. each) refrigerated crescent rolls

1. In a large skillet, cook beef and onion over medium heat until meat is no longer pink, crumbling meat, 5-7 minutes; drain. Add sauerkraut and cheese.
2. Preheat the air fryer to 350°. Unroll crescent roll dough and separate into rectangles; pinch seams to seal. Place ½ cup beef mixture in center of each rectangle. Bring corners to the center and pinch to seal. In batches, place the turnovers in a single layer on a greased tray in air-fryer basket. Cook until golden brown, 12-15 minutes.

NOTE In our testing, we find cook times vary dramatically among brands of air fryers. As a result, we give wider than normal ranges on the suggested cook times. Begin checking at the first time listed and adjust as needed.

2 TURNOVERS 634 cal., 35g fat (7g sat. fat), 63mg chol., 1426mg sod., 54g carb. (14g sugars, 2g fiber), 27g pro.

AIR-FRYER
BEEF TURNOVERS

PRESSURE-COOKER SHRIMP RISOTTO

Shrimp and risotto are two of my favorite dishes. But risotto takes a lot of time and attention when cooked on the stovetop. So I tried it in a pressure cooker, since it's such a timesaver. I think the flavor and texture of this speedy version is similar to the traditional method.
—*DonnaMarie Ryan, Topsfield, MA*

PREP: 30 min. • **COOK:** 5 min.
MAKES: 6 servings

- 1   lb. uncooked shell-on shrimp (16-20 per lb.)
- 4   Tbsp. butter, divided
- 1   carton (32 oz.) chicken stock
- 1   medium onion, chopped
- 2   cups uncooked arborio rice
- 3   garlic cloves, minced
- ¾   cup fresh or frozen corn
- ¼   cup oil-packed sun-dried tomatoes, chopped
- 2   tsp. minced fresh thyme or 1 tsp. dried thyme
- ¼   cup white wine, such as Sauvignon blanc
- ¾   cup grated Parmesan cheese
- ¼   cup heavy whipping cream
- ¾   tsp. kosher salt
- ¼   tsp. freshly ground pepper

PRESSURE-COOKER SHRIMP RISOTTO

1. Peel and devein the shrimp; reserve shells. In a small saucepan, melt 1 Tbsp. butter over medium heat. Add shells; cook and stir 2 minutes. Stir in stock. Bring to a boil; reduce heat. Simmer, covered, 10 minutes. Remove from heat and keep warm.
2. Meanwhile, select saute setting on a 6-qt. electric pressure cooker. Adjust for medium heat; add remaining 3 Tbsp. butter. When butter is melted, cook and stir shrimp until shrimp turn pink, 3-4 minutes. Remove shrimp with a slotted spoon and keep warm. Add onion to pressure cooker; cook and stir until crisp-tender, 2-3 minutes. Add rice and garlic; cook and stir until rice is coated, 1-2 minutes. Stir in corn, tomatoes and thyme. Add wine; cook and stir until absorbed, about 30 seconds, stirring to loosen browned bits from pan. Press cancel.
3. Drain broth mixture; discard shrimp shells. Stir drained broth into pressure cooker. Lock lid; close pressure-release valve. Adjust to pressure-cook on high for 5 minutes. Quick-release pressure.
4. Stir in the Parmesan cheese, cream, salt and pepper until combined; continue stirring until creamy. Stir in shrimp; heat through. If desired, top with additional fresh thyme and grated Parmesan cheese. Serve immediately.

1½ CUPS 499 cal., 16g fat (9g sat. fat), 132mg chol., 916mg sod., 63g carb. (3g sugars, 2g fiber), 24g pro.

TEST KITCHEN TIP
Keep a jar of minced garlic on hand to streamline dinner prep for this dish as well as other last-minute entrees.

GOES GREAT WITH …
Lemon Date Couscous (p. 301) is a fantastic and fast addition to this chicken.

AIR-FRYER ROTISSERIE CHICKEN

AIR-FRYER ROTISSERIE CHICKEN ✓

This air-fried whole chicken is so crispy yet succulent, just like the rotisserie chickens you get at Boston Market. I serve it straight up, but you can also shred and add it to tacos, soups, pasta salads and so much more.
—*Dawn Parker, Surrey, BC*

PREP: 5 min. • **COOK:** 65 min. + standing
MAKES: 6 servings

- 1 broiler/fryer chicken (3 to 4 lbs.)
- 1 Tbsp. olive oil
- 2 tsp. seasoned salt

Preheat air fryer to 350°. Brush outside of chicken with olive oil and sprinkle with seasoned salt. Place chicken, breast side down, on a tray in air-fryer basket; cook 30 minutes. Flip chicken and cook until a thermometer inserted in thickest part of thigh reads 170°-175°, 35-40 minutes longer. Remove chicken; let stand for 15 minutes before carving.

NOTE In our testing, we find cook times vary dramatically among brands of air fryers. As a result, we give wider than normal ranges on the suggested cook times. Begin checking at the first time listed and adjust as needed.

5 OZ. COOKED CHICKEN 313 cal., 19g fat (5g sat. fat), 104mg chol., 596mg sod., 0 carb. (0 sugars, 0 fiber), 33g pro.

TEST KITCHEN TIP ✗

We like to use air fryers with a 5-qt. capacity or larger. This recipe calls for a 3- or 4-lb. chicken, which should fit nicely. If your chicken is too big, you can cut the chicken into pieces and adjust the cooking time accordingly.

PORTOBELLO ROPA VIEJA

PORTOBELLO ROPA VIEJA

I created this version of a Mexican favorite for my family.
—*Arlene Erlbach, Morton Grove, IL*

PREP: 25 min. • **COOK:** 5 hours
MAKES: 6 servings

- 2 Tbsp. canola oil
- 1 medium onion, halved and thinly sliced
- 1 poblano pepper, thinly sliced
- 1 medium sweet red pepper, thinly sliced
- 1 jar (12 oz.) sofrito tomato cooking base
- 1 cup fire-roasted diced tomatoes
- 3 Tbsp. lime juice, divided
- 2 Tbsp. brown sugar
- ¾ tsp. garlic powder
- 6 large portobello mushrooms, thinly sliced
- 1 Tbsp. adobo seasoning
   Hot cooked rice
   Minced fresh cilantro

1. In a large skillet, heat oil over medium-high heat. Add onion; cook and stir until tender, 5-7 minutes. Add poblano and red peppers; cook and stir until crisp-tender, 3-4 minutes. Transfer to a greased 5- or 6-qt. slow cooker. Stir in the sofrito, tomatoes, 2 Tbsp. lime juice, brown sugar and garlic powder.

2. Toss the mushrooms with adobo seasoning; place on top of the pepper mixture. Cook, covered, on low until the mushrooms are tender, 5-6 hours. Stir in remaining 1 Tbsp. lime juice. Serve warm with rice and cilantro.

⅔ CUP 253 cal., 15g fat (0 sat. fat), 0 chol., 1449mg sod., 19g carb. (9g sugars, 4g fiber), 10g pro.

PRESSURE-COOKER PENNE WITH MEAT SAUCE

This is pressure-cooker pasta isn't just delicious but also super easy to make. I like to serve it with a chopped salad and Italian dressing. If you have leftovers, try them spooned into individual ramekins and baked with a little extra sauce and some cheese on top.
—*Virginia Butterfield, Cranberry Township, PA*

TAKES: 30 min. • **MAKES:** 6 servings

- 1 Tbsp. olive oil
- 1½ lbs. lean ground beef (90% lean)
- ¾ cup finely chopped onion
- 1 medium green pepper, chopped
- 12 oz. uncooked penne pasta
- 2¼ cups water
- 2 tsp. Italian seasoning
- ¾ tsp. salt
- ½ tsp. pepper
- 1 jar pasta sauce (24 oz.)
  Optional: shredded Parmesan cheese and torn fresh basil leaves

Select saute setting on a 6-qt. electric pressure cooker. Adjust for medium heat; add oil. When oil is hot, cook beef, onion and pepper until beef is no longer pink and the vegetables are tender, 8-10 minutes, breaking up beef into crumbles; drain. Press cancel; add the pasta, water and seasonings; cover with pasta sauce. Lock lid; close pressure-release valve. Adjust to pressure-cook on high for 6 minutes. Quick-release pressure. Remove the lid; stir to combine. If desired, sprinkle with Parmesan cheese and basil.

1½ CUPS 472 cal., 14g fat (4g sat. fat), 71mg chol., 775mg sod., 55g carb. (12g sugars, 5g fiber), 31g pro.

PRESSURE-COOKER PENNE WITH MEAT SAUCE

SLOW-COOKER CUBANO SANDWICHES
(PICTURED ON PAGE 225)

This recipe came about because I didn't have pepperoncinis for my usual Italian pork recipe so I used pickles instead. It reminded me of a Cuban sandwich so much that I added some ham and Swiss cheese to complete the dish. Instead of adding cheese to the slow cooker, you can also top the sandwiches with sliced cheese. Place under the broiler to melt.
—*Kristie Schley, Severna Park, MD*

PREP: 15 min. • **COOK:** 6½ hours
MAKES: 8 Servings

- 2 lbs. pork tenderloin
- 7 Tbsp. stone-ground mustard, divided
- 1 tsp. pepper, freshly ground
- 1 lb. fully cooked boneless ham steak, cut into ½-in. cubes
- 1 jar (16 oz.) whole baby dill pickles, undrained, sliced thick
- 2 cups shredded Swiss cheese
- 8 submarine buns, split

1. Rub pork with 3 Tbsp. mustard, season with pepper and place in a 5- or 6-qt. slow cooker. Add the ham and pickles, including pickle juice. Cover and cook on low 6 hours or until tender, turning halfway through.
2. Shred pork with 2 forks. Sprinkle cheese over the meat mixture; cover and cook until the cheese melts, about 30 minutes.
3. When ready to serve, slice rolls and toast lightly in a toaster oven or broiler. Spread remaining mustard evenly over both sides. Using a slotted spoon, top the rolls with the meat mixture. Serve immediately.
1 SANDWICH 526 cal., 20g fat (8g sat. fat), 118mg chol., 1941mg sod., 36g carb. (4g sugars, 3g fiber), 48g pro.

SAUERBRATEN SOUP

Sauerbraten and soup are both family favorites. This combines the two, without the long marinating time the traditional beef dish requires. You can substitute spaetzle or gnocchi for the egg noodles.
—*Jennifer Yerkes, Franklin Square, NY*

PREP: 15 min. • **COOK:** 4 hours
MAKES: 11 cups

- 2 Tbsp. olive oil
- 2 lbs. beef stew meat, cut into 1 in. pieces
- 1 Tbsp. mixed pickling spices
- 1 bay leaf
- 6 cups beef broth, divided
- 1 medium onion, chopped
- 1 jar (16 oz.) shredded sweet-and-sour red cabbage
- ½ tsp. ground ginger
- ¼ tsp. ground cloves
- 8 gingersnap cookies, crushed
  Cooked wide egg noodles

1. In a large skillet, heat oil over medium-high heat; brown the meat in batches. Transfer the meat to a 4- or 5-qt. slow cooker.
2. Place pickling spices and bay leaf on a double thickness of cheesecloth. Gather corners of cloth to enclose seasonings; tie securely with kitchen string. Add the spice bag, 4 cups broth, onion, cabbage, ginger and cloves to slow cooker. Cook, covered, on high 3 hours.
3. Meanwhile, in a saucepan, heat the remaining broth and gingersnaps over medium heat; cook and stir until thickened, about 10 minutes. Transfer to slow cooker; cook, covered, until meat is tender, about 1 hour longer. Discard spice bag. Serve with noodles.
1¾ CUPS 371 cal., 16g fat (5g sat. fat), 94mg chol., 1226mg sod., 22g carb. (13g sugars, 1g fiber), 32g pro.

CHAPTER 12
LOTSA PASTA

P. 265

P. 256

P. 267

P. 260

GOES GREAT WITH ...
Pita breads are lovely served with this pasta main course.

SMOKED SALMON PASTA

SMOKED SALMON PASTA

This pasta originally came to be from the miscellaneous ingredients in my fridge, and depending on whom I'm cooking for, the recipe changes a little bit each time I make it. It makes enough for a party or for leftovers, which is a bonus because it is excellent the next day whether you serve it cold or reheated.
—*Jackie Hennon, Boise, ID*

TAKES: 25 min. • **MAKES:** 8 servings

- 1 lb. uncooked spiral or penne pasta
- 2 Tbsp. olive oil
- 2 large tomatoes, diced
- 2 cups water-packed artichoke hearts, drained and chopped
- 1½ cups kalamata olives, pitted and halved
- 1 cup chopped oil-packed sun-dried tomatoes
- ¾ cup chopped onion
- 8 oz. smoked salmon fillets
- 2 Tbsp. sun-dried tomato pesto
- 2 tsp. dried basil
- ¾ tsp. crushed red pepper flakes
- ¼ cup grated Parmesan cheese
- ¼ cup crumbled feta cheese

1. In a large saucepan, cook pasta according to package directions for al dente. Meanwhile, in a Dutch oven, heat oil over medium-low heat. Add the next 5 ingredients. Break salmon into bite-sized pieces; add to tomato mixture. Stir in the pesto, basil and red pepper flakes. Cook, stirring occasionally, until vegetables are crisp-tender, 8-10 minutes.
2. Drain pasta. Add to salmon mixture; stir to combine. Top with cheeses.
¾ CUP 433 cal., 16g fat (3g sat. fat), 11mg chol., 924mg sod., 55g carb. (4g sugars, 4g fiber), 17g pro.

SAUSAGE & SWISS CHARD PASTA

SAUSAGE & SWISS CHARD PASTA
✓ spinach

I whipped up dinner with fresh produce from the farmers market, and the result was amazing.
—*Kate Stiltner, Grand Rapids, MI*

TAKES: 30 min. • **MAKES:** 6 servings

- 12 oz. uncooked orecchiette or small tube pasta (about 2½ cups)
- 1 Tbsp. olive oil
- ½ lb. bulk Italian sausage
- ½ cup chopped red onion
- 1 medium fennel bulb, chopped
- ½ lb. baby portobello mushrooms, chopped
- 3 garlic cloves, minced
- 1 bunch Swiss chard *(spinach)*, trimmed and chopped
- ½ tsp. salt
- ¼ tsp. pepper
- ¾ cup grated Parmesan cheese, divided
- ½ cup pine nuts or chopped walnuts, toasted

1. Cook pasta according to package directions for al dente. Meanwhile, in a large skillet, heat oil over medium heat. Cook sausage and red onion until no longer pink, 3-4 minutes, breaking sausage into crumbles. Add the fennel, mushrooms and garlic; cook until tender, 6-8 minutes. Add Swiss chard; cook and stir until wilted, 4-5 minutes longer.
2. Drain the pasta, reserving 1 cup pasta water. In a large bowl, combine pasta, sausage mixture, salt, pepper and ½ cup Parmesan cheese, adding enough reserved pasta water to coat pasta and create a creamy texture. Serve with remaining ¼ cup cheese and toasted pine nuts.
1⅓ CUPS 487 cal., 25g fat (6g sat. fat), 34mg chol., 726mg sod., 51g carb. (5g sugars, 4g fiber), 19g pro.

BOW TIES WITH SAUSAGE & ASPARAGUS

We love asparagus, so I look for ways to go green. This pasta dish comes together fast on hectic nights and always makes wonderful leftovers.
—*Carol A. Suto, Liverpool, NY*

TAKES: 30 min. • **MAKES:** 6 servings

3 cups uncooked whole wheat bow tie pasta (about 8 oz.)
1 lb. fresh asparagus, trimmed and cut into 1½-in. pieces
1 pkg. (19½ oz.) Italian turkey sausage links, casings removed
1 medium onion, chopped
3 garlic cloves, minced
¼ cup shredded Parmesan cheese
Additional shredded Parmesan cheese, optional

1. In a 6-qt. stockpot, cook the pasta according to package directions, adding asparagus during last 2-3 minutes of cooking. Drain, reserving ½ cup pasta water; return the pasta and asparagus to pot.
2. Meanwhile, in a large skillet, cook the sausage, onion and garlic over medium heat until no longer pink, 6-8 minutes, breaking sausage into large crumbles. Add to stockpot. Stir in ¼ cup cheese and reserved pasta water as desired. Serve with additional cheese if desired.

1⅓ CUPS 247 cal., 7g fat (2g sat. fat), 36mg chol., 441mg sod., 28g carb. (2g sugars, 4g fiber), 17g pro. **DIABETIC EXCHANGES** 2 lean meat, 1½ starch, 1 vegetable.

RAVIOLI WITH APPLE CHICKEN SAUSAGE

I love butternut squash ravioli but was never quite sure what flavors would best complement the squash. Turns out that creamy spinach, chicken sausage and a hint of sweet spice are the perfect go-alongs.
—*Mary Brodeur, Millbury, MA*

TAKES: 30 min. • **MAKES:** 4 servings

1 pkg. (18 oz.) frozen butternut squash ravioli
2 pkg. (10 oz. each) frozen creamed spinach
1 Tbsp. olive oil
1 pkg. (12 oz.) fully cooked apple chicken sausage links or flavor of your choice, cut into ½-in. slices
1 tsp. maple syrup
¼ tsp. pumpkin pie spice

1. Cook the ravioli according to package directions. Prepare spinach according to package directions. Meanwhile, in a large skillet, heat oil over medium heat. Add sausage; cook and stir until browned, 2-4 minutes.
2. Drain ravioli. Add ravioli, spinach, maple syrup and pie spice to sausage; heat through.

1½ CUPS 531 cal., 16g fat (4g sat. fat), 64mg chol., 1409mg sod., 69g carb. (19g sugars, 4g fiber), 26g pro.

BOW TIES WITH SAUSAGE & ASPARAGUS

**LEMONY SCALLOPS WITH
ANGEL HAIR PASTA**

LEMONY SCALLOPS WITH ANGEL HAIR PASTA

This delicate dish tastes so bright with a touch of lemon and tender sauteed scallops. Serve with crusty whole grain bread, and you have an impressive dinner that comes together in a flash.
—*Thomas Faglon, Somerset, NJ*

TAKES: 25 min. • **MAKES:** 4 servings

  8 oz. uncooked multigrain angel hair pasta
  3 Tbsp. olive oil, divided
  1 lb. sea scallops, patted dry
  2 cups sliced radishes (about 1 bunch)
  2 garlic cloves, sliced
  ½ tsp. crushed red pepper flakes
  6 green onions, thinly sliced
  ½ tsp. kosher salt
  1 Tbsp. grated lemon zest
  ¼ cup lemon juice

1. In a 6-qt. stockpot, cook the pasta according to package directions; drain and return to pot.
2. Meanwhile, in a large skillet, heat 2 Tbsp. oil over medium-high heat; sear scallops in batches until opaque and the edges are golden brown, about 2 minutes per side. Remove from skillet; keep warm.
3. In same skillet, saute radishes, garlic and pepper flakes in remaining 1 Tbsp. oil until radishes are tender, 2-3 minutes. Stir in the green onion and salt; cook 1 minute longer. Add to the pasta; toss to combine. Sprinkle with lemon zest and juice. Top with scallops to serve.

1½ CUPS 404 cal., 13g fat (2g sat. fat), 27mg chol., 737mg sod., 48g carb. (4g sugars, 6g fiber), 25g pro.

TEST KITCHEN TIP
Create a satisfying low-carb version of this dish by simply swapping cauliflower rice or shirataki noodles for angel hair pasta.

TORTELLINI WITH SAUSAGE & MASCARPONE

When I crave Italian comfort food on a busy night and don't have a lot of time to cook, this recipe is a lifesaver. This fast and yummy dish starts with a premade jarred sauce, but then makes it much more special with just a few key additions. You can have it on the table in less time than a takeout order.
—Gerry Vance, Millbrae, CA

TAKES: 20 min. • **MAKES:** 6 servings

1 pkg. (20 oz.) refrigerated cheese tortellini
8 oz. bulk Italian sausage
1 jar (24 oz.) pasta sauce with mushrooms
½ cup shredded Parmesan cheese
1 carton (8 oz.) mascarpone cheese
 Crushed red pepper flakes, optional

1. Prepare the tortellini according to package directions. Meanwhile, in a large cast-iron or other heavy skillet, cook sausage over medium heat until no longer pink, 6-8 minutes, breaking into crumbles; drain. Stir in the pasta sauce; heat through.
2. Drain the tortellini, reserving 1 cup cooking water. Add tortellini to sauce with enough reserved cooking water to reach desired consistency; toss to coat. Stir in Parmesan cheese; dollop with mascarpone cheese. If desired, sprinkle with red pepper flakes.
1 CUP 637 cal., 37g fat (17g sat. fat), 113mg chol., 1040mg sod., 57g carb. (11g sugars, 4g fiber), 24g pro.

TORTELLINI WITH SAUSAGE & MASCARPONE

ANGEL HAIR PRIMAVERA

I love to make pasta primavera when summer is in full swing and garden-fresh veggies are at their best. You can toss in any vegetable that's in season. At my house, this dish is rarely the same twice.
—*Tre Balchowsky, Sausalito, CA*

TAKES: 30 min. • **MAKES:** 4 servings

- 1 Tbsp. olive oil
- 2 medium zucchini, coarsely chopped
- 1 cup fresh baby carrots, halved lengthwise
- 1 cup fresh or frozen corn
- 1 small red onion, cut into thin wedges
- 1 cup cherry tomatoes, halved
- 2 garlic cloves, minced
- 1 pkg. (4.8 oz.) Pasta Roni angel hair pasta with herbs
- ½ cup chopped walnuts, toasted
- ¼ cup shredded Parmesan cheese
  Coarsely ground pepper

1. In a large skillet, heat oil over medium-high heat. Add zucchini, carrots, corn and onion; cook and stir until carrots are tender, 10-12 minutes. Stir in tomatoes and garlic; cook 1 minute longer.
2. Meanwhile, prepare the pasta mix according to the package directions. Add to the vegetable mixture; toss to combine. Sprinkle with walnuts, cheese and pepper.

NOTE To toast nuts, bake in a shallow pan in a 350°; oven for 5-10 minutes or cook in a skillet over low heat until lightly browned, stirring occasionally.

1½ CUPS 416 cal., 23g fat (7g sat. fat), 22mg chol., 603mg sod., 45g carb. (12g sugars, 6g fiber), 13g pro.

GREEK PASTA TOSS

My husband and I developed this bright pasta dish by tossing in our favorite Greek ingredients, such as olives, feta cheese and sun-dried tomatoes. Try it with shrimp or chicken too!
—*Terri Gilson, Calgary, AB*

TAKES: 30 min. • **MAKES:** 4 servings

- 3 cups uncooked whole wheat spiral pasta (about 7 oz.)
- ¾ lb. Italian turkey sausage links, casings removed
- 2 garlic cloves, minced
- 4 oz. fresh baby spinach (about 5 cups)
- ½ cup Greek olives, halved
- ⅓ cup julienned oil-packed sun-dried tomatoes, drained and chopped
- ¼ cup crumbled feta cheese
  Lemon wedges, optional

1. In a 6-qt. stockpot, cook the pasta according to package directions; drain and return to pot.
2. Meanwhile, in a large skillet, cook and coarsely crumble the sausage over medium-high heat until no longer pink, 4-6 minutes. Add garlic; cook and stir 1 minute. Add to pasta.
3. Stir in spinach, olives and tomatoes; heat through, allowing spinach to wilt slightly. Stir in cheese. If desired, serve with lemon wedges.

2 CUPS 335 cal., 13g fat (3g sat. fat), 35mg chol., 742mg sod., 36g carb. (1g sugars, 6g fiber), 19g pro. **DIABETIC EXCHANGES** 2 starch, 2 lean meat, 2 fat, 1 vegetable.

BROCCOLI-PORK STIR-FRY WITH NOODLES

BROCCOLI-PORK STIR-FRY WITH NOODLES ✓

I combined several recipes to come up with this dish that my family loves. It is not only quick and delicious but healthy too. I sometimes substitute boneless, skinless chicken breasts for the pork.
—Joan Hallford, Fort Worth, TX

TAKES: 30 min. • **MAKES:** 4 servings

6   oz. uncooked whole wheat linguine
2   Tbsp. cornstarch
3   Tbsp. reduced-sodium soy sauce
1½ cups reduced-sodium chicken broth
3   green onions, chopped
1½ tsp. canola oil
1   pork tenderloin (1 lb.), cut into bite-sized pieces
1   Tbsp. minced fresh gingerroot
3   garlic cloves, minced
1½ lbs. fresh broccoli florets (about 10 cups)
1   Tbsp. sesame seeds, toasted

1. Cook linguine according to package directions; drain and keep warm. Whisk cornstarch into soy sauce and broth until smooth; stir in green onion.
2. In a large nonstick skillet, heat oil over medium-high heat; stir-fry pork 3 minutes. Add the ginger and garlic; cook and stir until pork is browned, 2 minutes. Remove from pan.
3. Add broth mixture to skillet; bring to a boil. Cook and stir until thickened, 1-2 minutes. Add broccoli; reduce heat. Simmer, covered, until the broccoli is crisp-tender, 5-8 minutes. Stir in pork; heat through, 2-3 minutes.
4. Serve over linguine; sprinkle with sesame seeds.
1 SERVING 376 cal., 8g fat (2g sat. fat), 64mg chol., 595mg sod., 47g carb. (4g sugars, 9g fiber), 35g pro. **DIABETIC EXCHANGES** 3 lean meat, 2 starch, 2 vegetable, ½ fat.

COWBOY PASTA ✓

This pasta combines ground beef, bacon, corn, tangy buttermilk and Monterey Jack cheese for an easy but hearty weeknight dinner. Add more chili powder or a chopped jalapeno to give this delicious pasta dish more of an Old West kick.
—Taste of Home *Test Kitchen*

PREP: 15 min. • **BAKE:** 20 min.
MAKES: 10 servings

8   oz. medium pasta shells
5   bacon strips, chopped
1   lb. ground beef
1   medium red onion, chopped
1   medium green or sweet red pepper, chopped
2   garlic cloves, minced
2   cups frozen corn, thawed
1   can (14½ oz.) diced tomatoes, drained
1¼ cups buttermilk
4   oz. cream cheese, cubed
1   tsp. chili powder
½   tsp. salt
¼   tsp. pepper
1   cup shredded Monterey Jack cheese

1. Cook the pasta according to package directions. Drain; set aside.
2. Meanwhile, in a large skillet, cook bacon over medium heat until crisp, stirring occasionally. Remove with a slotted spoon; drain on paper towels. Discard all but 1 Tbsp. drippings.
3. In the same pan, cook the beef, onion and green pepper over medium heat until the meat is crumbly and no longer pink; drain. Add garlic; cook and stir until fragrant, 2 minutes. Add corn, tomatoes, buttermilk, cream cheese, chili powder, salt, pepper and cooked pasta; stir to combine.
4. Stir in Monterey Jack cheese and bacon pieces. If desired, sprinkle with additional chopped cooked bacon.
1 CUP 333 cal., 16g fat (8g sat. fat), 56mg chol., 456mg sod., 29g carb. (5g sugars, 2g fiber), 18g pro.

COWBOY PASTA

GOES GREAT WITH ...
Cap off this meal-in-one dish with Brownie Sundaes (p. 307).

CREAMY BEEF & ONION PASTA

This delicious pasta sauce originated after I noticed a box of onion soup packets in my cupboard. I could not believe how much flavor it added as a seasoning blend! To my delight, my whole family gave this dish rave reviews, including my infamously picky children. Now, it's my go-to dinner when I want to serve an easy, comforting dish after an especially difficult week or when the weather is cold and dreary.
—*Kristin Bowers, Gilbert, AZ*

TAKES: 30 min. • **MAKES:** 6 servings

3 cups uncooked spiral pasta
1 lb. ground beef
½ small onion, diced
1 cup heavy whipping cream
1 cup 2% milk
1 envelope onion soup mix
¼ cup shredded Gruyere cheese
¼ cup shredded Swiss cheese
 Optional: Chopped fresh thyme and green onions

1. Cook pasta according to package directions; drain. In a large skillet, cook beef and onion over medium-high heat, breaking up beef into crumbles, until the meat is no longer pink and onion is tender, 5-7 minutes; drain and return to the pan. Stir in the cream, milk and soup mix; bring to a boil. Reduce heat; simmer uncovered until mixture thickens, 8-10 minutes.
2. Remove from heat and stir in cheeses and cooked pasta. If desired, serve with thyme and green onion.

1 CUP 505 cal., 28g fat (15g sat. fat), 105mg chol., 521mg sod., 38g carb. (5g sugars, 2g fiber), 24g pro.

CREAMY BEEF & ONION PASTA

PESTO LASAGNA

1. Preheat the oven to 350°. In a large saucepan melt butter over medium heat; add onion. Cook and stir until tender, 4-6 minutes. Add garlic; cook 1 minute longer. Stir in flour and salt until blended. Gradually whisk in milk. Bring to a boil; cook and stir until thickened, about 1 minute. Stir in 2 cups mozzarella cheese, ½ cup Parmesan cheese, basil, oregano and pepper; set aside.
2. In a large bowl, combine ricotta cheese, parsley and remaining 2 cups mozzarella; set aside. Spread about 1½ cup cheese sauce into a greased 13x9-in. baking dish; top with 3 noodles and half each of the following: ricotta mixture, pesto and spinach. Repeat layers. Top with remaining noodles and cheese sauce. Sprinkle with the remaining ½ cup Parmesan.
3. Bake, uncovered, until heated through and the cheese is melted and the sauce is bubbly, 35-40 minutes. Let stand for 15 minutes before serving.

1 PIECE 452 cal., 27g fat (13g sat. fat), 65mg chol., 903mg sod., 31g carb. (7g sugars, 3g fiber), 23g pro.

TEST KITCHEN TIP
Like other vegetarian pasta recipes, you could add meat for a heartier lasagna. Try layering in cooked seasoned ground beef, Italian sausage, cubed chicken or shredded turkey. You could also add layers of roasted red peppers, Greek olives or chopped artichokes.

PESTO LASAGNA

The bright flavor of basil takes center stage in this pesto lasagna. Paired with a rich cheese sauce and layers of noodles, it's a potluck dish that will have guests asking you for the recipe.
—Taste of Home *Test Kitchen*

PREP: 25 min. • **BAKE:** 35 min. + standing
MAKES: 12 servings

- ⅓ cup butter, cubed
- 1 medium onion, chopped
- 1 garlic clove, minced
- ½ cup all-purpose flour
- 1 tsp. salt
- 3½ cups 2% milk
- 4 cups shredded part-skim mozzarella cheese, divided
- 1 cup grated Parmesan cheese, divided
- 1 tsp. dried basil
- 1 tsp. dried oregano
- ½ tsp. white pepper
- 1 carton (15 oz.) whole-milk ricotta cheese
- 1 Tbsp. minced fresh parsley
- 9 lasagna noodles, cooked and drained
- 2 pkg. (10 oz. each) frozen chopped spinach, thawed and squeezed dry
- 1 jar (8.1 oz.) prepared pesto

GARLIC-LEMON SHRIMP LINGUINE

The Cheesecake Factory has a really extensive menu, but I always seem to order their delicious fresh and citrusy Lemon-Garlic Shrimp with pasta. I'd enjoyed it enough times that I was confident I could recreate it to share with friends and family. Think I hit it spot on! When I have fresh basil from the garden, I use that instead of parsley.
—*Trisha Kruse, Eagle, ID*

TAKES: 30 min. • **MAKES:** 4 servings

- 8   oz. uncooked linguine
- 2   Tbsp. olive oil
- 1   Tbsp. butter
- 1   lb. uncooked shrimp (26-30 per lb.), peeled and deveined
- 3   garlic cloves, minced
- 1   Tbsp. grated lemon zest
- 1   Tbsp. lemon juice
- 1   tsp. lemon-pepper seasoning
- 2   Tbsp. minced fresh parsley

1. Cook linguine according to package directions for al dente. Meanwhile, in a large skillet, heat oil and butter over medium-high heat. Add shrimp; cook and stir 3 minutes. Add garlic, lemon zest, juice and lemon-pepper seasoning; cook and stir until shrimp turn pink, 2-3 minutes longer. Stir in parsley.

2. Drain linguine, reserving ⅓ cup pasta water. Add enough pasta water to shrimp mixture to achieve desired consistency. Serve with linguine.

1 SERVING 387 cal., 12g fat (3g sat. fat), 146mg chol., 239mg sod., 43g carb. (2g sugars, 2g fiber), 26g pro.

WEEKNIGHT PASTA SQUIGGLES

This zesty pasta dish is ideal for busy weeknights. It's low on ingredients and easy to prep, and it tastes so comforting when the weather turns cool. A salad on the side makes it a meal.
—*Stacey Brown, Spring, TX*

TAKES: 30 min. • **MAKES:** 8 servings

- 1   pkg. (19½ oz.) Italian turkey sausage links, casings removed
- 1   can (28 oz.) whole plum tomatoes with basil
- 1   can (14½ oz.) no-salt-added whole tomatoes
- 4   cups uncooked spiral pasta (about 12 oz.)
- 1   can (14½ oz.) reduced-sodium chicken broth
- ¼   cup water
- ½   cup crumbled goat or feta cheese

1. In a Dutch oven, cook and crumble sausage over medium-high heat until no longer pink, 5-7 minutes. Meanwhile, coarsely chop the tomatoes, reserving the juices.

2. Add tomatoes and reserved juices to sausage; stir in pasta, broth and water. Bring to a boil. Reduce heat to medium; cook, uncovered, until pasta is al dente, 15-18 minutes, stirring occasionally. Top with cheese.

1½ CUPS 278 cal., 7g fat (2g sat. fat), 34mg chol., 622mg sod., 38g carb. (5g sugars, 4g fiber), 16g pro. **DIABETIC EXCHANGES** 2½ starch, 2 medium-fat meat.

**SPAGHETTI &
MEATBALL
SKILLET SUPPER**

SPAGHETTI & MEATBALL SKILLET SUPPER

I developed this one-skillet spaghetti and meatball dish to cut down a little on cooking time for busy nights. The beans, artichokes and tomatoes bump up the nutrition factor, while the lemon and parsley make it pop with brightness.
—*Roxanne Chan, Albany, CA*

TAKES: 30 min. • **MAKES:** 6 servings

 1 Tbsp. olive oil
12 oz. frozen fully cooked Italian turkey
     meatballs
 1 can (28 oz.) whole tomatoes,
     undrained, broken up
 1 can (15 oz.) cannellini beans, rinsed
     and drained
 1 can (14 oz.) water-packed quartered
     artichoke hearts, drained
½ tsp. Italian seasoning
 1 can (14½ oz.) reduced-sodium
     chicken broth
 4 oz. uncooked spaghetti, broken into
     2-in. pieces (about 1⅓ cups)
¼ cup chopped fresh parsley
 1 Tbsp. lemon juice
     Grated Parmesan cheese

1. In a large skillet, heat the oil over medium heat; add the meatballs and cook until browned slightly, turning occasionally.
2. Add the tomatoes, beans, artichoke hearts, Italian seasoning and broth; bring to a boil. Stir in spaghetti; return to a boil. Reduce heat; simmer, covered, until spaghetti is tender, 10-12 minutes, stirring occasionally.
3. Stir in the parsley and lemon juice. Serve with cheese.
1⅓ CUPS 330 cal., 10g fat (2g sat. fat), 43mg chol., 1051mg sod., 38g carb. (5g sugars, 6g fiber), 20g pro.

ONE-POT SAUSAGE & BASIL PASTA

GOES GREAT WITH ...
Old-Fashioned Banana Cream Pie (p. 308) takes 10 minutes and makes a great dessert.

ONE-POT SAUSAGE & BASIL PASTA

There's nothing better than coming home and putting dinner on the table quickly. Add different kinds of sausage or seasonings to make it your own.
—*Erin Raatjes, New Lenox, IL*

TAKES: 30 min. • **MAKES:** 8 servings

- 1 pkg. (16 oz.) spaghetti
- 1 pkg. (13 to 14 oz.) smoked turkey sausage, thinly sliced
- 3 cups grape tomatoes, halved
- 2 cups fresh basil leaves, loosely packed
- 1 large onion, thinly sliced
- 4 garlic cloves, thinly sliced
- 4½ cups water
- 1 cup grated Parmesan cheese
- ¾ tsp. salt
- ½ tsp. pepper
- ¾ tsp. crushed red pepper flakes, optional

In a Dutch oven, combine the first 7 ingredients. Bring to a boil; reduce heat and simmer, uncovered, until pasta is al dente, 8-10 minutes, stirring occasionally. Add the Parmesan, salt and pepper; stir until cheese is melted. If desired, mix in crushed red pepper flakes and top with additional Parmesan cheese.

1 CUP 332 cal., 6g fat (3g sat. fat), 37mg chol., 862mg sod., 49g carb. (5g sugars, 3g fiber), 19g pro.

TEST KITCHEN TIP
Don't have turkey sausage on hand? Save time and money by stirring in leftover cooked chicken or ham instead.

SPICY CHICKEN & BACON MAC

SPICY CHICKEN & BACON MAC

I've been working to perfect a creamy, spicy mac and cheese for years. After adding smoky bacon, chicken, jalapenos and spicy cheese, this is ultimate! I use rotisserie chicken and precooked bacon when I'm pressed for time.
—*Sarah Gilbert, Beaverton, OR*

TAKES: 30 min. • **MAKES:** 6 servings

- 1½ cups uncooked cavatappi pasta or elbow macaroni
- 3 Tbsp. butter
- 3 Tbsp. all-purpose flour
- 1½ cups heavy whipping cream
- ½ cup 2% milk
- 1 tsp. Cajun seasoning
- ¼ tsp. salt
- ¼ tsp. pepper
- 2 cups shredded pepper jack cheese
- 2 cups shredded cooked chicken
- 6 bacon strips, cooked and crumbled
- 1 jalapeno pepper, seeded and chopped
- 1 cup crushed kettle-cooked potato chips or panko bread crumbs

1. Cook pasta according to package directions for al dente; drain. Preheat broiler.

2. In a 10-in. cast-iron or other ovenproof skillet, heat butter over medium heat. Stir in flour until blended; cook and stir until lightly browned, 1-2 minutes (do not burn). Gradually whisk in cream, milk, Cajun seasoning, salt and pepper. Bring to a boil, stirring constantly. Reduce heat; cook and stir until thickened, about 5 minutes. Stir in cheese until melted. Add pasta, chicken, bacon and jalapeno; cook and stir until heated through. Sprinkle chips over top.

3. Broil 3-4 in. from heat until chips are browned, about 30 seconds.

1 CUP 673 cal., 50g fat (28g sat. fat), 175mg chol., 705mg sod., 26g carb. (3g sugars, 1g fiber), 32g pro.

ITALIAN SAUSAGE LASAGNA ROLLS

It's the same wonderful flavor of lasagna but in a fun and interesting shape. I often make a pan of these and pop them in the freezer for future dinners.
—Hollie Lervold, Redding, CA

PREP: 30 min.
BAKE: 45 min. + standing
MAKES: 10 servings

- 1 Tbsp. olive oil
- 1 medium onion, finely chopped
- 2 garlic cloves, minced
- 1 can (28 oz.) crushed tomatoes, undrained
- 1 can (15 oz.) tomato sauce
- 1 can (6 oz.) tomato paste
- 1 tsp. each dried basil, marjoram, oregano, parsley flakes and thyme
- ½ tsp. pepper
- ¼ tsp. salt
- 1 can (2¼ oz.) sliced ripe olives, drained

- 10 uncooked lasagna noodles
- 1 pkg. (19 oz.) Italian sausage links
- 1 pkg. (6 oz.) fresh baby spinach
- 1 pkg. (8 oz.) cream cheese, softened
- 2 cups shredded part-skim mozzarella cheese

1. Preheat the oven to 350°. In a large saucepan, heat oil over medium heat. Add onion; cook and stir 4-6 minutes or until tender. Add garlic; cook 1 minute longer. Stir in tomatoes, tomato sauce, tomato paste and seasonings; bring to a boil. Reduce heat; simmer, uncovered, 40 minutes. Stir in olives.
2. Meanwhile, cook lasagna noodles according to package directions for al dente. Cook the sausages in a large skillet according to package directions; drain. Remove sausages and cut in half widthwise. In the same skillet, cook and stir spinach over medium-high heat for 2-3 minutes or until wilted; drain spinach and squeeze dry.

3. In a small bowl, combine cream cheese and spinach. Spread 3 cups sauce mixture into a 13x9-in. baking dish. Spread 2 Tbsp. cream cheese mixture on each noodle. Place a sausage half on a short end; carefully roll up. Cut in half widthwise; place ruffle side up in sauce mixture. Repeat with remaining noodles, cream cheese mixture and sausages.
4. Pour 1½ cups sauce mixture over rolls; sprinkle with mozzarella cheese. Bake, covered, 40 minutes. Bake, uncovered, 5-10 minutes longer or until the cheese is melted. Serve with remaining sauce mixture.

2 LASAGNA ROLL-UPS 504 cal., 32g fat (14g sat. fat), 78mg chol., 1090mg sod., 35g carb. (9g sugars, 4g fiber), 22g pro.

HAM & PEA PASTA ALFREDO

When I want a filling meal that even the kids enjoy, I simply toss ham and sugar snap peas with Romano cream sauce and pasta.
—C.R. Monachino, Kenmore, NY

TAKES: 25 min. • **MAKES:** 8 servings

- 1 pkg. (16 oz.) fettuccine
- 2 Tbsp. butter
- 1½ lbs. sliced fully cooked ham, cut into strips (about 5 cups)
- 2 cups fresh sugar snap peas
- 2 cups heavy whipping cream
- ½ cup grated Romano cheese
- ¼ tsp. pepper

1. Cook fettuccine according to package directions. Meanwhile, in a large skillet, heat butter over medium heat. Add ham and peas; cook and stir 5 minutes. Stir in cream, cheese and pepper; bring to a boil. Reduce heat; simmer, uncovered, 1-2 minutes or until sauce is slightly thickened and peas are crisp-tender.
2. Drain fettuccine; add to skillet and toss to coat. Serve immediately.

1¼ CUPS 582 cal., 32g fat (18g sat. fat), 151mg chol., 1032mg sod., 45g carb. (6g sugars, 3g fiber), 33g pro.

ITALIAN SAUSAGE LASAGNA ROLLS

**FIVE-CHEESE
ZITI AL FORNO**

**GOES GREAT
WITH ...**
Quick Garlic Toast
(p. 299) is a fast
fix for rounding
out this meal.

FIVE-CHEESE ZITI AL FORNO

After having the five-cheese ziti at
Olive Garden, I tried to make my own
homemade version—and I think I got
pretty close. I always double this and
freeze the second one for another meal.
—*Keri Whitney, Castro Valley, CA*

PREP: 20 min. • **BAKE:** 30 min. + standing
MAKES: 12 servings

- 1½ lbs. (about 7½ cups) uncooked ziti or
  small tube pasta
- 2 jars (24 oz. each) marinara sauce
- 1 jar (15 oz.) Alfredo sauce
- 2 cups shredded part-skim
  mozzarella cheese, divided
- ½ cup reduced-fat ricotta cheese
- ½ cup shredded provolone cheese
- ½ cup grated Romano cheese

TOPPING

- ½ cup grated Parmesan cheese
- ½ cup panko bread crumbs
- 3 garlic cloves, minced
- 2 Tbsp. olive oil
  Optional: Minced fresh parsley or
  basil

1. Preheat oven to 350°. Cook the pasta
according to the package directions for
al dente; drain.
2. Meanwhile, in a large Dutch oven,
combine the marinara sauce, Alfredo
sauce, 1 cup mozzarella and the ricotta,
provolone and Romano. Cook over
medium heat until the sauce begins
to simmer and cheeses are melted.
Stir in cooked pasta; pour mixture into
a greased 13x9-in. baking dish. Top with
remaining 1 cup mozzarella cheese.
3. In a small bowl, stir together the
Parmesan, bread crumbs, garlic and oil;
sprinkle over the pasta.
4. Bake, uncovered, until mixture is
bubbly and topping is golden brown,
30-40 minutes. Let stand 10 minutes
before serving. Garnish with fresh
parsley or basil if desired.

1 CUP 449 cal., 15g fat (8g sat. fat), 32mg
chol., 960mg sod., 59g carb. (11g sugars,
4g fiber), 21g pro.

VEGETABLE GNOCCHI

When we go meatless, we toss gnocchi (my husband's favorite) with vegetables and a dab of prepared pesto. I also use zucchini in this 30-minute dish.
—*Elisabeth Larsen, Pleasant Grove, UT*

TAKES: 30 min. • **MAKES:** 4 servings

2   medium yellow summer squash, sliced
1   medium sweet red pepper, chopped
8   oz. sliced fresh mushrooms
1   Tbsp. olive oil
¼   tsp. salt
¼   tsp. pepper
1   pkg. (16 oz.) potato gnocchi
½   cup Alfredo sauce
¼   cup prepared pesto
    Chopped fresh basil, optional

1. Preheat oven to 450°. In a greased 15x10x1-in. baking pan, toss vegetables with oil, salt and pepper. Roast 18-22 minutes or until tender, stirring once.
2. Meanwhile, in a large saucepan, cook gnocchi according to package directions. Drain and return to pan.
3. Stir in roasted vegetables, Alfredo sauce and pesto. If desired, sprinkle with basil.

1½ CUPS 402 cal., 14g fat (4g sat. fat), 17mg chol., 955mg sod., 57g carb. (12g sugars, 5g fiber), 13g pro.

VEGETABLE GNOCCHI

HAM & SWISS BAKED PENNE

As a kid I loved the hot ham and Swiss sandwiches from a local fast-food restaurant. With its melty, gooey goodness, this hot dish makes me think of them.
—Ally Billhorn, Wilton, IA

TAKES: 30 min. • **MAKES:** 6 servings

2⅓ cups uncooked penne pasta
3 Tbsp. butter
3 Tbsp. all-purpose flour
2 cups 2% milk
1 cup half-and-half cream
1½ cups shredded Swiss cheese
½ cup shredded Colby cheese
2 cups cubed fully cooked ham
TOPPING
¼ cup seasoned bread crumbs
¼ cup grated Parmesan cheese
2 Tbsp. butter, melted

1. Preheat oven to 375°. Cook pasta according to package directions for al dente; drain.
2. Meanwhile, in a large saucepan, melt butter over medium heat. Stir in flour until smooth; gradually whisk in milk and cream. Bring to a boil, stirring constantly; cook and stir until thickened, 1-2 minutes. Gradually stir in Swiss and Colby cheeses until melted. Add ham and pasta; toss to coat.
3. Transfer to a greased 11x7-in. baking dish. In a small bowl, mix topping ingredients; sprinkle over pasta. Bake, uncovered, until bubbly, 15-20 minutes.
1 CUP 559 cal., 30g fat (18g sat. fat), 116mg chol., 905mg sod., 41g carb. (7g sugars, 2g fiber), 31g pro.

WHITE CHEDDAR MAC & CHEESE

My mac and cheese is simple and has lots of flavor from the cheeses and ground chipotle chiles. I use conchiglie pasta because its large openings allow more melted cheese to pool inside. Yum!
—Colleen Delawder, Herndon, VA

TAKES: 25 min. • **MAKES:** 8 servings

1 pkg. (16 oz.) small pasta shells
½ cup butter, cubed
½ cup all-purpose flour
½ tsp. onion powder
½ tsp. ground chipotle pepper
½ tsp. pepper
¼ tsp. salt
4 cups 2% milk
2 cups shredded sharp white cheddar cheese
2 cups shredded Manchego or additional white cheddar cheese

1. In a 6-qt. stockpot, cook the pasta according to package directions. Drain; return to pot.
2. Meanwhile, in a large saucepan, melt butter over medium heat. Stir in the flour and seasonings until smooth; gradually whisk in the milk. Bring to a boil, stirring constantly; cook and stir until thickened, 6-8 minutes. Remove from heat; stir in cheeses until melted. Add to pasta; toss to coat.
1 CUP 650 cal., 35g fat (22g sat. fat), 101mg chol., 607mg sod., 55g carb. (8g sugars, 2g fiber), 27g pro.

EASY ASIAN BEEF & NOODLES

EASY ASIAN BEEF & NOODLES

I created this dish on a whim to feed my hungry teenagers. It's since become a dinnertime staple, and now two of my grandchildren make it in their own kitchens.
—*Judy Batson, Tampa, FL*

TAKES: 25 min. • **MAKES:** 4 servings

1   beef top sirloin steak (1 lb.), cut into ¼-in.-thick strips
6   Tbsp. reduced-sodium teriyaki sauce, divided
8   oz. uncooked whole grain thin spaghetti
2   Tbsp. canola oil, divided
3   cups broccoli coleslaw mix
1   medium onion, halved and thinly sliced
    Chopped fresh cilantro, optional

1. Toss beef with 2 Tbsp. teriyaki sauce. Cook spaghetti according to package directions; drain.
2. In a large skillet, heat 1 Tbsp. oil over medium-high heat; stir-fry the beef until browned, 1-3 minutes. Remove from pan.
3. In same skillet, heat remaining oil over medium-high heat; stir-fry coleslaw mix and onion until crisp-tender, 3-5 minutes. Add spaghetti and remaining teriyaki sauce; toss and heat through. Stir in beef. If desired, sprinkle with cilantro.
2 CUPS 462 cal., 13g fat (2g sat. fat), 46mg chol., 546mg sod., 52g carb. (9g sugars, 8g fiber), 35g pro.

SAUSAGE & ASPARAGUS PASTA WITH CAJUN CREAM SAUCE

I needed to use up some ingredients in my refrigerator, so I threw together this dish. It's delicious and everyone loves it. I only use Tony Chachere's Creole seasoning mix.
—*Angela Lively, Conroe, TX*

TAKES: 25 min. • **MAKES:** 8 servings

1   pkg. (16 oz.) spiral pasta
1   lb. fresh asparagus, trimmed and cut into 2-in. pieces
1   pkg. (14 oz.) smoked sausage, sliced
2   garlic cloves, minced
1   cup heavy whipping cream
½   cup shredded Parmesan cheese
1   Tbsp. Creole seasoning
¼   tsp. pepper

1. In a Dutch oven, cook pasta according to package directions, adding asparagus during the last 4 minutes of cooking. Meanwhile, in a large nonstick skillet, cook sausage over medium heat until browned. Add the garlic; cook 1 minute longer. Stir in cream, Parmesan cheese, Creole seasoning and pepper; cook and stir until slightly thickened, about 3 minutes.
2. Drain pasta mixture, reserving ½ cup cooking water; add to sausage mixture. Toss to coat, gradually adding enough reserved cooking water to reach desired consistency.
1¼ CUPS 496 cal., 26g fat (14g sat. fat), 71mg chol., 909mg sod., 46g carb. (4g sugars, 2g fiber), 18g pro.

TEST KITCHEN TIP
Beat the clock by replacing the cream and Parmesan with jarred Alfredo sauce.

GOES GREAT WITH ...
Toss some frozen mozzarella sticks into the air fryer for a fun side.

SAUSAGE & ASPARAGUS PASTA WITH CAJUN CREAM SAUCE

LEMONY SHRIMP & ARUGULA ORZO

What I love about this recipe is that it's so tasty and it can be eaten hot or cold. If you're allergic to shrimp, it also tastes fantastic with chicken.
—*Aleni Salcedo, East Elmhurst, NY*

TAKES: 30 min. • **MAKES:** 8 servings

- 2 Tbsp. olive oil
- 1 small onion, chopped
- 2 garlic cloves, minced
- 3½ cups reduced-sodium chicken broth
- 1 lb. uncooked whole wheat orzo pasta
- 1 cup water
- 1 lb. uncooked shrimp (31-40 per lb.), peeled and deveined
- 4 cups fresh arugula
- 3 Tbsp. lemon juice
- ½ tsp. salt
- ¼ tsp. pepper
- ½ cup Greek olives, halved
- 1½ cups crumbled feta cheese
  Fresh basil leaves

1. In a large skillet, heat oil over medium-high heat. Add onion; cook and stir until crisp-tender, 3-4 minutes. Add garlic; cook 1 minute longer. Stir in broth, orzo and water. Bring to a boil; reduce heat. Simmer, uncovered, until orzo is al dente, 8-10 minutes.
2. Stir in shrimp, arugula, lemon juice, salt and pepper. Cook and stir until the shrimp turn pink, 4-5 minutes. Stir in olives. Sprinkle with feta and fresh basil.

1 CUP 367 cal., 11g fat (3g sat. fat), 80mg chol., 808mg sod., 44g carb. (1g sugars, 10g fiber), 22g pro.

LEMONY SHRIMP & ARUGULA ORZO

GINGER VEGGIE BROWN RICE PASTA

Once I discovered brown rice pasta, I never looked back. Tossed with ginger, bright veggies and rotisserie chicken, it tastes like a deconstructed egg roll!
—*Tiffany Ihle, Bronx, NY*

TAKES: 30 min. • **MAKES:** 8 servings

- 2 cups uncooked brown rice elbow pasta
- 1 Tbsp. coconut oil
- ½ small red onion, sliced
- 2 tsp. ginger paste
- 2 tsp. garlic paste
- 1½ cups chopped fresh Brussels sprouts
- ½ cup chopped red cabbage
- ½ cup shredded carrots
- ½ medium sweet red pepper, chopped
- ½ tsp. salt
- ¼ tsp. ground ancho chile pepper
- ¼ tsp. coarsely ground pepper
- 1 rotisserie chicken, skin removed, shredded
- 2 green onions, chopped

1. In a Dutch oven, cook pasta according to package directions.
2. Meanwhile, in a large skillet, heat coconut oil over medium heat. Add red onion, ginger paste and garlic paste; saute for 2 minutes. Stir in the next 7 ingredients; cook until vegetables are crisp-tender, 4-6 minutes. Add chicken; heat through.
3. Drain pasta, reserving 1 cup pasta water. Return pasta to Dutch oven. Add vegetable mixture; toss to coat, adding enough reserved pasta water to moisten pasta. Sprinkle with green onion before serving.

1 CUP 270 cal., 7g fat (3g sat. fat), 55mg chol., 257mg sod., 29g carb. (2g sugars, 2g fiber), 21g pro. **DIABETIC EXCHANGES** 3 lean meat, 2 starch, 1 fat.

GARLIC CHICKEN RIGATONI

My family loves the scampi-inspired combination of garlic and olive oil in this delicious pasta. I love that it's guilt free!
—*Judy Crawford, Deming, NM*

TAKES: 30 min. • **MAKES:** 4 servings

- 8 oz. uncooked rigatoni or large tube pasta
- ¼ cup sun-dried tomatoes (not packed in oil)
- ½ cup boiling water
- ½ lb. boneless skinless chicken breasts, cut into 1-in. cubes
- ¼ tsp. garlic salt
- 2 Tbsp. all-purpose flour
- 2 Tbsp. olive oil, divided
- 1½ cups sliced fresh mushrooms
- 3 garlic cloves, minced
- ¼ cup reduced-sodium chicken broth
- ¼ cup white wine or additional reduced-sodium chicken broth
- 2 Tbsp. minced fresh parsley
- ¼ tsp. dried basil
- ⅛ tsp. salt
- ⅛ tsp. pepper
- ⅛ tsp. crushed red pepper flakes
- ¼ cup grated Parmesan cheese

1. Cook rigatoni according to package directions. In a small bowl, combine tomatoes and boiling water; let stand 5 minutes. Drain; chop tomatoes.
2. Sprinkle chicken with garlic salt; add flour and toss to coat. In a large skillet, heat 1 Tbsp. oil over medium-high heat. Add chicken; cook and stir 4-5 minutes or until no longer pink. Remove from the pan.
3. In same skillet, heat the remaining oil over medium-high heat. Add mushrooms and garlic; cook and stir until tender. Add the broth, wine, parsley, seasonings and chopped tomatoes; bring to a boil. Stir in chicken; heat through.
4. Drain rigatoni; add to chicken mixture. Sprinkle with cheese and toss to coat.

1½ CUPS 398 cal., 11g fat (2g sat. fat), 36mg chol., 290mg sod., 50g carb. (5g sugars, 3g fiber), 23g pro.

CHAPTER 13

BOWLS & ENTREE SALADS

P. 282

P. 292

P. 278

P. 290

GOES GREAT WITH ...
Keep the bread in the cabinet and serve flour tortillas with this meal instead.

ONE-DISH TURKEY DINNER

ONE-DISH TURKEY DINNER

This quick one-dish dinner helped keep my husband and me on track throughout the week while we were still learning to balance our busy schedules.
—Shannon Barden, Alpharetta, GA

TAKES: 30 min. • **MAKES:** 4 servings

- 1 lb. ground turkey
- 1 medium onion, chopped
- 1 shallot, finely chopped
- 3 garlic cloves, minced
- ¼ cup tomato paste
- 1 medium sweet potato, peeled and cubed
- 1 cup chicken broth
- 2 tsp. smoked paprika
- ½ tsp. salt
- ¼ tsp. pepper
- 3 cups chopped fresh ~~kale~~ *spinach*
  Dash crushed red pepper flakes
- 1 medium ripe avocado, peeled and sliced
  Minced fresh mint, optional

1. In a large skillet, cook turkey, onion, shallot and garlic over medium heat until turkey is no longer pink and vegetables are tender, 8-10 minutes, breaking up the turkey into crumbles; drain. Add tomato paste; cook and stir 1 minute longer.
2. Add the sweet potato, broth, smoked paprika, salt and pepper. Bring to a boil; reduce heat. Simmer, covered, until the sweet potato is tender, about 10 minutes, stirring occasionally. Add kale and red pepper flakes; cook and stir until ~~kale~~ *S* is wilted, about 2 minutes. Serve with avocado, and mint if desired.
FREEZE OPTION Once cool, freeze in freezer containers. To use, partially thaw in refrigerator overnight. Heat through in a saucepan, stirring occasionally; add broth or water if necessary. Serve with avocado, and mint if desired.
1⅓ CUPS 318 cal., 14g fat (3g sat. fat), 76mg chol., 628mg sod., 24g carb. (8g sugars, 5g fiber), 26g pro. **DIABETIC EXCHANGES** 3 lean meat, 2 fat, 1½ starch.

CARIBBEAN SHRIMP & RICE BOWL

CARIBBEAN SHRIMP & RICE BOWL

I had a similar rice bowl on vacation and re-created this lighter version at home. It takes me back to the islands every time I make it. Try grilling the shrimp for more beachy flavor.
—Lauren Katz, Ashburn, VA

TAKES: 20 min. • **MAKES:** 4 servings

- 1 medium ripe avocado, peeled and pitted
- ⅓ cup reduced-fat sour cream
- ¼ tsp. salt
- 1 can (15 oz.) black beans, rinsed and drained
- 1 can (8 oz.) unsweetened crushed pineapple, undrained
- 1 medium mango, peeled and cubed
- ½ cup salsa
- 1 pkg. (8.8 oz.) ready-to-serve brown rice
- 1 lb. uncooked shrimp (31-40 per lb.), peeled and deveined
- 1 tsp. Caribbean jerk seasoning
- 1 Tbsp. canola oil
- 2 green onions, sliced
  Lime wedges, optional

1. For avocado cream, mash avocado with sour cream and salt until smooth. In a small saucepan, combine beans, pineapple, mango and salsa; heat through, stirring occasionally. Prepare rice according to package directions.
2. Toss the shrimp with jerk seasoning. In a large skillet, heat oil over medium-high heat. Add shrimp; cook and stir until shrimp turn pink, 2-3 minutes.
3. Divide rice and bean mixture among 4 bowls. Top with shrimp and green onions. Serve with avocado cream, and lime wedges if desired.
1 SERVING 498 cal., 14g fat (2g sat. fat), 145mg chol., 698mg sod., 62g carb. (23g sugars, 9g fiber), 29g pro.

TEQUILA-LIME STEAK SALAD ✓

This recipe is one of my family's Fourth of July favorites. The adults can make margaritas from the rest of the tequila!
—*Laura Wilhelm, West Hollywood, CA*

PREP: 15 min. + marinating
GRILL: 10 min. • **MAKES:** 6 servings

- ¾ cup plus 1 Tbsp. lime juice, divided
- ¾ cup blanco tequila
- 2 Tbsp. garlic powder
- 1 Tbsp. ground cumin
- 1 Tbsp. Montreal steak seasoning
- 1 Tbsp. dried oregano
- ½ tsp. pepper
- ⅛ tsp. crushed red pepper flakes
- 2 lbs. beef flank steak
- 1 pkg. (9 to 10 oz.) hearts of romaine salad mix
- 3 Tbsp. olive oil
- 1 pint rainbow cherry tomatoes, halved
  Optional: Cotija cheese and lime wedges

1. In a large bowl, whisk together ¾ cup lime juice, tequila, garlic powder, cumin, steak seasoning, oregano, pepper and red pepper flakes. Place the steak in a shallow dish; add tequila mixture and turn to coat. Refrigerate, covered, 8 hours or overnight, turning once.
2. Drain beef, discarding marinade; pat dry. Grill, covered, over direct medium-high heat, turning once, until desired doneness (for medium-rare, a thermometer should read 135°; medium, 140°; medium-well, 145°), 10-15 minutes. Place beef on cutting board; cover and let rest 5-10 minutes. Thinly slice steak across the grain.
3. Place salad mix on serving platter; drizzle with olive oil and the remaining 1 Tbsp. lime juice. Place steak over romaine; top with tomatoes and, if desired, Cotija cheese and lime wedges.
4 OZ. COOKED STEAK WITH 1½ CUPS SALAD 257 cal., 11g fat (5g sat. fat), 72mg chol., 243mg sod., 8g carb. (2g sugars, 2g fiber), 31g pro. **DIABETIC EXCHANGES** 4 lean meat, 1½ fat, 1 vegetable.

TEST KITCHEN TIP
Remember this tequila marinade the next time you want to jazz up pork too.

TEQUILA-LIME
STEAK SALAD

POMEGRANATE, CHICKEN & FARRO SALAD

This salad recipe is special—simple, yet sophisticated—and never fails to win rave reviews. I use quick-cooking farro, which takes only 10 minutes on the stovetop. Many stores now carry packaged pomegranate seeds in the refrigerated section year-round.
—*David Dahlman, Chatsworth, CA*

PREP: 15 min. • **COOK:** 25 min. + cooling
MAKES: 8 servings

1½ cups uncooked farro, rinsed, or wheat berries
2 medium ripe avocados, peeled, pitted and chopped
3 cups shredded rotisserie chicken
¾ cup chopped dried apricots
½ cup thinly sliced green onions
½ cup chopped walnuts, toasted
1 Tbsp. chopped seeded jalapeno pepper, optional
¾ cup pomegranate seeds
⅓ cup olive oil
¼ cup orange juice
3 Tbsp. white wine vinegar
1 Tbsp. Dijon mustard
½ tsp. salt
½ tsp. pepper

1. Place farro in a large saucepan; add water to cover. Bring to a boil. Reduce heat; cook, covered, until tender, 25-30 minutes. Drain and cool.
2. Arrange the farro, avocados, chicken, apricots, green onions, walnuts, and jalapeno if desired, on a platter. Sprinkle with pomegranate seeds. For dressing, in a small bowl, whisk the remaining ingredients until blended. Serve the dressing with salad.
1 SERVING 482 cal., 24g fat (3g sat. fat), 47mg chol., 251mg sod., 44g carb. (9g sugars, 9g fiber), 23g pro.

POMEGRANATE, CHICKEN & FARRO SALAD

ASIAN NOODLE & BEEF SALAD

My Asian-inspired pasta salad is crunchy, tangy and light. If you have fresh herbs like basil or cilantro on hand, add them to the mix.
—*Kelsey Casselbury, Odenton, MD*

TAKES: 30 min. • **MAKES:** 4 servings

- ¼ cup reduced-sodium soy sauce
- ¼ cup lime juice
- 2 Tbsp. sugar
- 2 Tbsp. rice vinegar
- 1 Tbsp. grated fresh gingerroot
- 1 Tbsp. sesame oil
- 1 beef top sirloin steak (1 lb.)
- ¼ tsp. pepper
- 6 oz. thin rice noodles
- 1 cup julienned zucchini
- 2 medium carrots, thinly sliced
- 1 celery rib, sliced

1. For dressing, mix first 6 ingredients. Sprinkle the steak with pepper. Grill, covered, over medium heat until meat reaches desired doneness (for medium-rare, a thermometer should read 135°; medium, 140°), 6-8 minutes per side. Let stand 5 minutes before slicing.
2. Meanwhile, prepare the rice noodles according to package directions. Drain; rinse with cold water and drain again. In a large bowl, combine the noodles, vegetables and steak; toss with dressing.
1½ CUPS 399 cal., 8g fat (2g sat. fat), 46mg chol., 855mg sod., 50g carb. (11g sugars, 2g fiber), 29g pro.

CHICKEN RICE BOWL ✓

This is so easy to toss together on a busy weeknight, and I usually have the ingredients on hand. I start sauteing the onion and pepper first, then I prepare the instant rice. If you like, top it with shredded sharp cheddar cheese.
—*Tammy Daniels, Batavia, OH*

TAKES: 10 min. • **MAKES:** 4 servings

- 1 cup uncooked instant rice
- 1 cup chicken broth
- ½ cup chopped frozen green pepper, thawed
- ¼ cup chopped onion
- 2 tsp. olive oil
- 1 pkg. (9 oz.) ready-to-use grilled chicken breast strips
- ½ cup frozen corn, thawed
- ½ cup frozen ~~peas~~, thawed   *green bean*
- 1 tsp. dried basil
- 1 tsp. rubbed sage
- ⅛ tsp. salt
- ⅛ tsp. pepper

Cook rice in broth according to package directions. Meanwhile, in a large skillet, saute the green pepper and onion in oil for 2-3 minutes or until crisp-tender. Stir in the chicken, corn, peas, basil and sage. Cook, uncovered, for 4-5 minutes over medium heat or until heated through. Stir in the rice, salt and pepper.
1 CUP 239 cal., 5g fat (1g sat. fat), 42mg chol., 914mg sod., 30g carb. (3g sugars, 2g fiber), 19g pro.

TEST KITCHEN TIP
You can add fresh vegetables to the rice bowl if you prefer. We recommend using broccoli, bell peppers or avocado but feel free to experiment with whatever you have on hand.

LOW-CARB SHRIMP SUSHI BOWL

Sushi is one of our family's favorite treats. This easy-to-prepare version is ready in 30 minutes or less. It's low carb and packed with veggies. With all the flavor, no one misses the carbs. If you don't like shrimp, use cooked shredded chicken or firm tofu instead. If you prefer your food extra spicy, change the ratio of red curry paste to mayonnaise.
—*Kristyne Mcdougle Walter, Lorain, OH*

TAKES: 30 min. • **MAKES:** 4 servings

- 5 Tbsp. mayonnaise
- 2 tsp. red curry paste
- 2 pkg. frozen riced cauliflower (10 oz. each)
- 3 Tbsp. sesame oil
- 1½ lbs. uncooked shrimp (31-40 per lb.), peeled and deveined
- 2 garlic cloves, minced
- 1 tsp. seasoned salt
- 1 medium ripe avocado, peeled and sliced
- ½ medium cucumber, sliced
- ½ cup julienned carrots
- 2 green onions, thinly sliced
- 1 medium lime, quartered

1. In a small bowl, mix mayonnaise and red curry paste.
2. Prepare riced cauliflower according to package directions.
3. Meanwhile, in a large skillet, heat the oil over medium heat. Add the shrimp; cook until shrimp turn pink, 5-7 minutes. Add garlic and salt; cook 1 minute longer. Remove from heat.
4. Divide cauliflower among 4 bowls. Top each bowl with shrimp, avocado, cucumber, carrot and green onion. Drizzle with curry mayonnaise and garnish each bowl with a lime quarter.
1 BOWL 460 cal., 31g fat (5g sat. fat), 213mg chol., 783mg sod., 16g carb. (5g sugars, 7g fiber), 32g pro.

LOW-CARB SHRIMP SUSHI BOWL

CURRY POMEGRANATE PROTEIN BOWL

CURRY POMEGRANATE PROTEIN BOWL

This simple and beautiful recipe blends together a lot of unique flavors to create a taste sensation that is out of this world. You can substitute other roasted, salted nuts for the soy nuts.
—*Mary Baker, Wauwatosa, WI*

PREP: 25 min. • **COOK:** 25 min.
MAKES: 6 servings

3   cups cubed peeled butternut squash (½-in. cubes)
2   Tbsp. olive oil, divided
½   tsp. salt, divided
¼   tsp. pepper
½   small onion, chopped
1   Tbsp. curry powder
1   Tbsp. ground cumin
1   garlic clove, minced
1   tsp. ground coriander
3   cups water
1   cup dried red lentils, rinsed
½   cup salted soy nuts
½   cup dried cranberries
⅓   cup thinly sliced green onions
⅓   cup pomegranate molasses
½   cup crumbled feta cheese
½   cup pomegranate seeds
¼   cup chopped fresh cilantro

1. Preheat oven to 375°. Place squash on a greased 15x10x1-in. baking pan. Drizzle with 1 Tbsp. oil; sprinkle with ¼ tsp. salt and pepper. Roast for 25-30 minutes or until tender, turning once.
2. Meanwhile, in a skillet, heat remaining 1 Tbsp. oil over medium-high heat. Add onion; cook and stir until crisp-tender, 4-6 minutes. Add curry powder, cumin, garlic, coriander and remaining ¼ tsp. salt; cook 1 minute longer. Add water and lentils; bring to a boil. Reduce heat; simmer, covered, until lentils are tender and water is absorbed, about 15 minutes.
3. Gently stir in soy nuts, cranberries, green onion and the roasted squash. Divide among serving bowls. Drizzle with the molasses and top with feta, pomegranate seeds and cilantro.
¾ CUP 367 cal., 9g fat (2g sat. fat), 5mg chol., 327mg sod., 60g carb. (23g sugars, 9g fiber), 14g pro.

CALIFORNIA BURGER BOWLS

Burgers are a weekly staple at our house all year round. Skip the fries, chips and bun—you won't need them with these loaded bowls. To spice up the mayo, stir in a little chipotle powder.
—*Courtney Stultz, Weir, KS*

TAKES: 25 min. • **MAKES:** 4 servings

3   Tbsp. fat-free milk
2   Tbsp. quick-cooking oats
¾   tsp. salt
½   tsp. ground cumin
½   tsp. chili powder
½   tsp. pepper
1   lb. lean ground turkey
4   cups baby ~~kale~~ *spinach* salad blend
1½ cups cubed fresh pineapple (½ in.)
1   medium mango, peeled and thinly sliced
1   medium ripe avocado, peeled and thinly sliced
1   medium sweet red pepper, cut into strips
4   tomatillos, husks removed, thinly sliced
¼   cup reduced-fat chipotle mayonnaise

1. In a large bowl, mix milk, oats and seasonings. Add turkey; mix lightly but thoroughly. Shape into four ½-in.-thick patties.
2. Place burgers on an oiled grill rack over medium heat. Grill, covered, until a thermometer reads 165°, 4-5 minutes per side. Serve over salad blend, along with remaining ingredients.
1 SERVING 390 cal., 19g fat (4g sat. fat), 83mg chol., 666mg sod., 33g carb. (22g sugars, 7g fiber), 26g pro. **DIABETIC EXCHANGES** 3 lean meat, 2½ fat, 2 vegetable, 1 fruit.

CALIFORNIA
BURGER BOWLS

**GOES GREAT
WITH ...**
Tall glasses of
lemonade are
lovely alongside
these bowls.

GREEK BROWN & WILD RICE BOWLS

This fresh rice dish tastes like the Mediterranean in a bowl! It is short on ingredients but packs in so much flavor. For a hand-held version, leave out the rice and tuck the rest of the ingredients in a pita pocket.
—*Darla Andrews, Boerne, TX*

TAKES: 15 min. • **MAKES:** 2 servings

- 1 pkg. (8½ oz.) ready-to-serve whole grain brown and wild rice medley
- ¼ cup Greek vinaigrette, divided
- ½ medium ripe avocado, peeled and sliced
- ¾ cup cherry tomatoes, halved
- ¼ cup crumbled feta cheese
- ¼ cup pitted Greek olives, sliced
  Minced fresh parsley, optional

In a microwave-safe bowl, combine the rice mix and 2 Tbsp. vinaigrette. Cover and cook on high until heated through, about 2 minutes. Divide between 2 bowls. Top with avocado, tomatoes, cheese, olives, remaining dressing and, if desired, parsley.

1 SERVING 433 cal., 25g fat (4g sat. fat), 8mg chol., 1355mg sod., 44g carb. (3g sugars, 6g fiber), 8g pro.

TEST KITCHEN TIP

These otherwise healthy bowls are a bit high in sodium because of the prepared rice, salad dressing, feta cheese and Greek olives. Save on sodium by cooking rice from scratch and using a simple oil and vinegar dressing.

GREEK BROWN & WILD RICE BOWLS

SPINACH SALAD WITH TORTELLINI & ROASTED ONIONS

EASY CITRUS SEAFOOD SALAD

This super simple, deceptively delicious recipe was inspired by a seafood salad I had in the Bahamas that featured conch. I substituted crab and shrimp for the conch and like it even more!
—*Cindy Heyd, Edmond, OK*

TAKES: 15 min. • **MAKES:** 4 servings

- 1 medium orange
- 1 medium lemon
- 1 medium lime
- ½ lb. peeled and deveined cooked shrimp, coarsely chopped
- ½ lb. refrigerated fresh or imitation crabmeat, coarsely chopped
- 2 Tbsp. finely chopped sweet onion
- 2 Tbsp. finely chopped sweet red pepper
  Shredded lettuce
  Assorted crackers

Finely grate zest from the orange. Cut orange crosswise in half; squeeze juice from orange. Transfer zest and juice to a large bowl. Repeat with lemon and lime. Add shrimp, crab, onion and pepper; toss to coat. Serve on lettuce with crackers.
¾ CUP 128 cal., 2g fat (0 sat. fat), 141mg chol., 309mg sod., 6g carb. (3g sugars, 1g fiber), 22g pro. **DIABETIC EXCHANGES** 3 lean meat.

SPINACH SALAD WITH TORTELLINI & ROASTED ONIONS

Spinach and tortellini go so well together and this salad makes an easy meal with leftover cooked chicken. What really makes this special is the roasted onions that add some pizzazz to bottled Italian salad dressing.
—*Robin Haas, Hyde Park, MA*

PREP: 20 min. • **BAKE:** 20 min.
MAKES: 6 servings

- 2 cups chopped sweet onion (about 1 large)
- 1 Tbsp. canola oil
- 1 pkg. (9 oz.) refrigerated cheese tortellini
- ½ to ⅔ cup Italian salad dressing
- 1 Tbsp. red wine vinegar
- 10 oz. fresh baby spinach (about 12 cups)
- 2 cups cubed cooked chicken breast (about 10 oz.)
- 1 can (12 oz.) marinated quartered artichoke hearts, drained
- 1 can (2¼ oz.) sliced ripe olives, drained
- ½ cup julienned roasted sweet red peppers
- ½ cup shaved Parmesan cheese

1. Preheat oven to 425°. Toss onion with oil; spread into a foil-lined 15x10x1-in. baking pan. Roast until softened and lightly browned, 20-25 minutes, stirring occasionally.
2. Cook tortellini according to package directions. Drain and rinse gently with cold water; drain well.
3. Place ½ cup salad dressing, vinegar and roasted onion in a blender. Cover; process until blended, thinning with additional dressing if desired.
4. To serve, place the spinach, chicken, artichoke hearts, olives, peppers and tortellini in a large bowl; toss with the onion mixture. Top with cheese.
2 CUPS 448 cal., 22g fat (6g sat. fat), 59mg chol., 887mg sod., 33g carb. (9g sugars, 3g fiber), 24g pro.

GRILLED SUMMER SAUSAGE SALAD

It's not often you see sausage in a salad, but I say why not? The grilled links and garden vegetables make for a garlicky, fresh-tasting, super-filling salad. I'll even grill the romaine on occasion!
—*Noelle Myers, Grand Forks, ND*

TAKES: 30 min. • **MAKES:** 8 servings

- 1 lb. garlic summer sausage, casing removed and quartered lengthwise
- 2 small zucchini, cut in half lengthwise
- 2 yellow summer squash, cut in half lengthwise
- 1 medium sweet red pepper, halved and seeded
- 1 medium sweet orange pepper, halved and seeded
- 2 Tbsp. olive oil
- ½ tsp. salt
- ¼ tsp. pepper
- 1 pkg. (5 oz.) spring mix salad greens
- ½ English cucumber, chopped
- 2 celery ribs with leaves, chopped
- ½ cup Italian salad dressing

1. Brush the summer sausage, zucchini, yellow squash and peppers with olive oil; sprinkle with the salt and pepper. Grill the sausage and vegetables on an oiled rack, covered, over medium heat until crisp-tender, 5-6 minutes on each side. Remove to cutting board; coarsely chop vegetables and sausage.

2. Place the salad greens in a large bowl; add cucumber, celery, grilled vegetables and sausage. Drizzle with dressing; toss to coat. Divide among 8 bowls. If desired, sprinkle with additional black pepper.

2 CUPS 260 cal., 21g fat (6g sat. fat), 35mg chol., 1048mg sod., 10g carb. (4g sugars, 2g fiber), 10g pro.

GRILLED SUMMER SAUSAGE SALAD

BARBECUE CHICKEN COBB SALAD

I turned barbecue chicken into a major salad with romaine, carrots, sweet peppers and avocados. That's how I got my family to eat more veggies.
—*Camille Beckstrand, Layton, UT*

PREP: 30 min. • **COOK:** 3 hours
MAKES: 6 servings

- 1 bottle (18 oz.) barbecue sauce
- 2 Tbsp. brown sugar
- ½ tsp. garlic powder
- ¼ tsp. paprika
- 1½ lbs. boneless skinless chicken breasts
- 12 cups chopped romaine
- 2 avocados, peeled and chopped
- 3 plum tomatoes, chopped
- 2 small carrots, thinly sliced
- 1 medium sweet red or green pepper, chopped
- 3 hard-boiled large eggs, chopped
- 6 bacon strips, cooked and crumbled
- 1½ cups shredded cheddar cheese
  Salad dressing of your choice

1. In a greased 3-qt. slow cooker, mix barbecue sauce, brown sugar, garlic powder and paprika. Add the chicken; turn to coat. Cook, covered, on low 3-4 hours or until the chicken is tender (a thermometer should read at least 165°).
2. Remove chicken from slow cooker; cut into bite-sized pieces. In a bowl, toss chicken with 1 cup of the barbecue sauce mixture. Place the romaine on a large serving platter; arrange chicken, avocado, vegetables, eggs, bacon and cheese over romaine. Drizzle with dressing.
1 SERVING 571 cal., 26g fat (9g sat. fat), 192mg chol., 1314mg sod., 47g carb. (32g sugars, 7g fiber), 39g pro.

CHICKEN RAMEN NOODLE BOWL

This healthier take on ramen uses ingredients I usually have on hand. It is an easy, quick and satisfying lunch. You can also make this with leftover chicken or pork. Fresh lime and/or bean sprouts would be a nice garnish.
—*Alicia Rooker, Milwaukee, WI*

TAKES: 20 min. • **MAKES:** 2 servings

- 1 pkg. (3 oz.) chicken ramen noodles
- 1 cup frozen stir-fry vegetable blend
- 1 can (5 oz.) chunk white chicken, drained
- 2 medium fresh mushrooms, thinly sliced
- 1 garlic clove, minced
- ½ tsp. Sriracha chili sauce
- 2 soft-boiled large eggs
- 1 green onion, thinly sliced

Cook the noodles and stir-fry blend according to package directions. Stir the chicken, mushrooms, garlic, chili sauce and cooked stir-fry blend into noodles; heat through. Divide between 2 bowls. Serve with the soft-boiled eggs and green onion, and additional chili sauce if desired.
1½ CUPS 368 cal., 14g fat (5g sat. fat), 230mg chol., 1199mg sod., 36g carb. (4g sugars, 3g fiber), 24g pro.

GOES GREAT WITH ...

Tasty Chicken Skewers with Cool Avocado Sauce (p. 26) add flair to these bowls.

KIMCHI CAULIFLOWER FRIED RICE

KIMCHI CAULIFLOWER FRIED RICE

This is one of my favorite recipes, because it is customizable. If there's a vegetarian in the family leave out the bacon or add your favorite veggies.
—*Stefanie Schaldenbrand, Los Angeles, CA*

TAKES: 30 min. • **MAKES:** 2 servings

- 2 bacon strips, chopped
- 1 green onion, chopped
- 2 garlic cloves, minced
- 1 cup kimchi, chopped
- 3 cups frozen riced cauliflower
- 2 large eggs
- 1 to 3 Tbsp. kimchi juice
  Optional: Sesame oil and sesame seeds

1. In a large skillet, cook bacon over medium heat until partially cooked but not crisp, stirring occasionally. Add the green onion and garlic; cook 1 minute longer. Add kimchi; cook and stir until heated through, 2-3 minutes. Add cauliflower; cook and stir until tender, 8-10 minutes.
2. Meanwhile, heat a large nonstick skillet over medium-high heat. Break eggs, 1 at a time, into pan; reduce heat to low. Cook until whites are set and yolks begin to thicken, turning once if desired. Stir enough kimchi juice into cauliflower mixture to moisten. Divide between 2 serving bowls. Top with the fried eggs, additional green onions and, if desired, sesame oil and sesame seeds.
1 SERVING 254 cal., 17g fat (5g sat. fat), 204mg chol., 715mg sod., 13g carb. (6g sugars, 6g fiber), 15g pro. **DIABETIC EXCHANGES** 2 vegetable, 2 high-fat meat.

SHRIMP SALAD WITH HOT HONEY AVOCADO DRESSING

SHRIMP SALAD WITH HOT HONEY AVOCADO DRESSING

This main dish salad with shrimp uses avocado in place of oil in the dressing and hot honey for a kick. Mix and match your favorite toppings to make this salad your own. Sometimes I like to add black olives and green onion. Plain water can be used in place of the mango sparkling water.
—*Jeanne Holt, Mendota Heights, MN*

TAKES: 25 min. • **MAKES:** 8 servings

- ½ cup mango sparkling water
- ¼ cup cider vinegar
- ¼ cup hot chile-infused honey
- 3 Tbsp. lime juice
- 1 medium ripe avocado, peeled and cubed
- ¼ cup fresh cilantro leaves
- 1 garlic clove
- 8 cups chopped romaine
- 1 medium mango, peeled and cubed
- 1 medium sweet red pepper, chopped
- 2 lbs. peeled and deveined cooked shrimp (31-40 per lb.)
- ¼ cup salted pepitas

1. In a blender or food processor, combine the first 7 ingredients. Cover and process until smooth.
2. Place the lettuce in a large serving bowl. Top with mango, red pepper and shrimp. Drizzle with 1 cup dressing; toss to coat. Sprinkle with pepitas and serve with remaining dressing.
2 CUPS 243 cal., 7g fat (1g sat. fat), 172mg chol., 185mg sod., 21g carb. (16g sugars, 3g fiber), 26g pro. **DIABETIC EXCHANGES** 3 lean meat, 1½ fat, 1 starch, 1 vegetable.

HERBED TUNA & WHITE BEAN SALAD

This is a quick and delicious salad that can be made special for guests—or yourself—by grilling fresh tuna steaks instead of using canned.
—Charlene Chambers, Ormond Beach, FL

TAKES: 15 min. • **MAKES:** 4 servings

- 4   cups fresh arugula
- 1   can (15 oz.) no-salt-added cannellini beans, rinsed and drained
- 1   cup grape tomatoes, halved
- ½   small red onion, thinly sliced
- ⅓   cup chopped roasted sweet red peppers
- ⅓   cup pitted Nicoise or other olives
- ¼   cup chopped fresh basil
- 3   Tbsp. extra virgin olive oil
- ½   tsp. grated lemon zest
- 2   Tbsp. lemon juice
- 1   garlic clove, minced
- ⅛   tsp. salt
- 2   cans (5 oz. each) albacore white tuna in water, drained

Place first 7 ingredients in a large bowl. Whisk together oil, lemon zest, lemon juice, garlic and salt; drizzle over salad. Add tuna and toss gently to combine.
2 CUPS 319 cal., 16g fat (2g sat. fat), 30mg chol., 640mg sod., 20g carb. (3g sugars, 5g fiber), 23g pro. **DIABETIC EXCHANGES** 3 fat, 2 lean meat, 1 starch, 1 vegetable.

TEST KITCHEN TIP
Kalamata olives, though much stronger in flavor, would be a good substitute for Nicoise olives.

THAI SALMON BROWN RICE BOWLS

Turn to this salmon recipe for a quick and nourishing meal. The store-bought sesame ginger dressing saves time and adds extra flavor to this healthy dish.
—Naylet LaRochelle, Miami, FL

TAKES: 15 min. • **MAKES:** 4 servings

- 4   salmon fillets (4 oz. each)
- ½   cup sesame ginger salad dressing, divided
- 3   cups hot cooked brown rice
- ½   cup chopped fresh cilantro
- ¼   tsp. salt
- 1   cup julienned carrot
      Thinly sliced red cabbage, optional

1. Preheat the oven to 400°. Place the salmon in a foil-lined 15x10x1-in. pan; brush with ¼ cup dressing. Bake until the fish just begins to flake easily with a fork, 8-10 minutes. Meanwhile, toss rice with cilantro and salt.
2. To serve, divide rice mixture among 4 bowls. Top with the salmon, carrot and, if desired, cabbage. Drizzle with remaining dressing.
1 SERVING 486 cal., 21g fat (4g sat. fat), 57mg chol., 532mg sod., 49g carb. (8g sugars, 3g fiber), 24g pro.

**PRESSURE-COOKER
THAI SWEET CHILI PORK BOWLS**

PRESSURE-COOKER
THAI SWEET CHILI PORK BOWLS

My family loves pork tenderloin as well
as Thai food, so I decided to combine the
two in this easy pressure-cooker dish.
It's very simple to put together and is
perfect for a weeknight. Don't forget the
cilantro, lime and Sriracha sauce—they
really make the dish stand out.
—Debbie glasscock, Conway, AR

PREP: 20 min. • **COOK:** 20 min. + releasing
MAKES: 6 servings

- 2 pork tenderloins (1 lb. each)
- ½ lb. sliced fresh mushrooms
- 1 large sweet onion, cut into 1-in. pieces
- 1 large sweet red pepper, cut into 1-in. pieces
- 1 cup hoisin sauce
- ¾ cup sweet chili sauce
- ¼ cup reduced-sodium soy sauce
- 2 Tbsp. lime juice
- 2 garlic cloves, minced
- 1½ tsp. minced fresh gingerroot
- 1 tsp. rice vinegar
   Torn fresh cilantro leaves
   Julienned green onions
   Hot cooked rice, lime wedges and Sriracha chili sauce

1. Place the pork in a 6-qt. electric
pressure cooker. Top with mushrooms,
onion and red pepper. Whisk together
the hoisin sauce, chili sauce, soy sauce,
lime juice, garlic, ginger and rice vinegar;
pour over vegetables. Lock lid; close
the pressure-release valve. Adjust to
pressure-cook on high for 20 minutes.
Allow pressure to release naturally.
2. Remove the pork; shred with 2 forks.
Return the pork to pressure cooker; heat
through. Sprinkle with cilantro and green
onion; serve with rice, lime wedges and
chili sauce.
1 SERVING 384 cal., 7g fat (2g sat. fat),
86mg chol., 1664mg sod., 44g carb.
(33g sugars, 3g fiber), 34g pro.

FAJITA IN A BOWL

Pull out the skewers and take a stab at grilling peppers, onions and corn for an awesome steak salad that's all summer and smoke.
—*Peggy Woodward, Shullsburg, WI*

TAKES: 30 min. • **MAKES:** 4 servings

- 1 Tbsp. brown sugar
- 1 Tbsp. chili powder
- ½ tsp. salt
- 1 beef flank steak (1 lb.)
- 12 miniature sweet peppers, halved and seeded
- 1 medium red onion, cut into thin wedges
- 2 cups cherry tomatoes
- 2 medium ears sweet corn, husked

SALAD
- 12 cups torn mixed salad greens
- 1 cup fresh cilantro leaves
- ½ cup reduced-fat lime vinaigrette
Optional ingredients: Cotija cheese, lime wedges and tortillas

1. In a small bowl, mix brown sugar, chili powder and salt. Rub onto both sides of the steak.
2. Place peppers and onion on a grilling grid; place on grill rack over medium heat. Grill, covered, until crisp-tender, stirring occasionally, 9-11 minutes; add tomatoes during the last 2 minutes. Remove from grill.
3. Place the steak and corn directly on grill rack; close lid. Grill the steak until a thermometer reads 135° for medium-rare, 8-10 minutes on each side; grill corn until lightly charred, turning occasionally, 10-12 minutes.
4. Divide the greens and cilantro among 4 bowls. Cut corn from cobs and thinly slice steak across the grain; place in the bowls. Top with vegetables; drizzle with vinaigrette. If desired, serve with cheese, lime and tortillas.

1 SERVING 351 cal., 14g fat (5g sat. fat), 54mg chol., 862mg sod., 33g carb. (16g sugars, 7g fiber), 28g pro.

MEDITERRANEAN SHRIMP ORZO SALAD

Loaded with veggies and shrimp, this crowd pleaser is a tasty change from standard pasta salads.
—*Ginger Johnson, Pottstown, PA*

TAKES: 30 min. • **MAKES:** 8 servings

- 1 pkg. (16 oz.) orzo pasta
- ¾ lb. peeled and deveined cooked shrimp (31-40 per lb.)
- 1 can (14 oz.) water-packed quartered artichoke hearts, rinsed and drained
- 1 cup finely chopped green pepper
- 1 cup finely chopped sweet red pepper
- ¾ cup finely chopped red onion
- ½ cup pitted Greek olives
- ½ cup minced fresh parsley
- ⅓ cup chopped fresh dill
- ¾ cup Greek vinaigrette

1. Cook the orzo according to package directions. Drain; rinse with cold water and drain well.
2. In a large bowl, combine the orzo, shrimp, vegetables, olives and herbs. Add vinaigrette; toss to coat. Refrigerate, covered, until serving.

1½ CUPS 397 cal., 12g fat (2g sat. fat), 65mg chol., 574mg sod., 52g carb. (4g sugars, 3g fiber), 18g pro.

FAJITA IN A BOWL

TOFU SALAD

TOFU SALAD

To make the tofu extra crispy in this recipe, we recommend draining some of the liquid and cooking it in a generous amount of oil at high heat. It takes a little extra time, but it's worth it!
—Taste of Home *Test Kitchen*

PREP: 15 min. + marinating.
COOK: 10 min. • **MAKES:** 4 servings

- 1 pkg. (16 oz.) extra-firm tofu, cut into 1-in. cubes
- ¼ cup rice vinegar
- ¼ cup reduced-sodium soy sauce
- 2 Tbsp. sesame oil
- 2 Tbsp. Sriracha chili sauce or 2 tsp. hot pepper sauce
- 2 Tbsp. creamy peanut butter
- ¼ tsp. ground ginger
- 2 Tbsp. canola oil
- 6 cups torn romaine
- 2 medium carrots, shredded
- 1 medium ripe avocado, peeled and sliced
- 1 cup cherry tomatoes, halved
- ½ small red onion, thinly sliced
- 2 Tbsp. sesame seeds, toasted

1. Blot tofu dry. Wrap in a clean kitchen towel; place on a plate and refrigerate at least 1 hour. In a large shallow dish, whisk the vinegar, soy sauce, sesame oil, chili sauce, peanut butter and ginger until smooth. Add tofu; turn to coat. Cover and refrigerate for 3-5 hours, turning occasionally. Drain the tofu reserving marinade; pat dry.
2. In a large skillet, heat oil over medium-high heat. Add tofu; cook until crisp and golden brown, 5-7 minutes, stirring occasionally. Remove from pan; drain on paper towels.
3. In a large bowl, combine the romaine, carrots, avocado, tomatoes, onion and tofu. Pour the reserved marinade over salad; toss to coat. Sprinkle with sesame seeds. Serve immediately.

2 CUPS 414 cal., 31g fat (4g sat. fat), 0 chol., 1129mg sod., 24g carb. (12g sugars, 7g fiber), 15g pro.

10-MINUTE
SIDES & SWEETS

P. 309

P. 302

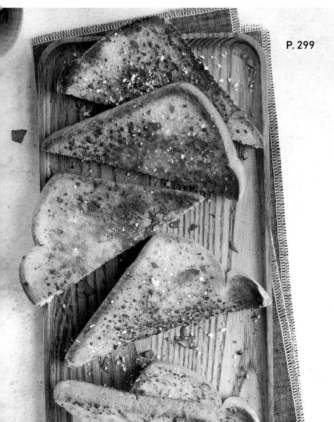

P. 299

P. 311

**BBLT CHOPPED
SALAD**

BBLT CHOPPED SALAD

My original salad recipe called for lettuce. One day I didn't have any, so I substituted spinach and then added broccoli. That's the extra "b" in the title!
—*Cindy VanBeek, Randolph, WI*

TAKES: 10 min. • **MAKES:** 4 servings

6 oz. (about 9 cups) fresh baby spinach, coarsely chopped
1 bunch broccoli, cut into small florets
2 cups grape tomatoes, halved
1 pkg. (2.52 oz.) ready-to-serve thick-cut fully cooked bacon, cut into 1-in. pieces
1 cup Miracle Whip
2 Tbsp. white vinegar
2 Tbsp. sugar

In a large bowl, combine the first 4 ingredients. In a small bowl, mix Miracle Whip, vinegar and sugar until blended. Just before serving, spoon dressing over salad; toss gently to coat.
2½ CUPS 356 cal., 22g fat (4g sat. fat), 39mg chol., 906mg sod., 29g carb. (19g sugars, 6g fiber), 14g pro.

OLD BAY CAULIFLOWER

Ready in 10 minutes, this bowl of veggies has three ingredients and a whole lot of flavor. If you ask me, it's the perfect cauliflower side dish.
—*Elizabeth Bramkamp, Gig Harbor, WA*

TAKES: 10 min. • **MAKES:** 4 servings

1 pkg. (16 oz.) frozen cauliflower
1 to 2 Tbsp. butter, melted
1 to 2 tsp. seafood seasoning

Prepare the cauliflower according to package directions; drain. Drizzle with butter; sprinkle with seafood seasoning.
1 CUP 53 cal., 3g fat (2g sat. fat), 8mg chol., 216mg sod., 5g carb. (3g sugars, 3g fiber), 2g pro. **DIABETIC EXCHANGES** 1 vegetable, ½ fat.

GRILLED NAAN

GRILLED NAAN

Indian food is my all-time favorite, and no meal is complete without some naan. I like to brush grilled or baked naan with lots of butter and garlic. Sometimes, I even add a little chopped cilantro.
—*Jerry Gulley, Pleasant Prairie, WI*

TAKES: 10 min. • **MAKES:** 4 servings

2 Tbsp. butter, melted
3 garlic cloves, minced
2 naan flatbreads

Stir butter and garlic together. Place naan on grill rack; grill over medium-high heat until bottom is golden brown, about 2 minutes. Flip and brush top with garlic butter. Grill until golden brown on bottom. Remove; cut each naan in half.
½ FLATBREAD 134 cal., 8g fat (4g sat. fat), 18mg chol., 286mg sod., 15g carb. (2g sugars, 1g fiber), 2g pro.

DILL & CHIVE PEAS

Growing my own vegetables and herbs helps keep things fresh in the kitchen. This side is a breeze to prepare.
—*Tanna Richard, Cedar Rapids, IA*

TAKES: 10 min. • **MAKES:** 4 servings

- 1   pkg. (16 oz.) frozen peas
- ¼   cup snipped fresh dill
- 2   Tbsp. minced fresh chives
- 1   Tbsp. butter
- 1   tsp. lemon-pepper seasoning
- ¼   tsp. kosher salt

Cook the peas according to package directions. Stir in remaining ingredients; serve immediately.

¾ CUP 113 cal., 3g fat (2g sat. fat), 8mg chol., 346mg sod., 16g carb. (6g sugars, 5g fiber), 6g pro. **DIABETIC EXCHANGES** 1 starch, ½ fat.

DILL & CHIVE PEAS

BLACK-EYED PEA SALAD WITH AVOCADO & JALAPENO

I have had a lot of compliments and requests for this recipe over the years. My husband loves it, and it's especially great on hot days. The salad dressing keeps the avocado from turning dark, even if you have leftovers which doesn't happen often! A fun alternative to pasta or potato salad.
—*Nancy Cariker, Bakersfield, CA*

TAKES: 10 min. • **MAKES:** 4 servings

- 1   can (15½ oz.) black-eyed peas, rinsed and drained
- 1   large tomato, diced
- 1   medium ripe avocado, peeled and diced
- ⅓   cup chopped green pepper
- 2   green onions, chopped
- 1   Tbsp. minced fresh cilantro
- 1   jalapeno pepper, seeded and chopped
- ⅓   cup Italian salad dressing

In a large serving bowl, combine all the ingredients; toss to coat. Serve with a slotted spoon.

NOTE Wear disposable gloves when cutting hot peppers; the oils can burn skin. Avoid touching your face.

¾ CUP 237 cal., 14g fat (2g sat. fat), 0 chol., 562mg sod., 22g carb. (4g sugars, 7g fiber), 7g pro.

BLACK-EYED PEA CORN SALAD Omit the tomato, avocado, green pepper and green onions. Add 2 cups corn and ¼ cup chopped red onion to the salad mixture.

QUICK GARLIC TOAST

QUICK GARLIC TOAST

Mom knew how to easily round out a meal with this crisp, cheesy garlic toast. We gobbled it up when she served it alongside slaw or salad—and used it to soak up gravy from her stew too.
—*Teresa Ingebrand, Perham, MN*

TAKES: 10 min. • **MAKES:** 12 pieces

- ⅓ cup butter, softened
- 12 slices bread
- ½ tsp. garlic salt
- 3 Tbsp. grated Parmesan cheese
  Chopped fresh parsley, optional

Spread butter on 1 side of each slice of bread. Cut each slice in half; place plain side down on a baking sheet. Sprinkle with garlic salt and Parmesan cheese. Broil the bread 4 in. from the heat until lightly browned, 1-2 minutes. If desired, sprinkle with parsley and additional Parmesan cheese.

1 PIECE 128 cal., 6g fat (4g sat. fat), 15mg chol., 287mg sod., 15g carb. (2g sugars, 1g fiber), 3g pro.

READER RAVES

"My mom used to make these when I was a kid, and now I do it for my kids. So easy and good!"

—**WADI2U, TASTEOFHOME.COM**

STIR-FRIED ZUCCHINI

I plant many vegetables to use in cooking. Zucchini is among our favorites and often in abundance. That's why this dish is so popular at our house.
—Deborah Elliot, Ridge Spring, SC

TAKES: 10 min. • **MAKES:** 8 servings

- 2 lbs. sliced zucchini
- 2 garlic cloves, minced
- ¼ cup olive oil
- 1 tsp. salt
- ½ tsp. Italian seasoning
- ¼ tsp. pepper

In a large cast-iron or other heavy skillet, saute the zucchini and garlic in oil until zucchini is crisp-tender, about 5 minutes. Sprinkle with the seasonings. Serve immediately.

½ CUP 77 cal., 7g fat (1g sat. fat), 0 chol., 299mg sod., 4g carb. (2g sugars, 1g fiber), 1g pro.

TEST KITCHEN TIP

You don't need to peel the zucchini for this recipe—just cut it up and throw the slices into the skillet.

STIR-FRIED ZUCCHINI

🕐 LEMON DATE COUSCOUS

Couscous is a fast and perfect base for bold flavors, colors and textures. Try adding lemon, dates, carrots, spinach and almonds.
—*Roxanne Chan, Albany, CA*

TAKES: 10 min. • **MAKES:** 4 servings

- ¾ cup uncooked couscous
- ½ cup fresh baby spinach
- ½ cup shredded carrots
- ¼ cup chopped dates
- 2 Tbsp. sliced almonds
- 1 tsp. lemon juice
- ¼ tsp. grated lemon zest
- ⅛ tsp. salt
- ⅛ tsp. lemon-pepper seasoning
  Thinly sliced green onions

1. Cook couscous according to package directions.
2. Meanwhile, in a small bowl, combine the spinach, carrots, dates, almonds, lemon juice, zest, salt and lemon pepper. Stir in the couscous. Garnish with the green onions.
NOTE Couscous can usually be found in the rice or pasta section of the grocery store. It is available in regular or quick-cooking forms.
¾ CUP 179 cal., 2g fat (0 sat. fat), 0 chol., 104mg sod., 37g carb. (9g sugars, 3g fiber), 6g pro. **DIABETIC EXCHANGES** 2½ starch.

🕐 🈺 WATERMELON-BLUEBERRY SALAD

People love the unique combination of flavors in the dressing that tops the fresh fruit in this salad. It's so refreshing on a hot summer evening.
—*Jenni Sharp, Milwaukee, WI*

TAKES: 5 min. • **MAKES:** 2 servings

- 1 Tbsp. honey
- ¾ tsp. lemon juice
- ½ tsp. minced fresh mint
- 1 cup seeded chopped watermelon
- ½ cup fresh blueberries

In a small bowl, combine the honey, lemon juice and mint. Add watermelon and blueberries; toss gently to coat. Chill until serving.
¾ CUP 78 cal., 0 fat (0 sat. fat), 0 chol., 2mg sod., 20g carb. (17g sugars, 1g fiber), 1g pro. **DIABETIC EXCHANGES** 1 fruit, ½ starch.

SIMPLE WALDORF SALAD ✓

This is my go-to salad when I need a quick little something for a meal. When I want a sweeter taste, I use whipped cream instead of yogurt.
—*Wendy Masters, East Garafraxa, ON*

TAKES: 10 min. • **MAKES:** 6 servings

- 2 large Gala or Honeycrisp apples, unpeeled and chopped (about 3 cups)
- 2 cups chopped celery
- ¼ cup raisins
- ¼ cup chopped walnuts, toasted
- ⅓ cup reduced-fat mayonnaise
- ⅓ cup plain yogurt

Combine the apples, celery, raisins and walnuts. Add mayonnaise and yogurt; toss to coat. Refrigerate, covered, until serving.

NOTE To toast the nuts, bake in a shallow pan at 350° for 5-10 minutes or cook in a skillet over low heat until lightly browned, stirring occasionally.

¾ CUP 140 cal., 8g fat (1g sat. fat), 6mg chol., 119mg sod., 17g carb. (12g sugars, 3g fiber), 2g pro. **DIABETIC EXCHANGES** 1½ fat, 1 fruit.

MINTY SUGAR SNAP PEAS

Fresh mint adds a lively touch to cooked sugar snap peas. The overall idea also works with green beans and carrots.
—*Alice Kaldahl, Ray, ND*

TAKES: 10 min. • **MAKES:** 4 servings

- 3 cups fresh sugar snap peas, trimmed
- ¼ tsp. sugar
- 2 to 3 Tbsp. minced fresh mint
- 2 Tbsp. butter

Place 1 in. water in a large skillet. Add peas and sugar; bring to a boil. Reduce heat; simmer, covered, until peas are crisp-tender, 4-5 minutes; drain. Stir in mint and butter.

¾ CUP 102 cal., 6g fat (4g sat. fat), 15mg chol., 45mg sod., 9g carb. (4g sugars, 3g fiber), 4g pro. **DIABETIC EXCHANGES** 2 vegetable, 1½ fat.

SIMPLE WALDORF SALAD

ORANGE & OLIVES SALAD
My grandmother made sure this salad was on our holiday table every year. We always celebrated the rustic Italian way, and she made lots of delicious food. This dish is simple to make, and so light that it didn't fill us up before one of her great meals. It also looks pretty on the table.
—*Angela David, Lakeland, FL*

TAKES: 10 min. • **MAKES:** 16 servings

4   large navel oranges, peeled and sliced
2   cans (6 oz. each) pitted ripe olives, drained
1   Tbsp. canola oil
⅛   tsp. pepper

Arrange orange slices on a large serving platter; top with olives. Drizzle with oil and sprinkle with pepper.
1 SERVING 54 cal., 3g fat (0 sat. fat), 0 chol., 185mg sod., 7g carb. (4g sugars, 2g fiber), 1g pro. **DIABETIC EXCHANGES** ½ fruit, ½ fat.

SALSA CORN
All you'll need for this corn salsa recipe is corn and pico de gallo—a simple and effective solution for a last-minute side.
—*Danielle Lee, Charleston, SC*

TAKES: 10 min. • **MAKES:** 4 servings

2   cups frozen corn (about 10 oz.)
¼   to ½ cup pico de gallo or salsa

Prepare corn according to package directions; drain. Stir in pico de gallo.
½ CUP 62 cal., 1g fat (0 sat. fat), 0 chol., 3mg sod., 15g carb. (2g sugars, 2g fiber), 2g pro. **DIABETIC EXCHANGES** 1 starch.

ORANGE & OLIVES SALAD

BLUEBERRY
CANTALOUPE
SALAD

MUSHROOM & SPINACH SAUTE

Mushrooms and spinach make a super fast combination that's perfect for two. And it's easy to double or even triple for a crowd.
—*Pauline Howard, Lago Vista, TX*

TAKES: 10 min. • **MAKES:** 2 servings

- 2 tsp. olive oil
- 2 cups sliced fresh mushrooms
- 2 garlic cloves, minced
- 1 pkg. (5 to 6 oz.) fresh baby spinach
- ⅛ tsp. salt
- ⅛ tsp. pepper

In a large skillet, heat oil over medium-high heat. Add mushrooms; saute until tender, about 2 minutes. Add garlic; cook 1 minute longer. Add spinach in batches; cook and stir until wilted, about 1 minute. Season with salt and pepper. Serve immediately.

¾ CUP 76 cal., 5g fat (1g sat. fat), 0mg chol., 208mg sod., 6g carb. (2g sugars, 2g fiber), 4g pro. **DIABETIC EXCHANGES** 1 vegetable, 1 fat.

READER RAVES

"Easy, great flavor and good for you too. A win-win."

—**MILLSTONE, TASTEOFHOME.COM**

BLUEBERRY CANTALOUPE SALAD

Add a fresh touch to any meal with these cute cups. The simple citrus dressing really jazzes up the fruit.
—*R. Jean Rand, Edina, MN*

TAKES: 10 min. • **MAKES:** 4 servings

- ¾ cup orange yogurt
- 1½ tsp. lemon juice
- ¾ tsp. poppy seeds
- ½ tsp. grated orange zest
- 2 cups diced cantaloupe
- 1 cup fresh blueberries

In a small bowl, mix yogurt, lemon juice, poppy seeds and orange zest. To serve, divide the cantaloupe and blueberries among 4 dishes; top with the yogurt dressing.

¾ CUP WITH 3 TBSP. DRESSING 76 cal., 1g fat (0 sat. fat), 1mg chol., 24mg sod., 17g carb. (15g sugars, 1g fiber), 2g pro. **DIABETIC EXCHANGES** 1 fruit.

BROCCOLI CRANBERRY SLAW

I need just four items to toss together this crunchy coleslaw that gets a sweet twist from dried cranberries. The shredded broccoli mixture is lightly coated with convenient prepared dressing.
—*Marie Siciliano, Westerly, RI*

TAKES: 10 min. • **MAKES:** 8 servings

- 1 pkg. (12 oz.) broccoli coleslaw mix
- 1 pkg. (3 oz.) dried cranberries
- 6 green onions, cut into ½-in. pieces
- ¼ cup coleslaw salad dressing

In a large bowl, combine the coleslaw mix, cranberries and onions. Add the dressing and toss to coat. Refrigerate until serving.

¾ CUP 81 cal., 3g fat (0 sat. fat), 4mg chol., 107mg sod., 14g carb. (10g sugars, 2g fiber), 1g pro.

QUICK MANGO SORBET

Last summer, I decided to try my hand at making a passion fruit and mango sorbet. But fresh fruits require more prep and are difficult to find ripened at the same time. So I experimented using frozen fruit and juice, and voila! Both are readily available and inexpensive too.
—*Carol A Klein, Franklin Square, NY*

TAKES: 5 min. • **MAKES:** 2½ cups

- 1 pkg. (16 oz.) frozen mango chunks, slightly thawed
- ½ cup passion fruit juice
- 2 Tbsp. sugar

Place all the ingredients in a blender; cover and process until smooth. Serve immediately. If desired, for a firmer texture, cover and freeze at least 3 hours.

½ CUP 91 cal., 0 fat (0 sat. fat), 0 chol., 2mg sod., 24g carb. (21g sugars, 2g fiber), 1g pro.

QUICK MANGO SORBET

CREAMY PINEAPPLE PIE

BROWNIE SUNDAES ✓

Here's a decadent brownie sundae recipe that's sure to appeal to the whole family! Topped with some ice cream and warm chocolate sauce, it makes a special treat.
—*Ruth Lee, Troy, ON*

TAKES: 10 min. • **MAKES:** 6 servings

- ¾ cup semisweet chocolate chips
- ½ cup evaporated milk
- 2 Tbsp. brown sugar
- 2 tsp. butter
- ½ tsp. vanilla extract
- 6 prepared brownies (3 in. square)
- 6 scoops vanilla or chocolate fudge ice cream
- ½ cup chopped pecans

1. In a large saucepan, combine the chocolate chips, milk and brown sugar. Cook and stir over medium heat for 5 minutes or until chocolate is melted and sugar is dissolved. Remove from the heat; stir in the butter and vanilla until smooth.
2. Spoon about 2 Tbsp. warm chocolate sauce onto each dessert plate. Top with a brownie and a scoop of ice cream. Drizzle with additional chocolate sauce if desired. Sprinkle with pecans.
1 SERVING 605 cal., 33g fat (13g sat. fat), 49mg chol., 276mg sod., 76g carb. (52g sugars, 3g fiber), 8g pro.

CREAMY PINEAPPLE PIE ✓

This light and refreshing pie is quick to make and impressive to serve. It's one of our favorite ways to complete a summer meal.
—*Sharon Bickett, Chester, SC*

TAKES: 10 min. • **MAKES:** 8 servings

- 1 can (14 oz.) sweetened condensed milk
- 1 can (8 oz.) crushed pineapple, undrained
- ¼ cup lemon juice
- 1 carton (8 oz.) frozen whipped topping, thawed
- 1 graham cracker crust (9 in.)
  Optional: Chopped toasted macadamia nuts and additional crushed pineapple

Combine milk, pineapple and lemon juice; fold in whipped topping. Pour into prepared crust. Refrigerate until serving. If desired, serve with toasted macadamia nuts and additional crushed pineapple.
1 PIECE 367 cal., 14g fat (9g sat. fat), 17mg chol., 185mg sod., 54g carb. (46g sugars, 1g fiber), 5g pro.

TEST KITCHEN TIP ✗

We recommend using fresh lemon juice for this dessert. Store-bought juice can be the slightest bit bitter—not a flavor you want in a refreshing pineapple pie.

COCONUT-LAYERED POUND CAKE

If you love chocolate, almonds and coconut, this cake is for you. It comes together in a flash and tastes just like an Almond Joy candy bar!
—*Linda Nichols, Steubenville, OH*

TAKES: 10 min. • **MAKES:** 8 servings

- 1 pkg. (7 oz.) sweetened shredded coconut
- 1 can (14 oz.) sweetened condensed milk
- ½ cup chopped almonds, toasted
- 1 loaf (16 oz.) frozen pound cake, thawed
- 1 cup chocolate fudge frosting

Mix coconut, milk and almonds. Cut the cake horizontally into 4 layers. Place the bottom layer on a serving plate; top with half the coconut mixture, 1 cake layer and ½ cup frosting. Repeat the layers. Refrigerate, covered, until serving.

NOTE To toast the nuts, bake in a shallow pan at 350° for 5-10 minutes or cook in a skillet over low heat until lightly browned, stirring occasionally.

1 PIECE 715 cal., 35g fat (19g sat. fat), 98mg chol., 426mg sod., 93g carb. (72g sugars, 3g fiber), 10g pro.

OLD-FASHIONED BANANA CREAM PIE

This fluffy no-bake pie is full of old-fashioned flavor, with only a fraction of the work. Because it uses instant pudding, it's ready in just minutes.
—*Perlene Hoekema, Lynden, WA*

TAKES: 10 min. • **MAKES:** 8 servings

- 1 cup cold 2% milk
- 1 pkg. (3.4 oz.) instant vanilla pudding mix
- ½ tsp. vanilla extract
- 1 carton (12 oz.) frozen whipped topping, thawed, divided
- 1 graham cracker crust (9 in.)
- 2 medium firm bananas, sliced
   Additional banana slices, optional

1. In a large bowl, whisk milk, pudding mix and vanilla for 2 minutes (mixture will be thick). Fold in 3 cups whipped topping.
2. Pour 1⅓ cups pudding mixture into pie crust. Layer with the banana slices and remaining pudding mixture. Top with remaining whipped topping. If desired, garnish with additional banana slices. Refrigerate until serving.

1 PIECE 311 cal., 13g fat (9g sat. fat), 2mg chol., 213mg sod., 43g carb. (34g sugars, 1g fiber), 2g pro.

CHOCOLATE & PEANUT BUTTER BANANA CREAM PIE Substitute 1 (9 in.) chocolate crumb crust for the graham cracker crust. Arrange banana slices on crust. In a microwave-safe bowl, mix ¾ cup peanut butter and 2 oz. chopped chocolate; microwave on high for 1-1½ minutes or until blended and smooth, stirring every 30 seconds. Spoon over bananas. Pour pudding mixture over top. Garnish with remaining whipped topping. Just before serving, garnish with 2 Tbsp. chopped salted peanuts or chopped peanut butter cups.

WATERMELON
FRUIT PIZZA

WATERMELON FRUIT PIZZA

Fruit pizza is an easy and refreshing way to end a meal. Top it with any fruit you may have on hand, and add other toppings like fresh mint leaves, toasted shredded coconut or chopped nuts.
—Taste of Home *Test Kitchen*

TAKES: 10 min. • **MAKES:** 8 servings

- 4 oz. cream cheese, softened
- 4 oz. frozen whipped topping, thawed
- ½ tsp. vanilla extract
- 3 Tbsp. confectioners' sugar
- 1 round slice of whole seedless watermelon, about 1 in. thick
   Assorted fresh fruit
   Fresh mint leaves, optional

1. In a small bowl, beat cream cheese until smooth. Gently fold in the whipped topping, then vanilla and confectioners' sugar until combined.
2. To serve, spread watermelon slice with cream cheese mixture. Cut into 8 wedges and top with your fruit of choice. If desired, garnish pizza with fresh mint.

1 PIECE 140 cal., 7g fat (5g sat. fat), 14mg chol., 45mg sod., 17g carb. (16g sugars, 0 fiber), 1g pro. **DIABETIC EXCHANGES** 1½ fat, 1 fruit.

CONTEST-WINNING EASY TIRAMISU

CONTEST-WINNING EASY TIRAMISU

Sweet little servings of tiramisu, dusted with a whisper of cocoa, end any meal on a high note. What a fun use for pudding snack cups!
—Betty Claycomb, Alverton, PA

TAKES: 10 min. • **MAKES:** 2 servings

- 14 vanilla wafers, divided
- 1 tsp. instant coffee granules
- 2 Tbsp. hot water
- 2 snack-size cups (3½ oz. each) vanilla pudding
- ¼ cup whipped topping
- 1 tsp. baking cocoa

1. Set aside 4 vanilla wafers; coarsely crush remaining wafers. Divide wafer crumbs between 2 dessert dishes.
2. In a small bowl, dissolve the coffee granules in hot water. Drizzle over wafer crumbs. Spoon pudding into the dessert dishes. Top with the whipped topping; sprinkle with cocoa. Garnish with the reserved vanilla wafers.

1 SERVING 267 cal., 9g fat (4g sat. fat), 4mg chol., 219mg sod., 41g carb. (28g sugars, 1g fiber), 3g pro.

FRESAS CON CREMA

FRESAS CON CREMA

This refreshing dessert is so wonderful when berries are in season. Media crema is a rich, unsweetened cream found in the baking aisle or ethnic food section of the grocery store. It's similar to creme fraiche and sour cream, although sour cream is quite a bit tangier.
—Taste of Home Test Kitchen

TAKES: 10 min. • **MAKES:** 4 servings

- 1 can (7.6 oz.) media crema table cream
- 3 Tbsp. sweetened condensed milk
- 1 tsp. vanilla extract
- 3 cups chopped fresh strawberries
  Fresh mint leaves, optional

In a small bowl, whisk crema, sweetened condensed milk and vanilla. Divide the strawberries among 4 serving dishes. Top with the milk mixture. Garnish with fresh mint if desired.

¾ CUP 241 cal., 17g fat (10g sat. fat), 43mg chol., 58mg sod., 21g carb. (14g sugars, 2g fiber), 2g pro.

TEST KITCHEN TIP

Fresas con crema, also known as strawberries and cream, is an authentic Mexican dessert. Just like the name implies, fresas con crema consists of fresh strawberries served in a sweet cream.

GLAZED PEAR SHORTCAKES

Family and friends will savor every last crumb of this easy dessert. The pound cake absorbs the apricot flavor and warm sweetness of the pears.
—*Frances Thomas, St. James City, FL*

TAKES: 10 min. • **MAKES:** 4 servings

- 2 medium pears, sliced
- 2 Tbsp. butter
- 4 tsp. apricot spreadable fruit
- 8 thin slices pound cake
- 4 tsp. chopped walnuts
- 4 Tbsp. whipped topping

1. In a small cast-iron skillet, saute pears in butter until tender. Remove from the heat; stir in spreadable fruit.
2. Place cake slices on 4 dessert dishes; top with pear mixture, walnuts and whipped topping.
1 SERVING 256 cal., 14g fat (8g sat. fat), 81mg chol., 161mg sod., 32g carb. (11g sugars, 3g fiber), 3g pro.

GLAZED PEAR SHORTCAKES

CHERRY CREAM CHEESE TARTS

It's hard to believe that just five ingredients and few minutes of preparation can result in these delicate and scrumptious tarts!
—*Cindi Mitchell, Waring, TX*

TAKES: 10 min. • **MAKES:** 2 tarts

- 3 oz. cream cheese, softened
- ¼ cup confectioners' sugar
- ⅛ to ¼ tsp. almond or vanilla extract
- 2 individual graham cracker crusts
- ¼ cup cherry pie filling

In a small bowl, beat the cream cheese, confectioners' sugar and extract until smooth. Spoon into the crusts. Top with the pie filling. Refrigerate until serving.
1 TART 362 cal., 20g fat (10g sat. fat), 43mg chol., 265mg sod., 42g carb. (29g sugars, 1g fiber), 4g pro.

PEANUT BUTTER CHOCOLATE FONDUE

Whenever the family wanted to do a little celebrating over the years, I would make this fondue. It's fun gathering around the table to get a taste of it.
—*Beverly Olthaus, Cincinnati, OH*

TAKES: 10 min. • **MAKES:** 12 servings

- 1   cup semisweet chocolate chips
- ½   cup sugar
- ½   cup 2% milk
- ½   cup creamy peanut butter
- 4   large firm bananas, cut into ¾-in. slices
- 1   pint whole strawberries
     Optional: Shortbread cookies and large marshmallows

In a heavy saucepan, cook and stir chocolate chips, sugar, milk and peanut butter over low heat until smooth. Transfer to a fondue pot and keep warm. Serve with banana slices, strawberries and, if desired, cookies and marshmallows.

¼ CUP 218 cal., 10g fat (4g sat. fat), 1mg chol., 57mg sod., 32g carb. (27g sugars, 3g fiber), 4g pro.

READER RAVES

"So easy and fast to prepare! My family just loved it!"

—CINDYPAL, TASTEOFHOME.COM

PEANUT BUTTER CHOCOLATE FONDUE

WHAT'S FOR DINNER?
HOW ABOUT....?

INSTANT POT®SPECIALTIES

MEATLESS DINNERS

ALPHABETICAL INDEX